Praise for *Ethical Ed Tech*

"*Ethical Ed Tech* refuses easy narratives about AI and education and instead offers educators something more useful: clarity grounded in values and practice. It helps K-12 educators move beyond hype or fear toward deliberate, context-aware decisions. Its strength lies in connecting ethical reflection, classroom reality, and system-level thinking in ways that make change both possible and responsible."

—**Lance Eaton, Ph.D.**

"Priten Soundar-Shah has an impressive ability to move between big-picture, philosophical questions about educational ethics and down-to-Earth, practical questions about what educators can do right now to make their classrooms more ethical spaces. *Ethical Ed Tech* is a great book that (I hope) pushes the conversation about ethics, Artificial Intelligence, and education in a more nuanced direction."

—**Jason Gulya,**
Professor of English and
Communications at Berkeley College

"As a parent, an educator, and a school leader, I've watched schools lurch from one tech trend to another without stopping to ask the fundamental questions Priten poses in this brilliant book: Just because we can, does that mean we should?

Our children deserve better than the hollow victory of 'getting their first'. They deserve to 'get their prepared.' Soundar-Shah's framework for deliberative decision-making transforms technology choices from reactive scrambling into intentional, values-driven leadership that grounds itself in the development of the whole person. It is a book that every parent and educational decision-maker should read."

—**Joseph Carver,**
Head of School, Academy of the
Sacred Heart Bloomfield Hills

"If you're a school leader, please don't waste your time trying to read 100 other books and articles to understand the AI landscape and how to make wise decisions under uncertainty. Simply read this book first. Priten's depth of thought, scope of research, and wise care for all stakeholders come through masterfully, as does his ability to crisply organize a ridiculous amount of information from dozens of disciplines. For example, he elegantly translate what philosophers call meta-ethical frameworks into very practical questions (i.e., translating 'deontology' to 'What lines will we never cross?'; 'consequentialism' to 'How will we evaluate the outcomes of our decisions?'; and 'virtue ethics' to 'What kind of people do we want to be?') On every page, he preserves nuance without getting lost in the weeds. This book is both a primer and a deep dive and is actionable on almost every page for those who need to make decisions quickly. Do yourself a favor and read it!"

—**Nate Otey,**
Educator and Philosopher

"At a time when technology in education is too often lauded rather than scrutinized, *Ethical Ed Tech* is both urgently relevant and enduringly significant—a courageous guide to the ethical complexities of modern education that will outlast any individual tool or trend. Priten Soundar-Shah's rare combination of philosophical grounding, classroom experience, and sustained engagement with leading voices in AI and education means he moves effortlessly between theory, policy, and practice with genuine authority. This is not an outsider's commentary, but an insider's honest reckoning."

—**Tamsyn Smith**,
Digital Learning, University of Southampton

"Priten Soundar-Shah bridges philosophy, ethics, policy, and classroom practice with exceptional clarity, providing not just principles but practical tools for deliberate decision-making about technology in our schools. It is a timely and necessary guide for any educator looking to integrate AI and educational technology with intentionality and care."

—**Keith Yi**,
former HS Principal and Adjunct Professor,
Inha University

"Priten Soundar-Shah is a thought leader who brings a rare combination of skills and experiences to make ethical thinking accessible and practical. His intellectual rigor and understanding of education as a dynamic and deeply human field informs his framework for clear decision-making that sees through the messiness of real school settings to sustain the core values of community. The case studies Soundar-Shah presents are a platform for conversations that unearth the essential questions for pioneering the field of Ethics and AI in classrooms."

—**Anne L'Hommedieu Sanderson**,
Executive Director, ThinkerU.org; Associate,
Harvard Department of Philosophy

"At a time when educational technology feels overwhelming and inevitable, Soundar-Shah offers educators something precious: agency. Soundar-Shah's latest book illuminates how to reclaim moral authority over the tools we use and the learning environments we create, foster, and facilitate. His framework transforms technology decisions from compliance exercises into opportunities for ethical leadership. This should be required reading for anyone with an interest, stake, or belief in the future of education."

—**Ajay Nair, Ph.D.**,
President of Arcadia University

"Most ed-tech books tell you what to adopt. This one teaches you how to decide—and who should be in the room when you do. Soundar-Shah has written the ethical playbook that K-12 has been waiting for."

—**Anand Rao**,
Director of the Center for AI and the Liberal Arts at
the University of Mary Washington and Professor of Communication

"Books are meant to endure for a while. Ed tech changes, it seems, daily. So won't a book about this latest version of ed tech be obsolete before it's even published? In this case, the answer is NO! Priten Soundar-Shah's *Ethical Ed Tech* truly gets to desperately needed foundational principles, questions, and strategies that may guide us through this, and the next, and the next incarnation of ed tech, so that we are anchored in five fundamental principles, from which we derive policies, and finally specific practices. We'll be ready to make tough decisions, whatever comes our way in the realm of education, knowing the high stakes for all."

—**Susan Blum**, Professor of Anthropology, The University of Notre Dame; Author of *Schoolishness: Alienated Education and the Quest for Authentic, Joyful Learning*

"As a district technology specialist and instructional coach navigating the rapid incursion of AI into the educational space with teachers, administrators, and policymakers, I often return to one guiding principle from this book: First, do no harm. Soundar-Shah's insights provide a clear North Star for how our communities must thoughtfully and ethically engage with AI's growing presence in the classroom and this book contains the roadmap educators need to navigate the future of instruction, and I heartily recommend it to anyone wrestling with the 'what now?' questions we're all facing at this pivotal moment in modern education."

—**Jason R. Williams**, Award-Winning Educator, Teacher-Leader and Licensed Administrator

Ethical Ed Tech

Ethical Ed Tech

HOW EDUCATORS CAN LEAD ON AI AND DIGITAL SAFETY IN K-12

PRITEN SOUNDAR-SHAH

JB JOSSEY-BASS™
A Wiley Brand

Copyright © 2026 by John Wiley & Sons, Inc. All rights reserved, including rights for text and data mining and training of artificial intelligence technologies or similar technologies.

Published by John Wiley & Sons, Inc., Hoboken, New Jersey.

No part of this publication may be reproduced, stored in a retrieval system, or transmitted in any form or by any means, electronic, mechanical, photocopying, recording, scanning, or otherwise, except as permitted under Section 107 or 108 of the 1976 United States Copyright Act, without either the prior written permission of the Publisher, or authorization through payment of the appropriate per-copy fee to the Copyright Clearance Center, Inc., 222 Rosewood Drive, Danvers, MA 01923, (978) 750-8400, fax (978) 750-4470, or on the web at www.copyright.com. Requests to the Publisher for permission should be addressed to the Permissions Department, John Wiley & Sons, Inc., 111 River Street, Hoboken, NJ 07030, (201) 748-6011, fax (201) 748-6008, or online at http://www.wiley.com/go/permission.

The manufacturer's authorized representative according to the EU General Product Safety Regulation is Wiley-VCH GmbH, Boschstr. 12, 69469 Weinheim, Germany, email: Product_Safety@wiley.com.

Trademarks: Wiley and the Wiley logo are trademarks or registered trademarks of John Wiley & Sons, Inc. and/or its affiliates in the United States and other countries and may not be used without written permission. All other trademarks are the property of their respective owners. John Wiley & Sons, Inc. is not associated with any product or vendor mentioned in this book.

Limit of Liability/Disclaimer of Warranty: While the publisher and author have used their best efforts in preparing this book, they make no representations or warranties with respect to the accuracy or completeness of the contents of this book and specifically disclaim any implied warranties of merchantability or fitness for a particular purpose. Certain AI systems have been used in the creation of this work. No warranty may be created or extended by sales representatives or written sales materials. The advice and strategies contained herein may not be suitable for your situation. You should consult with a professional where appropriate. Further, readers should be aware that websites listed in this work may have changed or disappeared between when this work was written and when it is read. Neither the publisher nor author shall be liable for any loss of profit or any other commercial damages, including but not limited to special, incidental, consequential, or other damages.

For general information on our other products and services or for technical support, please contact our Customer Care Department within the United States at (800) 762-2974, outside the United States at (317) 572-3993 or fax (317) 572-4002.

Wiley also publishes its books in a variety of electronic formats. Some content that appears in print may not be available in electronic formats. For more information about Wiley products, visit our website at www.wiley.com.

Library of Congress Cataloging-in-Publication Data is Available:

ISBN: 9781394369621 (Paperback)
ISBN: 9781394369645 (ePub)
ISBN: 9781394369638 (ePDF)

Cover Art and Design: Paul McCarthy

To my teachers, who showed me what love can teach; to my students, who remind me why care matters; and to everyone working to keep learning a human endeavor in an increasingly technological age.

Contents

Dear Reader   xvii

Chapter 1   **Our Ethical Imperative**   1
    Cycles of Adoption   2
    Dangers of Speed   2
    Multiple Ends   3
    Schools' Difficult Role   4
    Diverse Visions   5
    Philosophy-Policy-Practice   6
    Deliberative Ethics   7
    An Invitation   8

Section A   **Philosophy**   11

Chapter 2   **Educational Ethics**   13
    Tragic Choices   14
    Practical Wisdom   15
    Shared Commitments   16
    Case Study Method   17
    Approaching Practice   18
    A Path Forward   19

Chapter 3   **Ethical Principles**   21
    Building the Five Principles   22
    Beneficence   24
    Non-Maleficence   25
    Autonomy   25
    Care   26
    Justice   27
    Tensions   28
    Carrying Our Principles   29

Chapter 4	**Ethical Approaches**	**30**
	Why Three?	31
	Defining Limits	31
	Weighing Consequences	33
	Building Virtues	34
	Using Our Approaches	34
Chapter 5	**Stakeholders**	**36**
	The Role of Stakeholders	37
	Students	38
	Educators	41
	Parents/Guardians	44
	Other Stakeholders	46
	Relational Decision-Making	47
Chapter 6	**Stakes**	**49**
	Stakes of Purpose: The Ends	50
	Economic Aims	51
	Civic Aims	53
	Personal Aims	55
	Stakes of Process: The Means	56
	Opportunity	57
	Voice and Recognition	58
	Balancing the Stakes	59
Chapter 7	**Reasoning Heuristics**	**61**
	Framing	62
	Weighing	64
	Validating	66
	Thinking Habits	68
Chapter 8	**Ed Tech Defined**	**69**
	Historical Foundations	70
	Contemporary Technology	72
	Future Horizons	75
	Never Neutral	77

Chapter 9	**Ed Tech Themes**	**79**
	Promises	80
	Measurements	87
	Justifications	91
	Beyond the Buzz	94
Chapter 10	**Inherent Risks of Tech**	**95**
	Design Risks	96
	Systemic Risks	102
	From Recognition to Response	106
Section B	**Policy**	**109**
Chapter 11	**Philosophy to Praxis**	**111**
	Practice System	112
	Policies as Anchors	115
	Ethics as Habits	116
Chapter 12	**External Constraints**	**118**
	Data Constraints	119
	Governance Constraints	122
	Access Constraints	123
	Why Not Just Laws	126
	Ethical Baselines	127
Chapter 13	**Designing Ethical Schools**	**129**
	Normative Infrastructure	130
	Procedural Infrastructure	132
	Cultural Infrastructure	134
	Phased Implementation	136
Chapter 14	**Sustaining Ethical Practices**	**138**
	Grand Rounds & Committees	139
	Agendas	139
	Facilitation	140
	Evaluation	140

Assessments ... 141
Revision ... 142
Potential Roadblocks ... 142
Starting Small ... 143

Chapter 15 Classroom Policies — 145
Classroom Policies & Decisions ... 146
Lived Policies ... 150
Ground-Up Policymaking ... 152

Chapter 16 Ed Tech Governance — 153
Ethical Lens for Technology ... 154
Governance Architecture ... 155
New Technology Policies ... 156
Operational Policies ... 158
Beyond Infrastructure ... 160

Section C   Practice — 161

Chapter 17 Cases in Learning — 163
Case Study 1: Ms. Patel & Balancing Learning & Privacy ... 163
Case Study 2: Mrs. Vargas & Equity in Learning Solutions ... 167
Case Study 3: Mr. Martinez & The Question of Me or We ... 172

Chapter 18 Cases in Assessment — 176
Case Study 4: Mr. Zan & Who Really Wrote What ... 176
Case Study 5: Mrs. Long & Her New Grading Assistant ... 181
Case Study 6: Mrs. Greene & How Risk Becomes a Category ... 185

Chapter 19 Cases in Safety — 190
Case Study 7: Dr. Walsh & Help with Critical Support ... 190
Case Study 8: Ms. Nguyen & The Decision to Speak ... 194
Case Study 9: Ms. Cipriano & Between Two Fears ... 199

Chapter 20 Cases in Policy — **204**
    Case Study 10: Mr. Khan & AI for All — 204
    Case Study 11: Mrs. Sierra & Cellphone Exceptions — 209
    Case Study 12: Dr. Rivera & Defending Enrollment — 213

Chapter 21 Our Ethical Reality — **218**
    Definite Constraints — 218
    Possible Critiques — 219
    What's Next? — 220
    We Are Not Alone — 220

Bibliography — **223**

About the Author — **249**

Acknowledgments — **251**

Index — **253**

Dear Reader

This book began with a feeling I could not ignore: fear. I fear that our students will inherit a world where their humanity has even less space to flourish. I fear that our future civic society will be even more fractured and ineffective at creating just institutions. And, I fear that our schools, in the rushed quest for relevancy, will become forever irrelevant.

Thus, I write this book with the hope that it serves as a starting place for the important conversations that educators must have in the coming years to avoid these outcomes. This book is an invitation to reclaim moral agency in how we build, teach with, and govern technology in education. We must think deeply, reflect intentionally, and deliberate jointly to ensure that we shape our educational institutions into sites of humanity that serve our students' interests in their own economic, civic, and personal growth.

Before we begin, I hope to answer some questions that will help orient you for the journey ahead.

What Experiences Have Shaped the Book's Strategy and Content?

This book is the result of many paths that I have taken through education. I draw influences from the argumentation skills of competitive debate, from the philosophical thinking of my undergraduate years, from the practical policy considerations of my graduate program, from my technical expertise gained working on the ideas of changemakers, from our work at Academy 4 Social Civics reimagining education for timely civic leadership, from our advocacy at The Boarding School to increase youth representation in educational institutions, and from my own teaching experiences from tutoring in high school to teaching at College Unbound. These experiences come together to shape the knowledge, skills, and dispositions this book seeks to reflect and impart.

What Is This Book Trying to Be?

I am well aware that in bridging those worlds, I have not done justice to any one of those. It is not a philosophical manifesto, a policy handbook, or a beautiful narrative of human experiences.

I remind myself, and my readers, that the purpose of this book is to lead conversations among educators globally that enable them to act more ethically in their daily practice. This inevitably means I must accept the confines of an unjust system, make arguments that will be effective for educators working across contexts and generations, and leave out some aspects that I wish we could devote more energy and effort to, all in service of being a primarily pragmatic endeavor.

Who Is This Book For?

The book is written primarily for educators within our schools, including teachers, counselors, technology & curriculum coordinators, and administrators, because they are best positioned to make immediate, informed decisions about educational technology. Thus, all of the questions, dilemmas, and policies explored in this book focus on issues that are within their spheres of influence.

Does the Book Want to Change How You Think?

I approach this endeavor through the lens of transformative learning first introduced to me through analogy by my first philosophy professor, Gina Schouten. On our first day of class, she described our worldviews as apartments with preexisting furnishings: wallpapers, lamps, couches, and vases.

She explained that her goal was to present us with new pieces of furnishing, making us reflect on how or if we would integrate them into our homes. We might realize that the new furnishing fits perfectly well into our preexisting decorative style and choose to incorporate it. Or, we might consider the new furnishing but decide that ultimately it does not fit into our aesthetic design and choose to do without it. Finally, we might decide that the new furnishing does not match, but we love it so much that we might have to redecorate our apartment to make room for it.

All three of these outcomes were markers of success for her, as they are for me. I invite you to consider the arguments in this book and decide what role they will or will not play in your own worldview. That act of consideration is the most I ask of you, and it is the starting point for meaningful ethical decision-making in education and technology.

I hope readers take the book in small doses and spend time reflecting on each chapter. The exit tickets are meant to encourage that slowing down, and the online resources that accompany each chapter will help deepen your understanding. Ethical decision-making is not learned overnight, and this book is not meant to be a binge read. You will get the most from it if you allow yourself the time and space to intentionally decorate your apartments.

What Role Did Artificial Intelligence Play in My Writing?

AI was used at multiple stages of the research and writing process to aid my own thinking, argumentation, and writing. During the research stage, it was used for compiling reading lists, drafting email outreach, transcribing audio interviews, and finding gaps in my structure. During the writing process, it was used to compile notes into outlines, reword complex sentences into readable prose, and break writer's block by providing temporary paragraphs before I could return to gather my own thoughts. And, in the editing process, it was used to critique the book through different perspectives, suggest areas of refinement and weakness, and improve my grammar and syntax when it detracted from readability.

The interactions with my manuscript were done with APIs from OpenAI and Anthropic that were used to power a custom platform. The platform, and larger process, was built to aid my work without giving up control over my thinking or writing. Screenshots of the platform and details of how it works are available on the book companion site.

This book was inherently a human project both in its creation and its purpose, so great care was taken to ensure the ideas and final expression in the book are my own both in authorship and responsibility.

Why Is the Book General to Education Sometimes and Specific to Educational Technology at Other Times?

There are two primary reasons for this natural occurrence. First, we cannot think about what ethical usage of educational technology is without thinking about what ethics are within the context of education. Without the general theorizing and policymaking, we risk artificially siloing our concerns and arguments to a domain that is one part of a larger set of practices. Second, while I am primarily concerned with technology in my current work, I hope that the urgency and newness of these issues help provoke deeper conversations about our work as educators that improves our institutions far beyond what technology touches, from how we make disciplinary policies to how we design curricula and assessment.

What Resources Exist Beyond the Book?

This book aims to provide a complete framework for ethical ed tech decision-making for practitioners. To keep it accessible and focused, I have moved supplementary materials to an online companion site. There you will find:

- Philosophy guides to further explain and apply the concepts.
- Policy templates, worksheets, and assessment tools.
- Simulations and an AI-powered case discussion tool to accompany each case study.
- Discussion guides for task forces and reading groups.
- Annotated bibliographies for additional reading and a Zotero export of all references.
- Audio recordings from interviews when permission was given.
- Additional case studies (including for higher education, boards of education, students, etc.).
- Regular updates as technology and my thinking evolve.

You can access the book companion site at: ethicaledtech.org. The book is complete without the online materials, but I highly recommend you take advantage of them!

If fear begins this journey, hope sustains it: the hope that thoughtful educators, acting together, can humanize the spaces that shape our students' futures, that we can embrace technology when it serves that end and reject it when it detracts from it, and that we can, together, do right by our students, and so ourselves, as we face the challenges that rapidly come our way.

With that hope,

Priten Soundar-Shah

CHAPTER 1

Our Ethical Imperative

In late 2024, I had the opportunity to present on the topic of AI in education to a group of teachers at the Science Centre Singapore. Afterward, my wife and I stumbled on an exhibit about bioethics as we discussed the receptiveness of the audience to thinking critically about the role of AI in teaching. As a psychiatrist and philosopher duo, we were very excited to venture through the hallway and see our worlds collide. Above all the gizmos and gadgets was a simple sentence that stuck with me: "Just because we can, doesn't mean we should." I glanced over at my wife and saw her knowingly looking back; that short sentence, displayed in big, bold letters, summed up what I was trying to convey during my presentation in big, bold letters.

This tension is one that educators worldwide are experiencing: the gap between technological possibility and educational wisdom. The bioethics exhibit reminded me that similar questions arise whenever powerful new technologies emerge: nuclear energy, genetic engineering, and now, artificial intelligence. In each case, society must confront the fundamental question of how to harness innovation responsibly and not solely because it is possible. Educators in particular have an onerous burden to answer those questions with intentionality as the decisions we make about technology directly shape the young minds of future citizens who go on to build, regulate, and use the technologies of the future.

The last few decades have seen a consistent surge in technological innovation, and with those surges have come new, flashy, and seemingly promising interventions that claim to solve the problems that have plagued education systems across generations and contexts. A lot of times, educators, students, parents, and administrators are attracted both to the novelty and the promise and jump on board the latest technological fad. And of course, there is merit in remaining nimble in our pedagogy and adding to our collection of tools, but there is also merit in pausing and asking ourselves "Why?"

Cycles of Adoption

This cycle of technological adoption in schools follows a familiar pattern. A new technology emerges with promises of transformation. As documented in studies of computers in classrooms, as early adopters embrace it enthusiastically, other schools and districts quickly implement the technology, fearing they might fall behind, often without sufficient planning or critical assessment.[1] Teachers receive minimal training and are expected to integrate it seamlessly. Students become unwitting participants in what amounts to a massive ongoing experiment. Then, before the impacts of this technology can be fully understood, the next innovation arrives, and we enter the cycle again.

We see this pattern continue with interactive whiteboards, learning management systems, tablet initiatives, and now with artificial intelligence. While each new innovation brings genuine possibilities, this potential is paired with exaggerated claims, commercial pressures, and insufficient ethical consideration.

The pace of technological change in education has accelerated dramatically. What once evolved over decades now transforms in months. The COVID-19 pandemic further compressed this timeline and forced schools to adopt remote learning technologies overnight.[2] Now, the rapid growth of artificial intelligence has introduced many of the same problems.[3] This acceleration leaves little time for thoughtful consideration of long-term implications, unintended consequences, or alignment with our core educational values.

Amid this technological acceleration, educators and school leaders find themselves making consequential decisions with incomplete information, minimal guidance, and intense pressure from vendors, parents, students, and policymakers. And, the stakes of these decisions extend far beyond learning outcomes and into the realms of student privacy, equity, well-being, and the fundamental purpose of education.

Before we adapt our classroom instruction to every new technological breakthrough, we ought to spend some time thinking about the "why" so we can answer the other follow-up questions of "what," "how," "when," "where," "who," and "for whom."

In this book, I hope to equip educators and school leaders with the resources to ask those necessary questions with rigor, nuance, and precision. Doing so requires drawing from a robust tradition of asking such questions: philosophy.

Dangers of Speed

At this point, it will be helpful to ask ourselves why engage in this navel-gazing activity? After all, we have real students with acute needs that cannot afford to wait for us to translate thousands of years of philosophy into policies and practice. While it is true that we will trade off expediency with this process, the danger is too much for us to continue operating

---

[1] Cuban, *Oversold and Underused*.
[2] Jacob and Stanojevich, "Rewiring the Classroom."
[3] Furze, *Practical AI Strategies*.

without establishing ethical frameworks that help us minimize the harm. These dangers include threats to:

Student development: Students' use of technology impacts their learning, but along with it, it also affects their identity, agency, and cognitive development. We must ensure our decisions are respecting their autonomy, supporting their well-being, and protecting their sense of self.[4]

Equity: Technology can both aggravate and repair the large gaps we have in our educational systems. We must evaluate our decisions to measure whether we are further exacerbating these problems or making progress toward solving them.[5]

Democracy: As society becomes increasingly reliant on technology, so too do our democratic processes. Public discourse, civic engagement, and entire bureaucratic systems are being reshaped by technology. We must prepare our students to navigate these spaces in ways that protect their civic agency as individuals and our democratic norms as a society.[6]

Economic: While these technologies are infiltrating our schools, they are even more rapidly infiltrating our workspaces. We must shape our curricula knowing that the careers that our students will have available to them when they graduate will be dramatically different from the ones we are preparing them for.[7]

Cultural: Technology also impacts the way our students develop their attention, navigate their relationships, and understand and participate in culture. We must help our students build healthy habits that build positive, fruitful relationships with their peers and society.[8]

Multiple Ends

The dangers are real, and this is further complicated by the unique complexity of ethical challenges in education. Education serves multiple purposes simultaneously: developing autonomy, preparing students for economic participation, fostering civic capabilities, and promoting personal flourishing.[9]

Our decisions in education must be evaluated against this full spectrum of educational aims, not merely academic outcomes or engagement metrics. The autonomy, privacy rights, and

---

[4] Idrees et al., "Associations Between Problem Technology Use, Life Stress, and Self-Esteem Among High School Students"; Dienlin and Johannes, "The Impact of Digital Technology Use on Adolescent Well-Being."
[5] OECD, "Digital Divide in Education"; Moore et al., "The Digital Divide and Educational Equity: A Look at Students with Very Limited Access to Electronic Devices at Home," August 2018.
[6] Noveck, "Artificial Intelligence Can Help Us Create a More Efficient Government"; Noveck, "Digital Mirror to Our Deliberation."
[7] Parker, "U.S. Workers Are More Worried Than Hopeful About Future AI Use in the Workplace"; West, *The Future of Work*.
[8] Laird et al., "Hand in Hand: Schools' Embrace of AI Connected to Increased Risks to Students"; Andoh, "Many Teens Are Turning to AI Chatbots for Friendship and Emotional Support."
[9] Allen, *Education and Equality*; Gutmann, *Democratic Education* Levinson, *The Demands of Liberal Education*; Brighouse, *On Education*; Brighouse et al., *Educational Goods*.

developmental needs of the youth affected differ from adults, and these stakes are unfolding in educational contexts with unique responsibilities and power dynamics. But the challenges of educational technology are even more complex because they also involve rapidly evolving technologies.

Consider just a few of the dilemmas educators face daily:

- ◆ A math department must decide whether to adopt an AI-powered personalized learning platform that promises improved outcomes but requires extensive in-class screen time.
- ◆ A middle school principal must create policies for student-owned smartphones that balance educational use, social development, distraction concerns, and family communication needs.
- ◆ A high school English teacher must determine whether AI writing tools represent a threat to learning or an opportunity for modern instruction.
- ◆ A district technology coordinator must evaluate ed tech products knowing that student data has become a valuable commodity in the digital marketplace.

Each of these dilemmas reveals a common pattern: what initially appears straightforward becomes complex when we consider the full range of stakeholders and outcomes involved. Oftentimes, the answer might seem obvious to us: "Of course, we should use the new tool that students are all raving about," or "We cannot possibly restrict student access to this technology they are already using outside of the school." Other times, we are sold on promises of "revolutionary," "magical," and "engaging" tools that are hard to resist when we feel the pain of the status quo.

However, in not slowing down and asking the right questions, we do a disservice to our students who are often adversely affected by such decisions. But, we also do a disservice to ourselves by expending time and energy on technology that does not truly serve our goals.

What makes these decisions particularly challenging is that they involve genuine tensions between legitimate values, not simple choices between right and wrong. Privacy must be balanced with personalization. Engagement must be weighed against potential distraction. Innovation must be considered alongside equity concerns. Efficiency gains must be evaluated against relationship impacts.

When faced with such complex ethical questions, simplistic approaches prove inadequate. Blanket policies either embracing or rejecting technology fail to address the reality of educational contexts. Purely technical solutions ignore the human and ethical dimensions of technology implementation. Meanwhile, isolated and rushed decision-making overlooks the interconnected nature of our choices.

Schools' Difficult Role

Given these competing legitimate values and complex trade-offs, one might wonder whether ethical deliberation can provide any real guidance, or if we are simply choosing between equally valid options. The answer becomes clear when we consider the unique position schools occupy in society and the profound responsibility they carry.

Schools occupy a unique position of public trust that no other profession quite matches. Doctors treat patients who consent to care, lawyers represent clients who seek their services, and software engineers design products that people can choose to use or ignore. By contrast, teachers and administrators shape the lives of children who are legally required to attend, who are developmentally vulnerable, and who depend on adults to make decisions on their behalf. This is why philosophers are uniquely challenged by questions of ethics that deal with schooling and parenting.

We must balance loyalty to the community (what is good for society) with loyalty to students (what is good for each student). We must make decisions that stand up to public scrutiny, both from community members and parents. And we must make decisions that have long-lasting future consequences based on the limited information we have in the present.

The compulsory relationship means that schools carry responsibilities beyond the individual well-being of each student. They are entrusted with preparing future citizens, transmitting cultural and social values, and balancing competing community expectations. Their choices affect democratic trust, economic opportunity, and social cohesion for generations. This combination of vulnerability, compulsion, and civic responsibility makes the ethical stakes in our schools distinctively important.

This distinctive position of trust and vulnerability intensifies the need for systematic ethical reasoning. It is why ethical paralysis in claiming that if harm is unclear, we might as well act in the name of urgency, ease, or fad, is unacceptable. Our responsibility is far too great and the implications far too long lasting and wide reaching for us to not concern ourselves with maximizing the morality of our decisions.

Diverse Visions

The ethical complexity of educational technology decisions is further complicated by the diverse stakeholders involved, each bringing legitimate but sometimes conflicting perspectives.

Students experience educational technology most directly, yet often have the least formal voice in decisions affecting them. Their perspectives vary dramatically based on age, socioeconomic background, learning needs, and technological access. Some students embrace technology as a means of personalization and engagement; others experience it as surveillance or distraction. Some have 24/7 access to the latest devices; others rely entirely on school-provided technology.

Teachers implement technology in the complex reality of their classrooms. Their professional judgment about pedagogical appropriateness, classroom management implications, and student needs represents crucial expertise. Yet teachers often find themselves caught between administrative mandates, vendor promises, student expectations, and their own teaching philosophies.

School leaders must make system-wide decisions balancing educational goals, budget constraints, technical capabilities, policy requirements, and community expectations. They face pressure to demonstrate innovation while ensuring equitable implementation, data security, and measurable outcomes.

Parents entrust schools with their children's education and development, bringing their own values and concerns to technology decisions. Parental perspectives are informed by their own wide spectrum of technological literacy and access. While many embrace technology's potential to prepare students for future careers, others worry about screen time, privacy, or emotional well-being.

Technology companies create tools that shape the educational experience while operating within commercial incentives that may not perfectly align with educational values. Their expertise in technology development must be balanced against educators' expertise in learning and development.

Policymakers establish the regulatory context for educational technology, often with limited understanding of classroom realities or technological complexities. Their decisions about data privacy, internet access, device funding, and curriculum standards create the framework within which local decisions occur.

Each of these stakeholders brings valid priorities and concerns to the conversation. The challenge is creating decision-making processes that meaningfully incorporate multiple viewpoints while remaining grounded in core educational values.

Thus, in this book, I ask you to slow down with me. Draw on ancient and modern philosophical traditions, think about the policies that can serve as our foundations, and practice the kind of deliberate decision-making that will both safeguard our pedagogical spaces from the dangers of a rapidly evolving technological landscape and bolster them with the advances that stand to benefit our students in ways we may have never imagined in the past.

Philosophy-Policy-Practice

This book is organized into three sections connecting philosophical foundations to daily practice and provides a pathway from philosophical principles to concrete implementation decisions.

PHILOSOPHY: THE FOUNDATION

The philosophical level addresses fundamental questions about values, purposes, and principles. It asks: What matters most in education? What are our non-negotiable commitments? What are we trying to achieve through technology integration? What kind of educational experience do we want for our students?

Without clarity at this foundational level, technology decisions risk being driven by fashion, fear, or false promises rather than educational values. Section A, thus, explores these philosophical foundations, key ethical frameworks, core value commitments, and the historical and ethical context of educational technology that should guide implementation.

When schools lack clarity about these things, technology decisions tend to follow the path of least resistance. This means adopting what is popular, what is marketed most aggressively, or what seems easiest to implement rather than what best serves education's purposes.

POLICY: THE STRUCTURE
The policy level translates philosophical foundations into concrete guidelines, procedures, and commitments. Well-crafted policies can provide guardrails that enable stakeholders to make daily decisions without prescribing universal answers for every situation. As such, they create the structured context for individual decisions, ensuring consistency while allowing appropriate flexibility. Effective policies serve multiple functions: they articulate institutional commitments, establish evaluation criteria, create decision-making processes, delineate responsibilities, and provide guidance for addressing both typical and exceptional situations. Rather than constraining professional judgment, well-designed policies can create the conditions for thoughtful practice.

To this end, Section B examines how to develop policies that remain faithful to philosophical foundations while addressing the practical realities of school environments and current regulatory frameworks. This includes guidelines for evaluating technology tools, approaches to student data and privacy, building a culture of ethical deliberation, and processes for involving all relevant stakeholders in these decisions.

PRACTICE: THE APPLICATION
The practical level involves applying philosophical principles and policy frameworks to specific situations that mirror the daily decisions educators make about technology integration. This is where abstract values and formal policies meet the messy reality of classrooms.

Section C explores this practical level through detailed case studies. Each case examines how principles and policies might guide decisions in specific contexts. These demonstrate that ethical practice requires both fidelity to foundational values and sensitivity to particular circumstances.

This practice strengthens the capacity to recognize what matters ethically in specific situations and determine appropriate action.

Deliberative Ethics
To be clear, this book will not provide definitive answers to every technology question schools might face. Given the pace of technological change and the diversity of educational contexts, such an approach would quickly become obsolete.

Rather, this book seeks to develop our collective capacity for ethical reasoning about technology: the ability to ask important questions, consider multiple perspectives, apply relevant principles, and make thoughtful decisions in specific contexts. The core argument of this book is that ethical technology implementation requires community alignment across three domains: philosophy (what we value), policy (what we commit to), and practice (what we do).

But, my fear with presenting philosophical concepts as deliberation tools rather than didactic rules to follow is that it sends the message that ethics is based on our individual personal whims. In fact, our philosophy, policy, and practice framework makes ethical decision-making more rigorous, not less.[10]

First, it highlights *shared values* that are central to education and schooling. Schools not only have a diversity of stakeholders (parents, students, teachers, administrators, community), but they also have diversity within those groups. Each member of a school's community has their own value systems that define how they approach moral decision-making. They might draw from their cultural history, religious belief, family values, political values, and lived experiences. All of these stakeholders need a shared framework to talk to each other on common grounds about a joint endeavor: educating our children. To help build that common ground, we need to highlight the values that we all have in common when we discuss education.

Second, it provides *shared vocabulary* for us to speak to each other. In this book, I draw from a variety of schools of thoughts and thinkers to provide vocabulary for describing those values. Thus, Section A builds the fluency to talk about the guiding principles, relevant stakeholders, and important stakes that support our decision-making. This allows us to draw from a shared bank of concepts when we think about a course of action; and it begins to build a culture of ethical reflection in education. With that as a starting point, we can all ask ethical questions and shape ethical practices together much more easily.

Third, it centers the importance of *iteration* as we learn new information. Theoretical discussions and guiding principles will only get us so far. We have to test them in the real world and engage in reflective equilibrium to find the balance between our principles and our judgments. This makes the flexibility of our framework, its strength. If we commit too rigidly to concrete rules, we lose the ability to modify them based on our professional experience, group deliberations, and new questions and cases as they arise.

Finally, this approach allows for a process of answering ethical questions as they arise based on *contextual judgments*. With the general frameworks, policies that institutionalize them, and practice applying our principles, we build the knowledge and disposition to approach new situations as they arise. Especially in educational technology, where new ethical challenges seem to arise overnight, we need to be prepared to approach these swiftly and thoughtfully using our shared reasoning methods to balance competing values, justify our choices, and act with integrity even when clear precedents do not yet exist.

An Invitation

The technological landscape of education will continue to evolve in ways we cannot fully predict. New tools will emerge, offering both genuine possibilities and exaggerated promises. The ethical questions will shift in response to technological capabilities, social contexts, and educational priorities. What remains constant is the need for thoughtful engagement with these questions. We must keep asking not just whether we can implement a technology, but whether and how we should.

---

[10] Levinson, "We Need a Field of Educational Ethics"; Habermas, "Justification and Application"; Shapiro and Stefkovich, *Ethical Leadership and Decision Making in Education*; Gutmann, *Democratic Education*.

I invite you to approach this journey with both critical thinking and open-minded exploration. The ethical questions surrounding educational technology have no perfect answers, but we can thoughtfully approach the decisions in ways that respect the complexity of the issues and remain faithful to core educational values. My hope is that this book serves as a starting point for ongoing reflection, conversation, and action as we navigate the technological transformation impacting education together.

The bioethics exhibit that I started this chapter with offered wisdom that applies equally to educational technology: "Just because we can, doesn't mean we should." While I encourage critical reflection on technological integration, I do not argue that we ought not to integrate educational technology. In fact, I hope we can realize some of our largest goals of education by using these tools intentionally. The path forward lies not in wholesale adoption or rejection of technology, but in thoughtful integration guided by pedagogical priorities and human values. So perhaps we might also add: "Just because we haven't, doesn't mean we shouldn't." It is to that worthy challenge that this book is dedicated.

Exit Ticket

Reflect: Can you identify a technology your school adopted enthusiastically but later abandoned? What questions might have prevented this cycle?

Act: Identify one upcoming technology decision. Prepare three questions you might share with your colleagues, drawing from this chapter's argument.

Advocate: How could your school make more room for ethical reflection before major technology adoptions?

SECTION A

Philosophy

Before we approach what commitments we make (our policies) and how we make daily decisions (our practice), we must clarify, both for ourselves and our community, what our philosophical foundations are.

In this section I provide a crash course on thinking about the ethics of educational technology. While I draw extensively from academic philosophy, the goal here is not to provide an academic background in philosophy or ethics, but to outline the most useful theories, frameworks, and approaches that might help us make decisions in the real world.

To that end, in Chapter 2, I start by explaining the field of educational ethics. I explain what it means to think systematically about ethics in education and why it is necessary. Here, I answer questions such as: What makes a problem an ethical one? How can we approach ethics in education without universal rules and "right" answers? And, what are the overarching questions we are trying to answer by using philosophical thinking? I end the chapter by explaining why and how we approach this with case-based ethical reasoning.

Then, I draw upon academic philosophy to develop the vocabulary to define our: principles (what values?), stakeholders (who's affected?), stakes (what goals?), and heuristics (how to weigh?).

In Chapter 3, I build an ethical reasoning framework we adapt from bioethics, which defines a set of principles for approaching these cases.

In Chapter 4, I contextualize how to use this framework by drawing from multiple approaches to ethics. This helps us consider how the principles introduced apply in practice when there are conflicts.

In Chapter 5, I break down who we are trying to act ethically toward by using our framework. Now that we can ask if an action is ethical, for whom do we want to act ethically?

In Chapter 6, I raise the question of what ends we are aiming for. What do we owe students, teachers, parents, and the community that we are trying to prioritize in this decision-making process?

In Chapter 7, I provide ethical reasoning heuristics that help us navigate conflicts that emerge between various stakes and stakeholders. While no single heuristic can resolve the conflict, they help form the right habitus to deliberate on them.

Then, after we have built our general framework, we turn to the specific concerns of educational technology, such as its history, major themes, and inherent risks.

In Chapter 8, we start with a development that shaped modern education, the printing press, and then move on to personal computers and the internet. Next, I discuss some of the powerful developments that current day educators are grappling with, including cellphones, social media, and AI. Finally, I discuss some of the rapidly approaching developments that we should be prepared for from more advanced AIs and virtual reality to the growing use of biometrics and fringe developments like blockchain and the metaverse.

In Chapter 9, I dissect concepts that are typically framed as values for *educational technology*, including innovation, privacy, data, efficiency, standardization, access, and personalization in ethical decision-making, but raise deeper questions about our values for *education*.

In Chapter 10, I cover the inherent risks of introducing and using technology. This chapter explores the impact of technology beyond how educators decide to use it. We cover topics like bias, environmental risks, the black box effect, and job displacement. While we can often do little to directly mitigate these risks, we should weigh them in our ethical analysis when deciding to adopt technological solutions.

After we have built our framework and seen how it applies to educational technology, we are prepared to move onto thinking about how to apply it in our policy and practice.

CHAPTER 2

Educational Ethics

Everyone working in education, from administrators and principals to teachers and support staff, constantly makes decisions that have enormous ethical implications. Despite this, educational institutions rarely systematically think about ethics and ethical decision-making the way other fields like medicine and law do.[1] Scholars have recently begun to address this gap. For example, Meira Levinson has spent the last decade advocating for and advancing a field of educational ethics in order to help move education in the direction of these other disciplines.[2]

This does not mean no one in education thinks about ethics. In fact, most educators ask ethical questions of themselves and their peers all the time:

- Is it right for us to punish this student for tardiness when we know their family situation?
- Should we keep our schools open for students to attend in-person during a global pandemic?
- What is the point of teaching this material when students might not use it in their careers?
- Is this student conduct policy fair to all of our students?
- Did we make budget decisions in a way that reflects our values as a school and community?

These are just some questions that have likely come up at most schools across the world, all of which are ethical questions about why and how we should act toward our students. The problem, then, is not that we are not asking any right questions, but that we do not have a systematic, shared way of approaching these questions.

In other fields such systems are standard practice. Hospitals have institutional review boards and ethics committees. Courts have judicial ethics advisors and bar association ethics counsels.

---

[1] Levinson, "We Need a Field of Educational Ethics."
[2] Levinson, "Theorizing Educational Justice"; Levinson, "We Need a Field of Educational Ethics"; Levinson and Fay, *Dilemmas of Educational Ethics*.

Even technology companies are beginning to formally introduce ethical decision-making within their companies through Chief Ethics Officers and corporate social responsibility departments. These professional positions are also backed up by academic fields that study ethics: bioethics, legal ethics, and science & technology studies.

Education, however, has traditionally left both the practice of and study of these decisions to individuals. Without a formal field of educational ethics or educational ethicists to help inform everyday practice, the onus falls on individual leaders and educators to think intentionally about these questions.[3]

A second problem also appears. No universal rule fits every case. Individual circumstances quickly make any rule feel arbitrary, and multiple principles might give conflicting answers. Thus, we need not a rulebook on the "right decision," but instead a system for thinking about these questions in deliberate and intentional ways. For individuals working within education, this requires building the skills and dispositions to ask ethical questions and apply clear frameworks in real contexts. For schools, this means developing a clear process that respects facts, weighs values, and produces defensible judgments.[4] This book explores case-based reasoning as a way to help create that process to help educators and leaders build practical judgment by working through real decisions together.

Guiding Questions
- Which types of questions require ethical reasoning?
- Why do we need a deliberative framework over a set of rules?
- What commitments do we need in order for this approach to work?
- How do we use cases and particular judgments to shape our framework?

Tragic Choices

Before we can build a systematic approach, we must separate which questions actually require deep ethical reasoning and which do not.

Some questions may seem like ethical considerations at first glance but are more accurately compliance questions. For example, when we are asking "Does this decision meet this agreed upon standard?" we are evaluating whether the decision is right or wrong according to some previously established policy, not whether the decision is right or wrong *ethically*. However, the question of whether or not we should adhere to a particular policy is an ethical one, because now we are asking a more fundamental question of what is right or wrong. Questions of compliance require a very different set of skills from questions of ethics.

There are also questions that are ethically settled, but do not require extensive ethical reasoning. When the question of right or wrong does not involve a trade-off between competing values we can arrive at an ethical decision much more quickly. For example, if we ask, "Should

---

[3] Levinson, "We Need a Field of Educational Ethics"; Levinson and Fay, *Dilemmas of Educational Ethics*.
[4] Levinson, "We Need a Field of Educational Ethics"; Levinson and Fay, *Dilemmas of Educational Ethics*; Brighouse et al., *Educational Goods*; Brighouse et al., "Good Education Policy Making."

students be allowed to play video games on their VR headset for the entire day," the question, while being one of ethics by asking what someone *should* do, might not be complex enough to require reasoned deliberation.

So, not all questions in schools call for deep ethical reasoning, and we must distinguish between routine compliance, straightforward ethics, and genuinely complex dilemmas.

What, then, are some criteria that signal an ethically complex question?

- There are multiple values at stake (e.g., educational outcomes, privacy, student well-being, parental consent).
- There are resource constraints that limit our decisions (e.g., budgetary restrictions, limited instructional time, student resource access).
- There are power asymmetries that affect the outcomes (e.g., students versus teachers, parents versus institutions, wealthy versus poor districts).
- There is uncertainty about the outcome (e.g., nonexistent or unclear data, unknown variables, long timeframe).

A common thread among these signals is that there will likely be some form of harm we have to accept in each of the cases (e.g., leaving our students underprepared for new innovations or jumping too quickly on new technology, providing resources to one set of students at the expense of another, listening to parents' requests on curricula while not teaching our students core content). These are decisions that involve what legal theorists term tragic choices.[5] Our goal in these decisions is not to avoid tragedy altogether but minimize it through compromise.

To quickly identify these situations, we can focus on five key considerations. These questions can reveal hidden complexities in seemingly routine choices.

You should ask yourself, "By making this decision":

- Impacts: Who gains and loses and by how much?
- Values: Which values are being promoted and which ones lost?
- Stakeholders: Which stakeholders will accept the decision, and which ones will reject it?
- Evidence: What evidence am I using and is it enough?
- Future: What precedents am I setting for the future?

Practical Wisdom

Upon identifying a tragic choice, we need a way of reasoning that matches the weight and complexity of these situations. People sometimes come to ethics expecting either clear rules ("never do X") or research-based best practices ("studies show Y works"). But, when facing educational dilemmas, we need more than principles. We need to see all the relevant factors,

---

[5] Calabresi and Bobbitt, *Tragic Choices*.

weigh competing goods, and act decisively while remaining humble about our fallibility. We need to answer questions that are so tied to particular contexts (this student, this community, this moment) that abstract rules alone will not suffice.

Here, relying on Aristotle helps us conceptualize what ethics is if it's not rules or best practices.[6] He split knowledge into different categories, one of which is phronēsis, or practical wisdom that adapts judgments to context without abandoning values.[7] This means holding firm commitments while remaining open to new information, maintaining consistency while recognizing unique circumstances, and acting decisively while acknowledging fallibility. When a teacher relies on her *judgment* on when to bend a deadline and when to hold firm, she demonstrates a capacity that transcends both rulebook adherence and pedagogical technique.

Aristotle argues that because general principles cannot account for all relevant factors, ethics requires us to apply our own discernment that we must acquire through practice. So, unlike learning content through reading, phronēsis develops through what Aristotle calls "habituation," or gradually developing better judgment by repeatedly making decisions and reflecting on outcomes.[8]

Practice allows us to develop the intuitive awareness of relevant factors and the mental dispositions to ask the right questions. This ensures that we are nimble and flexible in our ethical decision-making, both now and in the future.

Practical wisdom, rather than rules, is also important because ethical decision-making in education occurs within systems that perpetuate existing inequalities. Our reasoning must, thus, grapple with how individual choices either reinforce or disrupt these patterns. The teacher who bends deadlines to account for students' unequal access to technology is not being "flexible" in a simplistic connotation of the word, they are making decisions about justice, equity, and the purpose of assessment itself.

Shared Commitments

The risk of this approach is that we might drift into ethical paralysis, thinking that since there is no universal answer, we cannot effectively think about the ethics of our actions at all. To avoid this, educators need shared commitments that anchor their reasoning process.

Generally, by being a part of a social system and community, we all agree on some shared commitments. Sometimes these are explicit in the forms of policies and mission statements, and other times they are implicit in the form of micro-decisions and cultural norms. Schools are no different. No matter how much one wants to depoliticize education and claim independence from any belief system, there are always underlying values that govern decision-making.

In the following chapters, I will attempt to highlight the shared values that I think both might and ought to underlie our education system. In doing so, I hope to create a basis for our understanding of our shared commitments that we can use in approaching our ethical decision-making.

---

[6] Levinson and Fay, *Dilemmas of Educational Ethics*.
[7] Kraut, "Aristotle's Ethics."
[8] Ibid.

After that, we can interrogate when our reasoning is based on these shared reasons and values, and when it is drifting from norms that are essential to a healthy school community.

Our shared commitments are not just what we value in education. We should also agree to norms of reasoning that will ensure that our decision-making process itself is clear. Here are some starting commitments, drawing from academic philosophy, which guide this project for me, and I believe ought to guide our ethical reasoning as a community:

Intellectual Humility: We must accept that we do not know all relevant information and actively seek out opposing viewpoints and contrary evidence.

Transparency: We must share how we arrive at our decisions with each other to build accountability and trust in our institutions.

Emotional Weighing: We must be honest about when our emotions would distract from reasoning or when it should inform it.

Error Correction: We must commit to quickly fixing our mistakes when new information or evidence arrives.

These commitments, and much of the book, draws heavily on Western philosophical thought, but ethical deliberation does not have to be confined to Eurocentric commitments and values. Schools around the world operate within their own rich moral traditions that might emphasize different parts of the framework or draw upon different commitments altogether.

The goal of this book is not to prescribe one universal moral code, but to provide a structure for shared reasoning that can accommodate diverse value systems. Communities may choose to reinterpret these through their own cultural lenses and context. The framework organizes dialogue, clarifies trade-offs, and supports transparent decision-making. In this sense, the shared commitments that anchor ethical reflection can come from any moral tradition. What matters is not which tradition we invoke, but that our reasoning rests on values we can articulate publicly, deliberate collectively, and justify to the communities we serve.

If we hold on to these commitments from our own context and communities, we can successfully approach these ethical questions with the right amount of adaptability and accountability to act ethically.

Case Study Method

In order to build practical knowledge, we need to have enough exposure to and practice with the kinds of relevant dilemmas that we might encounter in our classrooms.

Similar to the case-based method used in other professional fields (medicine, law, and business), we can use case studies that place us in realistic situations to develop and strengthen our ethical reasoning abilities. By examining realistic scenarios from multiple perspectives, readers develop insight into different stakeholder concerns and can carry them to new situations. By reasoning through cases that have no perfect solutions, readers can build comfort with the inherent tensions of ethical decision-making. And by thinking about detailed contexts rather than abstract principles, readers can develop the insight that bridges theory and practice.[9]

The case studies in this book were developed through conversations with educators, technologists, and students facing real ethical dilemmas in educational technology. While fictionalized to protect privacy and enable optimal learning, each case is grounded in authentic challenges schools face daily.[10] The cases were selected and crafted to highlight the most pressing ethical tensions across critical domains of educational technology: learning, assessment, safety, and policies.

The case studies in this book are chosen to help educators and leaders practice asking and answering ethical questions through narrative descriptions. They all contain a normative problem, a problem of what someone ought to do, and have no one correct answer. Depending on how we each weigh competing values, our own context, experience, and the policies that constrain our decisions, we might arrive at very different decisions. The goal, then, is to develop the skillset by which we come to these decisions, so that we can effectively consider the ethical values and principles and use them with fidelity in our schools.

Approaching Practice

The most valuable approach to these case studies is to resist the impulse to immediately identify the "right answer" and instead map the full ethical landscape of each scenario. This involves identifying all stakeholders and their interests, recognizing the values and principles at stake, considering all the factors that shape the situation, and exploring multiple potential approaches before forming judgments.

While individual reflection on these cases provides valuable practice in ethical reasoning, the cases are particularly powerful when discussed with colleagues. Collective engagement reveals different perspectives, challenges assumptions, and builds shared understanding, all of which help lay the groundwork for collaborative ethical decision-making in schools.[11]

In order to use the practice of these cases to form policies and inform our shared commitments, we will use a process John Rawls called "reflective equilibrium."[12] This involves moving between particular considered judgments, general principles, background theory, and empirical evidence until we reach a coherent, mutually-supporting position that balances all of those.

For example, we might think that every student must take the same tests under the same constraints for fairness. As such, we form the following principle: equality of testing environments is fair. However, in class we meet a student with dyslexia who needs adapted tests and extra time to demonstrate competency.

---

[9] Levinson and Fay, *Dilemmas of Educational Ethics*; Ta et al., "'The Power of Open Dialogue'"; Aamodt and Plaza, "Case-Based Reasoning"; Jonsen and Toulmin, *The Abuse of Casuistry*; Robeson and King, "Performable Case Studies in Ethics Education"; Thiel et al., "Case-Based Knowledge and Ethics Education."
[10] Geron and Levinson, "The Ethics of World-Building in Normative Case Studies."
[11] Ta et al., "'The Power of Open Dialogue.'"
[12] Rawls, *A Theory of Justice*.

Many educators would judge that the basic principle fails this student, so we must find ways to be more considerate of individual circumstances. Rather than treat it as a rigid rule, we should let our considered judgment about this case count as evidence that our principles need revision. We can also consult background theory on justice, equality of opportunity, and disability rights, empirical evidence from cognitive science, special education, and assessment research, and the relevant legal standards.

These sources give us the context to ask sharper questions: Are we thinking about fairness correctly? What duties do we have to students who have special learning needs? Answering them informs how we can modify our general principles or align our judgment with our principles.

This might lead us to a coherent, mutually supporting position that we should give students with disabilities extra time to work on their assignments.

This process of going back and forth between particular judgments, cases, theory, evidence, and our principles helps us refine our principles to serve us until they do not. The goal is to continue to develop a set of shared principles and values that fit the facts we face yet stay flexible enough for further revision.

The case studies in this book will help you go through this process for yourselves, and the resulting discussions will help us reform our shared commitments as a community.

A Path Forward

When we commit to engage in systematic ethical reasoning, we are developing the capacity to navigate inherent tensions between immediate pressures and long-term consequences, between individual student needs and institutional constraints, between personal values and systemic forces that may perpetuate inequality.

The teacher who learns to identify when a disciplinary policy reflects broader patterns of racial bias, or the administrator who recognizes how budget decisions today will shape educational opportunities for decades, is not engaging in an abstract philosophical exercise but in the essential work of moral professional practice. Thus, I start with philosophy not to armchair theorize, but to help inform how we carry out our fiduciary duties to our students and our communities with fidelity.

There are many implementation challenges to relying on philosophical reasoning in practice, ranging from time constraints and hierarchical structures to resource scarcity. While I address these throughout the book, especially in Section A and the concluding chapter, we should also recognize that they are precisely the conditions that make such reasoning necessary by creating injustices. In a profession where every decision dominoes through multiple lives and generations, the focus must be on prioritizing this ethical reasoning. We cannot afford the risk of additional harm from a rushed decision.

This cultivation of practical wisdom through deliberate practice with complex cases offers us a path toward more coherent, defensible, and ultimately more effective educational leadership. It honors both the weight of educational responsibility and the irreducible complexity of the contexts in which we must exercise that responsibility. To do so, we must build out the vocabulary to reason and deliberate effectively.

Exit Ticket

Reflect: Choose one decision you have faced or observed recently. Identify the ethical problem. Who was impacted? What did they gain or lose? What values were in conflict? Which stakeholders had different perspectives?

Act: Based on your reflection, identify one specific action you could take. What would you do differently? What evidence would you need to gather first?

Advocate: How would you explain your decision to someone who disagrees? What precedent would you want to set for others facing similar situations?

CHAPTER 3

Ethical Principles

In Chapter 2, I highlighted the need for shared systems and values that shape how we think about ethical decision-making in education. In this chapter, I start building the framework for discussing ethical questions in a systematic way. Here, I discuss principles and theories that will provide us with vocabulary to define exactly which things are of ethical value to us.

Even without a framework, we make decisions on these dilemmas every day. We decide whether to suspend a student, adopt new technology, or reallocate resources. Yet, too often, rapid instinct, habit, or compliance with policy guides these choices. Instead, a framework can move us from instinct and private judgment to deliberation and public reasoning. It shifts the burden from the vague notion of making right decisions to a more concrete idea of the right *process* for making these decisions.

One field that has built this already is medicine. Bioethics was formed to guide how medical professionals exert their authority responsibly over vulnerable patients. Within bioethics, one framework that emerged early on to accommodate the contextual flexibility was principlism.[1] Principlism centers on four principles: beneficence, non-maleficence, autonomy, and justice. Throughout our discussions, these will serve as lenses that reveal ethical tensions we might otherwise miss. The goal is not for them to function as a checklist to memorize, but rather, a set of tools to guide our reflection.

While principlism was designed for healthcare, the challenge it addresses is not unique to medical professionals. Educators, too, make decisions in unpredictable situations that affect the lives of those who depend on them. Because of this overlap, I borrow their framework as a starting point, though not as a full transplant.

After introducing principlism, I introduce a fifth principle to our framework: care, which I will argue is necessary for educational ethics, because of education's inherently relational nature.

Bringing in multiple principles always risks relativism, or sending the message that every choice is equally valid depending on whom you ask. But the aim here is to sharpen our

---

[1] Beauchamp and Childress, *Principles of Biomedical Ethics*.

judgment and understand the ethical tensions. Each lens has strengths and weaknesses, and by comparing across them, we can gain a fuller picture of ethical concerns and values. Thus, I offer a pluralist framework to build a disciplined practice of approaching these decisions.

By the end of this chapter, you will have a set of principles to ask sharper questions, to see tensions more clearly, and to make choices that are both thoughtful and defensible.

Guiding Questions
- What principles should guide how we approach ethical decision-making?
- How can we use the five principles to examine what ethical dilemmas we face?
- What are common tensions that might appear among our principles?

Building the Five Principles

Beauchamp and Childress presented four principles for medical ethics: beneficence, non-maleficence, autonomy, and justice.[2] There are three features that make principlism a good starting point for our framework.

First, both frameworks involve asymmetric power relationships where one group has authority over a vulnerable population that cannot exit the relationship easily. In most cases, patients must rely on medical care and students must attend school. Second, they both require balancing multiple goods that cannot be easily reduced to a single metric, though bioethicists have tried.[3] For example, in medicine there is longevity and quality of life, and in education, we care about current safety and long-term happiness.

Finally, there is the practical overlap that both fields involve making decisions in a variety of different contexts, with a high degree of uncertainty, and with many, rapidly moving factors. Medicine has to make decisions that are specific to a particular patient's medical history and current diagnosis, and education has to cater to individual students with a variety of lived experiences, learning needs, and family backgrounds. This overlap in the complexity of challenges makes principlism an appealing starting point.

However, there are also major differences that we have to account for. Education involves multiple stakeholders at all times; we must account for students, parents, society, and policymakers, because they all have valid stakes in educational outcomes. Also, students might be developing capacities for very different outcomes based on their idea of a "good life," and what that capacity looks like is very different for each individual. Whereas in medicine, there are some objective markers of health (e.g., blood pressure, heart rates, and brain functioning). To account for this, I incorporate stakeholder involvement in Chapter 5 and a discussion of the different capacities and stakes in Chapter 6.

There are also the length and impact of our relationships. Nearly all educator–student relationships are longer both in total time spent and in total length of the relationship than ones

---

[2] Ibid.
[3] Neumann, "The Death of QALYs Is Greatly Exaggerated–Center for the Evaluation of Value and Risk in Health"; Weinstein and Stason, "Foundations of Cost-Effectiveness Analysis for Health and Medical Practices."

shared by a patient and doctor. And, beyond individual relationships, students certainly spend more time in educational settings than most patients do in medical settings. Each relationship a student has with an educator plays a formative role in the development of a child.[4] To help us distinguish these, we add "care" from Noddings's work on the need for an ethics of relationships, especially in education.[5] Without care as a central principle, we risk treating educational relationships as neutral channels for delivering benefits and avoiding harms, rather than as goods in themselves.

Noddings argued that we should center care as the only form of ethics in education, both for making the ethical decisions ourselves and for helping our students become caring individuals.[6] Here, I incorporate it as a primary principle amongst many to ensure that we have the shared framework and vocabulary to discuss the varied values that educators themselves hold.

Together, these principles will provide us with a starting point for evaluating educational decisions. We will use them as a series of lenses that help us think about our decisions to figure out *what* core tension between values we need to resolve.

First, we will use the principle of **beneficence** to ask, "Are we doing something good for someone?" Our goal here is to make sure our action benefits someone, either by promoting good or preventing harm.

Second, we will turn to **non-maleficence** to ask, "Are we harming anyone?" We will aim to avoid causing harm needlessly and to think about the potential ways our actions might hurt someone.

Third, we apply **autonomy** and ask, "Are we respecting everyone's agency?" We want to use our authority ethically, especially with vulnerable populations, and protect the freedom to make your own informed choices about your life.

Then, we think about **care** and ask, "Are we maintaining and strengthening our relationships?" We consider whether we are truly listening to and understanding the needs of those affected, responding with genuine concern, and nurturing the relational bonds that make education meaningful.

Finally, we aim for **justice** by asking, "Is what we are doing fair?" We will consider whether the allocation of costs, benefits, and risks is just.

In an ideal world, every decision we make would have five quick answers. Yes, we are benefitting someone. No, we are not hurting anyone. Yes, we are respecting everyone's agency. Yes, we are attending to relationships with care. Yes, what we are doing is fair.

Unfortunately, the most interesting decisions, and the ones that need the kind of thinking this book calls for, will not be so simple. Instead, the decisions will require us to balance these

---

[4] Wentzel et al., "Social Supports from Teachers and Peers as Predictors of Academic and Social Motivation"; Skipper and Douglas, "The Influence of Teacher Feedback on Children's Perceptions of Student–Teacher Relationships"; Rucinski et al., "Teacher–Child Relationships, Classroom Climate, and Children's Social–Emotional and Academic Development."; Birch and Ladd, "The Teacher-Child Relationship and Children's Early School Adjustment"; Abry et al., "Are All Program Elements Created Equal?"

[5] Noddings, *Caring*; Noddings, "An Ethic of Caring and Its Implications for Instructional Arrangements."

[6] Bioethicists, especially feminist philosophers, have also critiqued principlism for not accounting for relational ethics, specifically as related to autonomy. Sherwin and Stockdale, "WHITHER BIOETHICS NOW? THE PROMISE OF RELATIONAL THEORY"; Gary, "Relational Approaches in Bioethics"; Gilligan, *In a Different Voice*.

principles against each other. For example, what happens if a decision we make both helps and harms someone? What if it helps one person and harms another? What if it helps someone, but they are not the ones who need our help?

The advantage, and disadvantage, of this framework is that it does not claim a hierarchy between these principles. We cannot rely on following algorithmic rules like "non-maleficence doesn't matter if there is beneficence." Instead, the goal is to maximize all five principles. And to do this, we will have to figure out when we are willing to sacrifice some aspect of one principle for gains in another.

Another advantage, and disadvantage, is that it allows us the flexibility to adhere to these principles based on how we define our values. We can choose how we define good, agency, harm, care, and fairness, and iteratively adapt it based on our reflections and deliberations. But it also might lead to confusion if we do not come to shared understanding of the values that underpin those principles.

Before thinking about those values in the following chapters, I will break down how we will use them in our decision-making principles.

Beneficence

We start by asking if our decision will benefit someone. After all, why would we do something if no one benefited? When evaluating benefits, we need to think about the following things.

Definition: In education, defining a "benefit" is complex. Education exists to create goods that students cannot easily secure alone. But, there are various perspectives on how to define those goods, including academic achievement, emotional well-being, college readiness, and civic preparation.[7]

Internal Trade-Offs: Even if it is a combination of goods, we might still have conflicts. A decision that maximizes academic achievement might undermine social development and what prepares students for economic success might not prepare them for democratic participation.[8]

Temporal Factor: We also need to think about whether the benefit is now or later. There are situations in which we defer benefits to the students as children so that they benefit as adults. For example, we do not allow students to experience the joy of playing outside all day, because structured learning during childhood will allow them to pursue a fulfilling life as adults. At the same time, we do want to also ensure that children are enjoying some of the goods of childhood and experiencing the joy, curiosity, and freedom that being a child brings.[9]

---

[7] Brighouse, *On Education*; Brighouse et al., *Educational Goods* Dewey, *Democracy and Education - An Introduction to the Philosophy of Education*; OECD, "Public Returns from Education"; Levinson, *The Demands of Liberal Education*; Nussbaum, "Education and Democratic Citizenship."

[8] Allen, *Education and Equality*; Gutmann, *Democratic Education*; Levinson, *The Demands of Liberal Education*; Brighouse, *On Education*; Brighouse et al., *Educational Goods*.

[9] Brighouse et al., *Educational Goods*.

Ethical Principles

Measuring: Unfortunately, we have yet to distill all the benefits we want in education to a single metric, so we have to consider how to measure the benefits and what serves as evidence of it. That might be quantitative evidence and measurements or qualitative evidence and narratives.[10]

Subject: We also want to think about who benefits. We have to weigh the benefits to students, parents, our communities, and our teachers against each other.

Because these questions all rely on value judgments about who matters and what the aims of education are, we cannot answer them without further defining our values, which we will discuss in Chapters 4 and 5. For now we will simply carry "doing good" as the lens and postpone a precise definition of what good is to later chapters. The temporary vagueness here is intentional. It gives us room to understand where values matter before we decide which values to endorse.

Non-Maleficence

Harm appears deceptively more straightforward to define than benefit. However, when we start to break down our decisions, we notice that education involves a lot of "productive struggle"[11] Education would be very different without the discomfort of intellectual challenges, social friction, and confronting failures. Yet, schools can do real harm through policy, process, or technology even when intentions are good.

Then, to truly think about the kind of harm we want to avoid, we have to distinguish between productive distress and real dangers. We can think of destructive harms in roughly four categories.

Psychological harms affect mental health (e.g., if a new technological tool causes loneliness or anxiety).

Reputational harms affect social standing (e.g., a behavior chart displayed publicly that causes embarrassment).

Physical harms cause bodily injury (e.g., a virtual-reality headset causes motion sickness).

Opportunity harms limit what someone can do (e.g., a predictive algorithm puts students into lower-level classes and reduces their access to advanced coursework).

A lot of the same questions raised when asking about benefit are relevant to our discussion of harm. Who is being harmed? When? What if there are conflicts among harms? What if we harm one person? What if we harm a whole group? What if the harm is on a marginalized group? Here again, we will carry "do no harm" as a guiding principle and return to these unresolved issues in later chapters. For now, the point is to notice where harms may occur, even before we settle on a final account of which harms matter most.

Autonomy

Educating children almost always restricts autonomy in some way. That is for good reasons but introduces complexities.

---

[10] Beach, "Why We Can't Measure What Matters Most in Education."
[11] Sparks, "What Teachers Get Wrong About 'Productive Failure'—and How to Get It Right."

Developmental: If we allow a kindergartener full autonomy to decide how they spend their day, they might not always make decisions that are in their best interest. By the same token, we would hesitate to dictate exactly which classes a senior in high school takes and which books they read. So, respecting autonomy is different at different levels of development.

Subjects: We also want to consider the autonomy of families, parents, and teachers. If we decide autonomy is important for these groups, we must clarify what it means to respect it. We also want to define what informed consent looks like and how we will judge capacity.

Objects: The next consideration is autonomy over *what* matters. Letting that kindergartner choose which book to read from the library is very different than letting them choose whether to learn to read or not.

Growth: And, within education, we want to think not only about their current autonomy, but also their future autonomy. As we will discuss further in Chapter 6, autonomy is an important goal of education. Thus, if our actions limit our students' abilities to be autonomous later, that, too, should be a factor in ethical decision-making.[12]

One distinction that will help as we continue is the difference between positive and negative autonomy.[13] **Negative** autonomy is when we avoid directly restricting someone's choice. When we prevent them from doing something (i.e., limit the decisions they are allowed to make), we sacrifice negative autonomy.

Positive autonomy, on the other hand, is when we actively help someone develop and exercise their choice. When we offer guidance and resources that help someone understand all their options and the implications of those options, we are promoting this type of autonomy.

As we use these different lenses, we will want to consider which type, if any, is more important than the other. In practice, educational decisions almost always blend these two forms of autonomy: we limit some choices in order to build the capacities that will expand students' meaningful choices later.[14]

Care

In our framework, care helps us ask how our decisions shape the quality of relationships in educational spaces.[15] We are not only asking if we do good or avoid harm, but whether we are attending to, sustaining, and strengthening the relationships that make that good possible at all.

---

[12] Brighouse, *On Education*.

[13] Berlin, *Four essays on liberty*.

[14] This is not exactly how Berlin frames his argument, but I do borrow from him the types of liberties. His distinction offers a helpful way of distinguishing between removing constraints on student choice and building the capacities that make meaningful choice possible.

[15] Using Care as a principle is complicated for two reasons. First, Noddings specifically wants to avoid reducing ethics to a checklist approach. I believe that the way I have advocated for building a vocabulary of deliberation through these principles rather than a singular approach to questions hopefully brings it closer to her argument. Second, care ethics is normally used as an alternative to other ethical traditions (the ones that appear in Chapter 4), but for my purposes here, Care works more effectively as a principle than as an ethical approach. The framework in Chapter 3 is designed to identify categories of ethical concern rather than to present complete moral theories. Care fills a conceptual gap the four bioethical principles leave open by drawing attention to the relational dimensions of education, which are central to how educational goods are created and distributed. Positioning care as a principle preserves the pluralist structure of the framework and ensures relational concerns are considered alongside beneficence, harm, autonomy, and justice.

In schools, caring relationships are not only instrumental to learning outcomes but also intrinsic goods that shape students' moral and emotional development.

Relationships: The ethics of care provides a relational approach to ethics that emphasizes the importance of caring relationships and the moral obligations that arise from these connections. This theory challenges the traditional ethical focus on universal principles and abstract reasoning, proposing instead that ethical actions stem from attentive, responsive care for another individual. We consider how our decisions affect trust, respect, and a sense of being known by someone else between students, teachers, and families.

Holistic: In educational settings, this means prioritizing the development of empathetic, nurturing relationships between educators and students. The application of care ethics in education involves recognizing the unique needs, circumstances, and potential of each student, and responding in a manner that supports their holistic well-being and growth. We want to recognize the student as a whole person with emotional, social, and academic needs, not reduce them to performance or outcomes.

Caregiving: Care ethics encourages us to view our role as caregivers playing a crucial role in their students' emotional and moral development. It prompts us to consider how our actions, curriculum choices, and interaction styles affect the student-teacher relationship and the overall culture of care within the classroom. Thus, we do not only want to act as an evaluator and information deliverer, but also as a caregiver who is responsive to students' vulnerabilities and needs.

By fostering an environment where students feel valued, understood, and supported, we can help students develop the confidence, empathy, and ethical sensibility needed to navigate their own relationships and moral dilemmas.

Of note is that when relational caregiving does happen in educational contexts, it is often done by women, and the framework's call for centering care ought to be a shared obligation. This is because of structural expectations within schools, not because the work itself is inherently gendered.[16]

In our framework, we will use the principle of care to center the students' relationship both with each other and with their educators, and what our decisions might do to benefit or harm them.

Justice

Thinking about justice requires us to zoom out. We consider the larger implications of our decision and how it fits into other decisions we and others have made. We evaluate the fairness in who gets costs and benefits, at what time, and by what process.

What is fair is not an easy question to answer for education. Is providing an advantage to one person knowing someone else does not have it fair? Is it fair to prioritize a certain group over another? What do we do when our decisions keep adding up against one group or even person?

---

[16] Olson et al., "Gendered Emotion Management and Teacher Outcomes in Secondary School Teaching."

To think comprehensively about justice, we need to examine it from various dimensions. We want to distribute our resources (money, time, care) in the fairest ways. We want our procedures for how we make decisions to be fair. We want to recognize everyone and value them fairly. We want to repair the harms we have caused before. We want to transform our systems and practices to make them fairer over time.

This gives us dimensions to evaluate fairness, but not definitions of fairness itself. I use fair here because it avoids committing us to a particular definition of justice too quickly. Fairness, for example, could require equality and the same treatment for everyone or equity and distribution based on need. It might be a combination of both. We also want to think about who we are being fair to. At what level are we asking the questions of fairness? Is it within our classroom, our school, our community, or our nation's history?

As with benefit and harm, this deliberate openness is a feature. It allows us to use fairness as a prompt for reflection while we build a more detailed account of justice in Chapter 6.

Tensions

The situations that will require the use of these principles will almost always be ones where there is tension between at least two of these principles.

> **Beneficence & Non-Maleficence:** When we try to achieve something good, but we risk some form of harm by doing so.
>
> **Beneficence & Autonomy:** When we know some action will produce good outcomes for a stakeholder, but doing so would require going against their will.
>
> **Beneficence & Justice:** When we are producing some good, but only for some individuals.
>
> **Beneficence & Care:** When acting for a stakeholder's long-term good requires doing something that strains or weakens the relationship in the short term.
>
> **Non-Maleficence & Autonomy:** When we provide a choice, but some of the choices are more likely to cause harm than others.
>
> **Non-Maleficence & Justice:** When the harm from our action will only affect some folks.
>
> **Non-Maleficence & Care:** When preserving a supportive relationship risks allowing harmful patterns to continue because addressing them directly may cause emotional strain.
>
> **Justice & Autonomy:** When allowing individual choices results in unequal outcomes.
>
> **Justice & Care:** When prioritizing relationships with individual students comes at the expense of treating students equitably.
>
> **Care & Autonomy:** When caring for a stakeholder leads to us being overly protective, undermining their ability to make independent choices.

For instance, imagine a school considering a new data system that can identify students at risk of dropping out. It may increase beneficence by allowing earlier support, but it also raises concerns about autonomy and justice if students are labeled in ways they cannot contest or that reinforce existing biases. This kind of situation pushes us to weigh which principles we are willing to compromise, and why.

These are the kinds of conflicts that require us to think deeper about our ethical values and commitments. Because, as helpful as these principles are for identifying what the ethical dilemmas are, they leave many questions unresolved. So, in Chapter 4 we turn to approaches to ethics that can help us answer them. We will also examine who we want to apply these lenses to and to what we ultimately aim in Chapters 5 and 6, respectively.

Carrying Our Principles

My goal at this point is not that you memorize the five principles or pledge loyalty to a single way of thinking about ethics in schools. Instead, you should be able to enter the ethical dilemmas we will encounter with multiple lenses in hand. Beneficence, non-maleficence, autonomy, care, and justice will give us a way to map the tensions at stake and ask the right questions.

Ethics in education is about cultivating the judgment to balance competing goods, to recognize hidden harms, to center relationships, and to envision fairer systems. When we face a choice about student discipline, curriculum design, technology adoption, or resource allocation, we can now ask: What does each principle reveal? Which trade-offs are unavoidable? Which are unacceptable?

This pluralist framework does not guarantee easy answers, but it equips us to ask better questions. And, asking better questions is the first step toward acting more ethically. That said, pluralism has limits. We cannot invoke contradictory principles simultaneously. When principles conflict, we must make judgments about priority, and that is precisely what the ethical approaches in Chapter 4 help us do.

This chapter is dense with new questions, and it may feel overwhelming at this juncture. Remember that these are meant to serve as a foundation for the kind of thinking we will do in Section C. As we apply this framework to various case studies, the kinds of questions and reasoning the framework requires will become second nature.

You will have plenty of opportunities to use the lenses to see ethical tensions clearly, question the stakes and values deeply, and think systematically using these frameworks. The decisions will not get easier, but you will make them better. The next step in building our framework, then, is to learn how to reason about these principles in practice.

Exit Ticket

Reflect: Apply all five principles to a tool that you use regularly in your classroom. What tensions come up?
Act: Based on your reflections above, what is one change you would make?
Advocate: What system or building level support or changes would help you use this tool more ethically?

CHAPTER 4

Ethical Approaches

While the principles in Chapter 3 offer a starting place to reveal ethical tensions, that is not enough on its own. This chapter gives us the approaches that help interpret those tensions and make decisions about them.

To gain clarity on these questions, we will borrow from three traditional approaches to ethics: deontology, consequentialism, and virtue ethics. Each one will help us further define and clarify what we mean when we say we will evaluate beneficence, non-maleficence, autonomy, care, and justice.

Deontology, or thinking about ethics as a set of duties, will help us define our hard constraints and our non-negotiable commitments. Consequentialism, or thinking about what our actions might lead to, provides a method for weighing benefits and harms when principles conflict. And, virtue ethics, or focusing on what kind of people we want to be, reminds us that ethics concerns character-formation, not just isolated acts.

Together, they prevent the framework from collapsing into either rigid rule-following or vague aspiration. They help us refine what we mean when we ask whether our actions promote good, avoid harm, respect autonomy, sustain caring relationships, or uphold justice. They also give us tools for interpreting and balancing those principles when they come into tension.

This is important for two reasons.

First, principles alone can sometimes feel like vague commitments without actionable next steps to navigate the tensions. Naming beneficence, non-maleficence, autonomy, care, and justice shows us the ethical tension, but when the tension appears, we still need a way of navigating them. These ethical traditions fill that need. They give us ethical perspectives for reasoning, not just values to consider.

Second, drawing from multiple traditions prevents us from collapsing complex educational decisions into a single moral lens. A purely deontological approach risks rigidity in a field where context matters. A purely consequentialist approach risks excusing serious harms if the "numbers work out." A purely virtue-based approach may fail to guide specific policy choices. My pluralist approach here is about developing a fuller framework to draw from.

The following three sections will help us see how we might approach those questions in practice. The nuance of the ethical approaches (duty, outcomes, virtue) will help us deepen our understanding of what those tensions mean in practice and how we will understand and balance them.

Guiding Questions
- What are our hard limits that we will never cross?
- How will we weigh costs and benefits when there is ambiguity?
- How can we make decisions by asking what kind of people we want to be?

Why Three?

Of course, readers familiar with philosophy might feel uneasy with more pluralism. As we discussed in Chapter 3, pluralism reflects the reality of educational decision-making rather than a theoretical ideal. Here, we build on that idea by showing how different ethical approaches can coexist without collapsing into relativism.

First, more pluralism reflects moral reality. In actual school decisions, teachers and leaders already reason with mixed lenses: duties to students, concern for outcomes, care for relationships, and attention to fairness often show up in the same sentence. Naming these approaches reveals the messy complexity that was already there to offer a path toward consensus building.

Second, pluralism does not mean every principle carries equal weight in every situation. Context and judgment are what will determine weight. In a scenario involving marginalized youth, beneficence and justice may have greater force; or, in a scenario involving sensitive student data, autonomy and non-maleficence may dominate. The point is to give ourselves disciplined ways to navigate these conflicts.

Third, pluralism gains coherence through practice. As we apply the principles and approaches across cases, we will revise those principles in light of cases and revise our case judgments in light of principles. Multiple perspectives will enrich our judgment rather than replace it. Over time, these adjustments bring us closer to a working harmony between our values, our judgments, and our lived experience.

Thus, we should not expect these principles to remain static or perfectly aligned. Instead, we should expect them to adapt as we use them. Their value lies in helping us see ethical dimensions that might otherwise remain hidden.

Defining Limits

To clarify our non-negotiable constraints, we begin with duty-based ethics, or deontology, most commonly associated with Immanuel Kant.[1] Deontological ethics holds that some actions are morally required or forbidden regardless of their consequences. What grounds these duties is

---

[1] Johnson and Cureton, "Kant's Moral Philosophy."

the recognition that all human beings have inherent dignity and must not be treated merely as a means to some external end. We can derive these duties by focusing on generating universal laws that dictate what we should do independent of the consequences. To find these laws, we might ask "what if everyone did this?" Kant calls these rules categorical imperatives.[2]

To be clear, the categorical imperative does not have to be general to the point of uselessness. For example, we can start with the maxim that one must never lie (because if everyone lied, social trust would cease to exist). Upon confronting a situation where lying would save a life, this maxim becomes complicated. We might have another maxim that if we can save a life, we always should. To resolve this conflict, we can modify our honesty maxim to say, "one must never lie, unless it is to save a life." This operates on the understanding that if everyone lied only in these situations, the world would be better off.

For our principles, it offers us a way to identify what any hard limits are in our decision-making. There are some harms that we should never accept, no matter what the other principles say. For example, a student's bodily autonomy should never be harmed by our decision. We might also think that lying to parents is never moral no matter what benefit it provides or how much it protects the students' interests. The lenses of autonomy and justice prevent us from focusing only on consequences when it comes at the cost of our other duties, namely, to respect agency and to build fair systems.

Thus, defining what these duties are toward all relevant stakeholders will help us clarify our ethical framework by clarifying what limits we can never cross. It results in a set of hard limits that we define.

In this way, duty-based reasoning strengthens four of our principles.

Non-maleficence: It helps us specify forms of harm that are categorically unacceptable, such as violations of bodily integrity, exploitative data extraction, or discriminatory targeting. These harms are wrong independent of their impact on test scores or institutional efficiency.

Autonomy: It clarifies that autonomy is not only about choice, but about meaningful participation and protection from coercion because everyone has inherent dignity that we have to protect. This includes developmentally appropriate consent, clear communication, and respecting the agency of educators and families.

Care: It grounds seeing care as part of our duty as caregivers and not just a component of the benefits or harms. It clarifies the obligation to think about our role as someone with whom the student has a relationship, and not just an independent actor.

Justice: It emphasizes equality of moral standing. If a decision replicates patterns of unequal treatment, avoids due process, or relies on biased assumptions that undermine the equal dignity of all students, it is wrong.

We will not use deontology to answer every question; but, it does help us define which actions and policies remain off-limits no matter how attractive their downstream benefits appear. It protects students, families, and educators from being sacrificed to short-term gains, institutional pressures, or technological enthusiasm.

---

[2] Johnson and Cureton, "Kant's Moral Philosophy."

Thinking through what your hard limits are for each principle can bring some clarity for future decision-making. And, it will serve as the ethical floor for all further reasoning.

Weighing Consequences

Once we have our non-negotiable rules, we need a system to weigh the different principles when there is not a clear answer. For this, we can turn to consequentialism, advanced by various moral philosophers, including John Stuart Mill.[3] Consequentialism judges actions by their outcomes.[4] An action is right if it produces the best consequences overall.

Consequentialism's core argument is that actions are moral when they maximize well-being or minimize suffering. Thus, we must think about all the people who will be affected by our actions and tally up the amount of good it causes versus harm it does. As long as we do more good than harm, our action is moral.

In our framework, this theory can help us weigh competing benefits and harms that are not attached to the duty-based ethical values. For example, when deciding where to spend more money, we might think decisions that provide the most benefit to the most students are better than one that only helps one student.

This kind of reasoning plays an important role in educational ethics. First, it forces us to pay attention to outcomes. It is not enough that we mean to help students. We must ask whether a decision actually advances one of the aims of education. Second, it gives us a way to address questions of resource allocation. When we cannot fund every program we wish we could, consequentialism helps us ask which investments will do the most good, especially for those who need it most. It is important to remember that consequentialism is not only about maximizing the number of people benefited.

For example, imagine we have five books to give, and the option to give them all to one child or give them to five different children. Initially, we might think that consequentialism would tell us to give them to five different children. However, if we look deeper and see that the five children already have hundreds of books at home that they have not read, while the one child has access to no books. Consequentialism would weigh giving the book to that one child more because the net increase in utility would be greater for that one child than the other five children combined.

In our framework, consequentialism helps us weigh beneficence and non-maleficence when both are in play. It reminds us to consider the broader implications of justice, not only in terms of equal treatment, but also in terms of the actual impact on our students. It does not tell us everything, but it gives us one disciplined way to ask, "If we must choose among imperfect options, which choice does the most good and the least harm for those we serve?" We will further develop our ability to reason about these considerations in Chapter 7 where we incorporate reasoning heuristics.

---

[3] Mill and Crisp, *Utilitarianism*.
[4] Although consequentialism includes many variations ranging from act to rule approaches and from maximizing to satisficing interpretations, the shared core is that the moral evaluation of an action depends on its outcomes.

Building Virtues

While weighing the consequences is one way to reason through the principles, it might still not provide a clear example. For example, if an action is likely to produce some harm and some benefits, it might be unclear how to weigh the two sides. In these situations, it is often more helpful to ask a different kind of question: What kind of educator, and what kind of community, are we becoming if we choose this path?

This is the approach of virtue ethics, often attributed to Aristotle.[5] Virtue ethics shifts our focus from isolated decisions to character over time. It asks not only, "is this action right?" but "what does repeatedly choosing this action do to the kind of person I am and the kind of school we are building?"

Thus, we might think about which traits we consider virtuous (e.g., compassion, integrity, courage, humility, open-mindedness), and how we need to act to foster that trait. We develop these virtues not by reading about them, but by practicing them. We become more just by making just decisions regularly. We become more caring by consistently attending to others with attention and concern.

This makes ethics in these situations a question of practical wisdom (or phronēsis). Our approach in this book is built on this vision of ethics. There is no algorithm that can tell us exactly how to apply beneficence, non-maleficence, autonomy, care, and justice in every case. We need the capacity to notice what matters in a situation, to judge which considerations carry more weight, and to act with conviction.

In doing so, we will arrive at real judgments based on a variety of lenses and our practical experience. By repeatedly asking how our choices affect beneficence, non-maleficence, autonomy, care, and justice, we practice seeing the world through those values. Over time, this practice can help make ethical attention less of an effortful add-on and more of a professional habit.

This makes ethics not just about the principles we apply but the people we are shaping ourselves and our students to become. In fact, each principle of principlism supports virtues that an ethical educator would embody. For example, virtue ethics connects directly to the principle of care. Caring is not simply a feeling, but a pattern of attentive, responsive action. A school that habitually prioritizes relational connection when making decisions is building a culture of care. It is cultivating the disposition to ask, "how will this affect trust and belonging?" before asking, "will this make our school look better?"

Using Our Approaches

With these three traditions in mind, our framework gains depth. Deontology clarifies our limits. Consequentialism helps us weigh competing goods and harms. Virtue ethics reminds us that every decision is also shaping who we and our students are becoming. Taken together, the five principles tell us what is ethically at stake in a decision, and the three ethical approaches help us decide how to act when those values come into tension.

---

[5] Luckowski, "A Virtue-Centered Approach to Ethics Education"; Aristoteles and Barnes, *The Nicomachean Ethics*.

This chapter is sparse by philosophy standards for explaining traditions of ethics, but I have pulled the most relevant arguments to help educators reason together about the kinds of issues we will talk about in this book. To deepen your understanding of these approaches, I have included further readings with the online resources.

In the chapters that follow, I bring this framework into closer contact with practice. Chapter 5 clarifies to whom these principles and approaches are owed by examining the stakeholders whose lives are shaped by educational decisions. Chapter 6 turns to the aims of education that give our principles direction. Later chapters then offer reasoning strategies and heuristics for using this framework to navigate concrete cases.

Exit Ticket

Reflect: Which approach seems to guide *you* most strongly: duty to rules and rights, attention to outcomes, or concern for character?

Act: Identify one hard limit you would treat as non-negotiable, one outcome you would want to track, and one virtue you would want to cultivate.

Advocate: Name one policy change that would make it easier for you to honor your duties, weigh outcomes responsibly, or cultivate the virtues.

CHAPTER 5

Stakeholders

Ethics in education is relational: every decision affects and obligates multiple groups at once. Our questions in Chapters 3 and 4 provide us a framework for what we should consider when we think about our ethical values in education. In Chapter 5, we will ask, "to whom do we have ethical obligations?" Our principles are only meaningful when applied to actual lives.

While students are and will remain our primary focus for decision-making in education, decisions made in schools involve other stakeholders as well: teachers, parents, school leaders, and the broader community. Building on the ethical lenses, we will examine how the principles of beneficence, non-maleficence, autonomy, care, and justice apply to all these stakeholder groups.

When we think about stakeholders in education, we can think about them from either end of the moral relationship. They can either be the party that must *act* ethically or *toward* whom someone else should act ethically. For example, not only do educators owe something to students, but students also owe something back to their educators. However, in this book, we will focus on ethical decision-making by educators, so we do not directly address the ethical obligation that students, parents, and society have toward education. We do, however, address how those perspectives ought to shape decisions made by educators in schools.

As we apply these perspectives in later cases, we will think about how to incorporate these diverse and, oftentimes, conflicting claims on education into our decision-making framework. We will think about how parents' interests in their children's education must be balanced with respect for student privacy and autonomy. And, we will think about how the impacts of technology choices made in classrooms shape the shared social and civic life of communities.

Beyond the stakeholders above, there are others who are in a position to act and be acted upon ethically. We will also think about what role ed tech vendors, policymakers, administrators, and future generations play in our ethical reasoning.

When the impact is high and the issues are complex, a commitment to understanding and balancing stakeholder interests is a necessary first step. By surfacing tensions, finding common ground, and deciding intentionally between these perspectives, we can ensure that our decision-making is accounting for all our ethical obligations.

Guiding Questions
- Who is directly or indirectly affected by decisions in schools?
- What type of obligations do educators owe each group?
- How do we honor one obligation without violating another?

The Role of Stakeholders

Education is inherently about multiple stakeholders.[1] Unlike business, where the primary motive is profit, or medicine, where the primary duty is to the patient, education has to simultaneously act ethically toward multiple constituencies, with sometimes overlapping, but also sometimes conflicting interests. It has to consider students' current and future well-being, parents' values and concern for their children, teachers' professional and personal identities, society's stake in citizens and workers, and future generations' role in the world that current students will lead. But because there will inevitably be disagreements among stakeholders, the ethical challenge is this: When stakeholders want different things, and all have legitimate claims, how do we decide?

This book generally takes the following deliberative approach: ethical decisions require meaningful input from all stakeholders through processes that respect their distinct relationships to education. This aligns with Gutmann's work on the ethical decision-making in pluralist societies and the need to account for what role each of the different stakeholders ought to play in democratic schooling.[2] Deliberative processes allow us to engage stakeholders on their actual perspectives, rather than presume we can persuade them to fully agree with us.

This deliberative approach avoids several alternatives that prove inadequate for educational ethics. One example is proportional representation, or taking a democratic stance, where we act under the assumption that those who are affected the most should have the most representation in the decision-making. We could use a fiduciary stance, where we center our role as students' guardians, and center the individual students' interests above all else, excluding parental voices and community good. Or, we might have ethical principles, such as egalitarianism, that ground all decisions regardless of what the relevant stakeholders in each decision think. But, a deliberative approach avoids the risk of tyranny of the majority, centering an individual student over the school or larger community and requiring commitments to theories of justice that real decision-makers disagree about.

For a deliberative view of stakeholder engagement to be ethical, we have to account for asymmetric power dynamics.[3] Education creates such asymmetries because of political, developmental, and social forces, and so we must consider each stakeholder's powers and powerlessness.[4] Below, I address these dynamics, and throughout the book, I suggest individual actions and systemic changes that can help us create the conditions for authentic stakeholder engagement.

---

[1] Gutmann, *Democratic Education*.
[2] Ibid.
[3] Apple, *Education and Power*.
[4] Freire and Macedo, *Pedagogy of the Oppressed*.

And, even among stakeholder groups, power is also patterned by race, class, disability, and language background in ways that shape whose interests tend to be centered or ignored.[5] We must recognize that stakeholders enter deliberation from vastly different social positions that shape their interests and their capacity to articulate those interests in forums of dialogue. Naming this helps frame justice when we consider structural disadvantages some communities face in schooling.[6]

Here, we focus on students, teachers, and parents, and then cover a range of community members that are also impacted by and impact education. For each stakeholder, we will cover our ethical obligation, tensions that come up, and practical strategies for centering their interests.

Students

Students are in a unique position, because while they are impacted the most by our decision-making, they have the least institutional power. Students can resist authority, express their voice, and eventually choose to use or abandon the values and knowledge they gain in schools. However, they cannot exit compulsory schooling in most cases, have limited legal standing, and are developmentally vulnerable. As we think about how to incorporate student stakeholders, we must make sure that their interests, experiences, and voices are shaping how we make our decisions.[7]

CORE ETHICAL OBLIGATIONS

All five of our principles will affect how we think about our obligations toward students. We have an obligation to act for their well-being and growth, to protect them from avoidable harm, to respect their agency and emerging capacity for choice, to preserve our relationships with them, and to treat them all fairly.[8]

TENSIONS

Individualization Versus Collective Fairness

One barrier to effective integration of students' perspectives is that decisions are often made with the idea of "student" in mind, not actual students. This concept of "the average student" becomes the target of decision-making by all stakeholders.[9] This can be a policymaker making policies they think work best for "students," technology companies maximizing "student" well-being, and teachers keeping the interest of their "students" in mind.

This idea is built on the false assumption that we can act ethically toward students by making assumptions about what we think an average student needs.

---

[5] Lareau, *Unequal Childhoods*; MINOW, "Sources of Difference"; Okin, *Justice, Gender, and the Family*; Freire and Macedo, *Pedagogy of the Oppressed*.
[6] Young and Allen, *Justice and the Politics of Difference*.
[7] Gheaus, "Children's Vulnerability and Legitimate Authority Over Children."
[8] Gheaus, "Children's Vulnerability and Legitimate Authority Over Children"; Freire and Macedo, *Pedagogy of the Oppressed*; Gutmann, *Democratic Education*; Feinberg, "The Child's Right to an Open Future."
[9] Walker, "Dismantling the Myth of the 'Average' Student | NEA"; Rose, *The End of Average*.

The reality is that our students have diverse needs and wants, informed by their identities and shaped by their unique environments. In order to act ethically toward our students, we need to find ways to accurately assess what each student is owed, and how any advantages or disadvantages of our actions might specifically affect them.

However, we must also balance individual choices with collective fairness. If we tailor our approach to each student, how do we ensure that we are still being fair to everyone and not simply prioritizing the loudest voices or those with the most visible needs? The challenge lies in creating systems and policies that are flexible enough to accommodate individual differences, yet are robust enough to maintain a consistent standard of equity for all.

Developmental Needs Versus Autonomy

The second barrier to student involvement is their developmental stage. Philosophers of democracy have described how developmental appropriateness changes how we view the rights of students.[10] We would never think it appropriate if the government required adults to show up to a certain place at a certain time every day, but we recognize the appropriateness of that for children.

This means that not only do we have to figure out how to incorporate their voice, we have to also figure out when and how much. Because, while we want to help with their immediate desires, we also have an obligation to ensure their future well-being.[11]

Erik Erikson's stages of psychosocial development can provide a starting framework for understanding how students' capacity for autonomous decision-making evolves.[12] Elementary-age students might need structure and guidance to develop competence while being protected from overwhelming choices that could lead to feelings of inadequacy. Middle and high school students might require increasing opportunities for self-determination to form their identity, yet still within supportive boundaries that prevent harm while they explore who they are becoming.

Our approach to granting student autonomy must be carefully balanced against the authority we exercise as educators.[13] This equilibrium directly impacts our fundamental obligation to ensure student protection. We have a shared responsibility for the well-being and developmental trajectory of our students. This responsibility extends beyond merely preventing immediate harm. It also includes actively guiding students toward more fundamental, long-term objectives of building a fulfilling and meaningful life.[14]

Therefore, every decision regarding student autonomy must avoid an overemphasis on autonomy that can expose students to unnecessary risks, but also, avoid an overly restrictive approach that can stifle their capacity for self-direction.

---

[10] Feinberg, "The Child's Right to an Open Future," ed. Aiken and LaFollette; Gutmann, "Children, Paternalism, and Education"; Gutmann, *Democratic Education*.
[11] Feinberg, "The Child's Right to an Open Future."
[12] Erikson, *Childhood and Society*.
[13] Brighouse, *On Education*.
[14] Feinberg, "The Child's Right to an Open Future"; Brighouse et al., *Educational Goods*.

The question of what we want for our students and how that impacts our ethical decision-making is the subject of Chapter 6, where we think about what we should aim for our students.

Disability and Expanded Networks of Care

Education for students with disabilities often involves an expanded network: special education teachers, paraprofessionals, therapists, medical providers, and advocacy organizations. This expanded network creates unique tensions. Parents of students with disabilities often carry heightened advocacy burdens, needing to navigate complex systems while balancing their child's right to inclusion with needs for specialized support. Teachers may face conflicts between their legal obligations under Individualized Education Programs (IEPs) and practical classroom constraints. Students themselves may have their autonomy further complicated by questions of capacity and supported decision-making.

PRACTICAL STRATEGIES

There are ways we can incorporate student voice while mitigating these barriers. What we need is a way to present students with opportunities for genuine choice-making and real influence. This will likely be a combination of consulting students on their opinion to gain their perspective, involving students in joint decision-making, and giving them direct authority over certain decisions.[15]

Perspective Gathering

Students of all school-going ages can share something about their experience, desires, needs, and concerns. Thus, no matter what student population you are working with, there should always be some attempt to learn about and consider their perspective. This might include surveys, town halls, one-on-one conversations, and guided reflection opportunities. Through these tactics, we can learn what the student is currently thinking about a decision that must be made.

The worst thing we can do is ask them a set of questions and then do what we planned anyway. We must genuinely approach the student perspectives with the intellectual humility we committed to in Chapter 2. At the same time, student perspectives are not trump cards. Because many decisions will involve other stakeholders (including the students' future selves), we must focus on meaningfully gathering and reporting on their perspectives in relation to these other stakeholders.

Joint Decision-Making

There are some decisions that we can make jointly with our students, whether through discussion or collaboration.[16] For example, we can provide a set of choices and let them ultimately choose. We can also provide exit rights, so that we decide on a path forward, but let students opt out if they deem it necessary. For example, when we provide students a set of electives to

---

[15] Gheaus, "Children's Vulnerability and Legitimate Authority Over Children"; McCombs, "Developing Responsible and Autonomous Learners"; Freire and Macedo, *Pedagogy of the Oppressed*.

[16] Freire and Macedo, *Pedagogy of the Oppressed*.

choose from, we narrow the pool of what they can choose from, but we still allow them to make a final decision. Or, if we insist that our students try to use a particular tool for studying, we can also respect students who opt out of using it after exploration.

Direct Authority

Finally, we can provide genuine authority for students to make their own decisions especially as our students demonstrate more capacity for nuanced thinking about their education and schooling.[17] When we allow students to choose which book they use for a book report, we are providing them the option to pursue that decision based on what is of interest to them, rather than asserting our predetermined notion of what they *should* be interested in.

All three of these strategies only work if we genuinely work with our students to understand what their concerns are. This also means making sure that our students are informed enough to share an educated perspective with us. We should find ways to help them understand the decision, the risks and benefits, and what other factors besides their own voice will be incorporated into the final outcome.

We also have to remember that students are contributing expertise about their lived experiences, cultures, and learning processes.[18] Incorporating student knowledge production in how we teach and how much we encourage them to take the lead supports autonomy, care, and justice because it treats students as partners in shaping our educational communities.

We will cover policies that can help support these approaches in Section B.

KEY TAKEAWAY

Ethical education centers students' lived realities, not abstractions, and grants them real participation while safeguarding their development.

In our framework, we will often start with students for all five of the lenses. How does this decision benefit and harm our students? Have we respected their agency over their own lives and our relationships with them? And, are we being just to all of our students?

While we want to think about students and our impact on their future lives primarily, we ought not to think about students only. Other stakeholders have valid claims to our ethical decision-making too. Ethical schools depend as much on the well-being and judgment of teachers as on the empowerment of students.

Educators

While students often don't have a say in education decision-making, educators' own concerns are also rarely considered, even by educators themselves.[19] True ethical decision-making needs to consider the ethical ramifications on all related stakeholders, and given the central role

---

[17] Ibid.
[18] Ibid.
[19] Lefstein and Perath, "Empowering Teacher Voices in an Education Policy Discussion."

educators have in making and executing these decisions, we need to make sure we incorporate educator perspectives.

Educators have the benefit of professional expertise, day-to-day interactions with students, and discretion on the implementation of policies and curricula. However, overpowering administrative authority, vulnerability to parental complaints, and limitations imposed by policymakers all threaten their ability to exercise those powers.

CORE ETHICAL OBLIGATIONS

Our core five principles should be applied to educators. We have an obligation to create a safe and fulfilling work environment, to avoid placing unreasonable burdens, to respect their professional judgment, to allow them to cultivate strong relationships, and to ensure that there is workload equity.

TENSIONS

Loyalty to Students Versus Obedience to Systems

Educators operate at the boundary of two domains of education: public and private. They have to answer to the public domain by being mandatory reporters, assessors of academic progress, and teachers of state or district mandated curricula. They also have to answer to the private domain by thinking about a student's life outside of the school, balancing all students' competing needs, answering to parents about schooling, and being a (and sometimes "the") caring adult in a student's life. Supporting educators means acknowledging these competing asks while maintaining clear ethical expectations.

Autonomy Versus Standardization

Within education, we struggle with the balance between educator autonomy and standardization. While we want to encourage educators to bring their full selves, we also want to minimize how much variability there is in student experience in order to ensure that our students are getting similar educations. This requires us to consider the trade-off between student experience in both cases. Respecting educator autonomy allows us to make the most of the talent in our schools, maintain morale, and ensure that our educators can teach the way they know best.

Personal Judgment Versus Institutional Policies

We also want to think about what we ask educators to do and how that relates to their own moral judgment. When educators are required to drill students on rote test preparation rather than nurture authentic learning, many experience what philosophers call moral injury.[20] This concept describes the wound that occurs when professionals are compelled to act against their core ethical commitments. In schools, moral injury can take the form of feeling that one is complicit in harming children by reducing them to scores or by enforcing policies that conflict with an educator's sense of care and fairness. Moral injury for educators occurs when the principles of beneficence, justice, or care are violated by institutional demands.

---

[20] Levinson, "Moral Injury and the Ethics of Educational Injustice"; Oberg, "Moral Injury in Teaching."

The result is a fracture between personal values and institutional demands. Schools that fail to acknowledge this reality risk trust and integrity among their educators. An important ethical task, therefore, is to build mechanisms that allow for teachers to act in ways that align with their professional conscience.

PRACTICAL STRATEGIES
Shared Governance
The most obvious way to ensure that educators' perspectives are heard is by giving them all of the decision-making authority that does not need to be centralized. We can start by asking, "What decisions can be left to the individual teachers' own preferences, judgment, and experience?" There are likely more decisions in that pile than we currently actually allow teachers to make, including daily pedagogical strategies and curriculum decisions.

At the same time, educators want to feel supported and backed up by school leaders. There are times when teachers are searching for more guidance on the right decision, and in those cases providing it is obligatory. A simple mental heuristic for this is, "Are teachers asking for a policy?" or "Am I trying to control the situation by making a policy?" If the teachers want guidance and support over rules and restrictions, we should respect that.

Individual educator voices also gain strength through collective organization. Teachers' unions represent a critical stakeholder in educational ethics. They can amplify concerns about unfair burdens, advocate for conditions that enable ethical practice, and provide institutional pushback to administrative power.[21]

Protection for Ethical Dissent
Another dimension of educator vulnerability arises when teachers speak out against practices they believe are unjust. Whether this involves misuse of student data, discriminatory enforcement of policy, or unsafe school conditions, educators who raise concerns often face retaliation rather than protection. The fear of reprisal silences ethical dissent and leaves questionable practices unchallenged. In such circumstances, the duty to protect students comes into direct conflict with the need for self-preservation.

Schools that wish to act ethically must therefore create safeguards for dissent, provide clear channels for reporting concerns, and recognize that whistleblowing is an ethical obligation.[22] Without these protections, silence becomes the default, and systemic harm goes unaddressed. In line with our commitment to transparency in Chapter 2, we must allow for genuine feedback from teachers in our schools.

Recognition of Hidden Labor
Much of the most important work that teachers do is invisible to formal structures. This includes the daily acts of emotional support, cultural translation, and advocacy for families that fall outside of assessment rubrics and evaluation checklists. This labor is often gendered and racialized,

---

[21] Barnes, "Soft Systems Analysis: Digital Tool Selection in K-12 Classrooms."
[22] National Education Association, "Educator Rights to Report Wrongdoing | NEA."

with disproportionate burdens falling on educators who already navigate multiple roles within the school system.[23] Technology has not necessarily relieved this hidden labor; rather, in some cases has intensified it.[24] Learning platforms may track assignments and attendance, but they rarely capture the hours spent counseling a child in crisis, mediating family concerns, or providing encouragement that sustains a student's confidence. And, the learning platform might require educators to rewrite the curriculum, be more accessible to students and parents, and feel confined to the design of the system.

The ethical responsibility of schools is to recognize and value this unseen labor by building cultures that acknowledge it as integral to the educational mission. Ignoring it distorts our understanding of what teaching truly requires and unfairly burdens educators whose contributions are not formally recognized.

Professional Duties

Educators also operate under a set of professional duties that extend beyond written contracts.[25] These duties arise from the trust society places in them and the vulnerability of the students they serve. Teachers are expected to maintain competence by continually developing their pedagogical and technological skills so that students are not disadvantaged by outdated practice. They are also bound by a duty of care, which requires attention not only to academic progress, but to the well-being of students in all its dimensions. Fairness demands that they treat students equitably across differences of identity, circumstance, and ability, and resist biases that might compromise opportunity. Integrity requires that they preserve appropriate boundaries, particularly in digital spaces where the lines between public and private can blur. Finally, teachers have a duty of advocacy to speak on behalf of students when systemic pressures threaten their interests. Each of these duties reflects the ethical weight of teaching as a profession and underscores the need for institutional support that makes it possible for teachers to fulfill them.

KEY TAKEAWAY

The ethical challenge for educators is to honor their own agency and values. In our case analysis, we will center decision-making by the educator, but the decision being made by the educator is not enough for the ethical obligations to educators to be met. Ultimately, we must advocate for systemic changes that avoid shifting the harm disproportionately to teachers.

Parents/Guardians

Parents and guardians present another critical layer of educational ethics. They are the primary caregivers for children and have responsibility for their upbringing. Yet, we recognize that children also deserve the right to some self-determination.[26]

---

[23] Staudt Willet and He, "Educators' Invisible Labour"; Gordon et al., "Invisible Labor and the Associate Professor."
[24] Shah, "I Was an AI Optimist. Now I'm Worried It's Making Teacher Burnout Worse."
[25] NEA, "Code of Ethics for Educators | NEA."
[26] Feinberg, "The Child's Right to an Open Future"; Gheaus, "Children's Vulnerability and Legitimate Authority Over Children."

As such, we must ask ourselves: When does parental access constitute healthy involvement, and when does it verge on surveillance? When does advocacy become interference? What roles do educators have when parent actions conflict with educational aims?

Schools must navigate these questions with care. Parents do have legitimate rights to information, direction, and protection for their children, as well as the opportunity to pass on values and advocate for their interests.[27] Yet these rights are neither unlimited nor uniform.[28]

CORE ETHICAL OBLIGATIONS

In most of our ethical decision-making, our focus on parents will center on parental autonomy. We will discuss our obligation to communicate clearly about their children's learning and well-being, the role of informed consent from parents, and ensuring that all families, not just vocal or privileged ones, are heard.[29]

TENSIONS

Involvement Versus Interference

Parents have both the right and the responsibility to engage in their children's education. In fact, their involvement can create alignment between home and school. Yet, when involvement crosses into micromanagement or control, it can undermine professional judgment and student autonomy. The ethical task for schools is to invite collaboration without ceding educational authority.

Transparency Versus Confidentiality

Families deserve clear information about their child's progress, safety, and well-being. Transparency fosters trust and shared understanding. At the same time, educators hold sensitive information that can cause harm to students if disclosed. Transparency can also invite more scrutiny than schools have the capacity to respond to. Schools must, therefore, find out how to build partnerships without breaching trust.

Responsiveness Versus Consistency

Schools must remain responsive to individual family concerns, adapting to diverse needs, values, and cultural contexts. Yet, too much customization risks inconsistency. Ethical decision-making requires hearing and validating family perspectives while upholding standard principles that ensure all students are treated equitably.

Because families vary in structure, resources, and expectations, parents with greater time, money, or social capital often dominate school discourse, while those with fewer resources struggle to make their voices heard.[30] Thus, we must rely on proactive outreach and inclusive design so that participation does not mirror existing inequalities.

---

[27] Brighouse and Swift, "Legitimate Parental Partiality"; Brighouse and Swift, "Parents' Rights and the Value of the Family."
[28] Dietrich, "Critical Reflection and the Limits of Parental Authority"; Brake and Millum, "Parenthood and Procreation."
[29] Lareau, *Unequal Childhoods*.
[30] Okin, *Justice, Gender, and the Family*; Douglas, "Parental Partiality and the Intergenerational Transmission of Advantage"; Brighouse and Swift, "Legitimate Parental Partiality"; Lareau, *Unequal Childhoods*.

PRACTICAL STRATEGIES

Schools should adopt clear expectations for when and how educators communicate with families. When we communicate openly and consistently with parents, we demonstrate that accountability and care can coexist.

Communication must be about more than just sharing information. True informed consent requires making sure parents *understand* the information too. Families with limited time, language access, or familiarity with school systems often need guidance and resources to participate fully. Proactive outreach recognizes that silence does not mean consent and that the burden of inclusion lies with institutions.

Finally, when schools explain not only *what* decisions they make but *why*, they transform disagreement into dialogue. Framing choices around values helps parents see decisions as moral reasoning rather than bureaucratic control. Turning decision-making into a concrete, collaborative process can provide us with a shared vocabulary that strengthens trust even in moments of tension.

KEY TAKEAWAY

Ethical partnership with families will balance respect for parental care with the protection of student autonomy and equity among households.

Other Stakeholders

In addition to students, teachers, and parents, several other groups shape and are shaped by educational decisions. The concerns of the community, administrators, school boards, policymakers, technology vendors, employers, and future generations also enable or constrain our ethical practice. The brevity of their treatment here reflects the different nature of their relationship to educational practice. Often, their ethical obligations and our obligations to them often operate at the policy and systems level, which show up in Chapter 6 when we discuss the aims of education.

Communities expect schools to prepare students for participation in civic life and to ensure students are career ready. They also expect transparency in how decisions are made and stewardship in the use of public funds. Schools are sites of individual development, but they are also institutions embedded in broader communities. Decisions made within them shape civic life, economic opportunity, and collective trust.[31]

Acting ethically toward communities requires more than compliance with public-comment procedures or routine town-hall meetings. It involves genuine dialogue that signals a readiness to listen, respond, and adapt. It involves recognition that every community has members with diverse interests. And it involves foresight to consider how present choices affect not only today's community but future communities.

---

[31] Gutmann, *Democratic Education*; Levinson, *The Demands of Liberal Education*; Allen, *Education and Equality*; Dewey, *Democracy and Education - An Introduction to the Philosophy of Education*.

The community is also comprised of:

- **Administrators and school boards** who have the power to allocate resources, select technologies, set policies, and hire and evaluate educators. However, they also face risks of political backlash, rely on teacher and student cooperation, and are constrained by state and federal policy.
- **Policymakers** establish accountability frameworks that can either promote justice or impose onerous bureaucracy through changing mandates.
- **Technology vendors** design the tools that classrooms depend upon and must protect data and design tools with children in mind, even as commercial incentives push them toward practices that may undermine student well-being.
- **Employers** influence curriculum through their workforce demands, and schools must guard against reducing education to narrow vocational training.
- Finally, **future generations** form a hypothetical, but key stakeholder group.[32] To act ethically in education is to consider not only those present in the classroom, but also those who will inherit the world it helps to create. We address this concern more thoroughly in the next chapter.

Taken together, these stakeholders add to a web of relationships and responsibilities that extend beyond the school walls. Recognizing this wider network of stakeholders prepares us to see how educational choices carry broader consequences that we explore in the chapters ahead.

In our case studies, we will primarily discuss these stakeholders when we think about the potential benefits and harms of our decisions. We will also think about how to deal with the constraints imposed by some of these stakeholders (e.g., administrators, policymakers, and vendors) and how to navigate them.

Relational Decision-Making

This chapter aimed to show that ethical decision-making in education is fundamentally relational.[33] Our obligations are layered. We want to educate our students, support educators, cooperate with families, and stay accountable to communities.

While we want to consider all these roles, we should be reassured that they are often aligned. By focusing on shared values and aims, we can prevent zero-sum thinking that makes decisions about one stakeholder or another "winning."

But of course, there will be conflicts between stakeholder perspectives. Our work is to apply the principles of Chapter 3 with clarity and recognize when one principle or stakeholder justifiably carries more weight.

We must recognize schools as places where ethical relationships shape shared futures. Decisions about technology, policy, and practice extend far beyond classrooms. They shape

---

[32] Rawls, *A Theory of Justice*.
[33] Habermas, "Justification and Application."

public trust, define economic opportunities, and build the world that our students (current and future) will inherit.

The framework introduced in Chapter 3 is only useful when it is considered alongside the relevant stakeholders whom our decisions impact. With the stakeholders identified, the next chapter turns to the harder task: what are we all working toward anyways?

Exit Ticket

Reflect: Think of a recent educational decision. Which, if any, voices were missing from the decision-making process? How might their inclusion have changed the outcome?

Act: How might you use the practical strategies introduced above for involving students in your own classroom?

Advocate: Choose one systemic barrier that prevents meaningful stakeholder participation for a particular group. What could better support their involvement?

CHAPTER 6

Stakes

In the last chapter, we asked who is affected by decision-making in schools. In this chapter, we ask: What is at stake when we are making these decisions? We only care about the influence on stakeholders because education has real consequences for students and society. It shapes lives, builds opportunities, and defines our collective future.

Thus, in order to approach the question of what is ethical, we have to ask what is at stake when we make decisions about schooling? This often causes avoidance of the topic altogether. Is it really the business of teachers and staff to think about the role of education? Who gets to have a say and why? Why can we not just focus on teaching?

The reality is that every act in a school already takes a stance on the stakes of education. When we argue about school calendars, grading policies, or technology adoption, what we are really debating is which ends we think matter most. Without surfacing those ends, we risk talking past one another or worse, working against each other. By naming them, we can see more clearly where our agreements lie and where the real tensions begin.

Understanding what is at stake helps us interpret conflicts between our principles. When beneficence (helping students) conflicts with autonomy (respecting their choices), stakes tell us what kind of help and what kind of choices we are talking about. That changes how we weigh the tension. Stakes give moral weight to abstract principles by connecting them to concrete educational purposes.

So, rather than pretend that we can separate out pedagogical strategy from pedagogical aims, we need to accept that pedagogy is always value-laden, not neutral. Our efforts are better spent analyzing for ourselves what those values are and coming to a shared consensus about them before attempting to make decisions.

The first set of stakes is about the purpose: the ends or outcomes we aim to achieve through schooling. They concern what education is for. Across the history of educational thought, there are dozens of competing theories about the purposes of schooling. But in practice, most discussions among families, educators, and policymakers return to three central aims: economic success, civic participation, and personal fulfillment. Families, educators, and policymakers may not use the same vocabulary, but these three themes capture the hope we place in education, that it should prepare students for work, equip them for citizenship, and help them live meaningful lives.[1]

The second set is about the process: the consequences of how we pursue those aims. They concern the means of education rather than the ends. The processes, policies, and priorities we choose shape society as much as the outcomes themselves. If we prepare some students better than others for careers, what happens to equality and social mobility? If civic education tells only a positive story of the nation, what happens to democratic discourse? If we value academic performance more than belonging, what happens to students' well-being? These questions remind us that the ethics of education lies not only in what we pursue but also in how we pursue it.

We have to examine these stakes in order to make ethical decisions about educational technology. We cannot ask "what works?" without clarifying "what are we working toward?" More so, until we examine both sets of stakes, we risk pursuing good ends through unjust means or building ethical procedures that lead to hollow promises.

Ultimately, our decisions carry both ends and means, and ethics requires balancing competing goods among the economic, civic, and personal aims while honoring fairness and inclusion in the procedures.

Guiding Questions

- How should we think about the economic (career), personal (fulfillment), and collective (civic) aims of education?
- How do we define what counts as success or failure in schools along these aims?
- How do we balance all these competing goods?

Stakes of Purpose: The Ends

In this section, we will think about what education is ultimately for. Earlier, we identified three themes that come up: economic, civic, and personal. Each of these represents a different vision of what is valuable in the life of a human and what our shared obligations are when we decide to school our children. And, each brings its own set of questions and tensions about how we make decisions in education.

First, students, parents, educators, and the community acknowledge the importance of schooling for economic progress. How do we prepare our students for their future careers? How do we ensure that they have upward economic mobility? How do we help them contribute meaningfully to the economy?

Second, policymakers, the community, and educators emphasize the importance of education in preparing students to be active participants of a democratic nation. How can a society that relies on the expertise and judgment of its people function if their knowledge and skills are not developed in a shared, formal setting?

---

[1] Brighouse et al., *Educational Goods*.

Third, an aim that is often implicit in all conversations about education is that we want our students to be happy. We want them to have a sense of identity and purpose, healthy relationships with their peers and society, and the dispositions and skills to achieve whatever success means for them.

Of course, there is overlap between these aims. Being an economically productive member of society likely gives you some insight into the civic needs of the nation. Feeling like your voice and opinion are well-grounded and impactful likely brings joy and pride.

However, there are also times when these aims are not as symbiotic even though they sound complementary. In practice, they often conflict: Should we teach students to maximize their income or to consider the social impact of their careers? How do we handle competitive college admissions when it creates pressure for students to sacrifice well-being for credentials? Do we teach the full truth about environmental risks or moderate it to avoid anxiety?

These are some examples to highlight that these aims do not inherently complement each other. This tension is not evidence that schools have failed. It is a sign that education carries multiple responsibilities at once. The challenge is to manage it with honesty about the trade-offs we make.

We might think that with more data, resources, or consensus, we might be able to pursue all these aims jointly. However, the reality is that even in ideal circumstances we would inevitably have to make some trade-offs. There is limited learning that students can do in a day, only so much we can expect individual educators to be experts in, and only a finite amount of attention and energy that any school system can distribute at once.

To decide on these trade-offs, we need two things. First, we need to understand why we care about these things in the first place (this chapter). Second, we need reasoning heuristics to decide when one trade-off is better than another (the next chapter).

I do not expect that all these aims will be agreed upon by everyone. I myself do not think some of these *ought* to be our aims of schooling. However, for consensus building and talking to stakeholders, we still need the vocabulary to define the aims, why people care about them, and how each aim might overlap or interact with what others see as an aim of education.

Economic Aims

The economic aim of education is to prepare students to participate meaningfully in the economy: to earn a living, contribute to productivity, and access opportunities that lead to material security.

The economic aim of schooling is not a recent motivation. From the start of compulsory education in the United States, schools were seen as a means of preparing children for participation in the labor market. In the nineteenth and early twentieth centuries, this often meant cultivating habits of punctuality, obedience, and routine that aligned with industrial factory work.[2]

---

[2] Labaree, *Someone Has to Fail*.

We can see the impact of this aim when we see discussions about career readiness, share statistics about economic outcomes, and prioritize skills and knowledge that are appealing to employers or build national economic competitiveness.

But, why do we think schools are the best place for developing career readiness?

LABOR

First, there is the macroeconomic need for laborers who can competently take the jobs that sustain our industries.[3] Our education system needs teachers, hospitals need doctors, our legal system needs lawyers, and our newspapers need journalists. These, and countless other positions, are both important to the collective well-being of our society and require schools to prepare students to take these jobs.[4]

We also want an educated population that can pursue careers, because it means they can be self-sustaining members of society.[5] While we might question the fairness of such an economic system, here, we must operate with the reality that in order for most of our students to be best equipped to obtain their own food, shelter, and other necessities, they need to secure jobs.

SORTING

Beyond preparing students for these careers, schools also serve as a sorting mechanism for employers. Diplomas and standardized tests function as credentials that signal to employers which students are qualified for certain jobs. As the economy has shifted away from industrial jobs, we have seen the bar for educational qualifications also change. A high school diploma that once guaranteed entry into middle-class work now often yields only low-wage jobs, while college degrees and even graduate training are required for access to stable careers.[6] What this looks like as our economy adapts to new technological innovations is yet to be known.

This matters because it reveals that when we talk about schools preparing students for careers, we are not only talking about teaching skills. We are also talking about how schools rank, sort, and credential students. That raises its own ethical questions about fairness, mobility, and the reproduction of inequality when schools play this role.[7]

OPPORTUNITY

Finally, we might still question, why not place the burden of career preparedness on parents and caregivers? We have given the job of preparing students for jobs to schools, not because it is the only way to do so. Instead, we recognize that it is our best avenue to making sure everyone has a fair shot in our society no matter their background. For example, Rawls argues that

---

[3] Bernal, "Education Can Help Prepare Learners for Tomorrow's Demands."
[4] OECD, "Education Economic and Social Outcomes"; OECD, "Public Returns from Education"; OECD, "Education Economic and Social Outcomes."
[5] Ibid.
[6] Morgan, "Degree Inflation."
[7] Labaree, *Someone Has to Fail*.

fair equality of opportunity requires public education to counterbalance the unequal advantages children receive from their families, ensuring access to careers is not determined by birth.[8]

If the economic aim of education is ultimately about fair opportunity, the core ethical question becomes whether schools merely open doors or actually ensure that students can walk through them. If schooling were to be equitable, every student would leave schools with genuine access to economic opportunities regardless of their background. The reality is that our students leave with very different prospects, despite our best attempts.

READINESS

Even if we agreed that schools must prepare students for economic participation, we still have to ask: what counts as readiness? A narrow definition emphasizes vocational training and specific job skills. A broader definition emphasizes adaptability, problem-solving, teamwork, and creativity. The broader vision also reflects the reality that students are preparing for jobs that may not yet exist.

Who gets to decide this definition also matters. Employers may want immediately employable graduates. Policymakers may want schools to supply a competitive workforce. Parents may want stability for their children. Students themselves may want freedom to shape their futures. The aim of career readiness is not self-explanatory, and it requires negotiation across the stakeholders we identified earlier.

If we define readiness narrowly, we risk reducing schools to pipelines into jobs. If we define it broadly, we risk promising skills without guaranteeing pathways to stable employment. Both these choices shape the fairness and adequacy of opportunity that students actually experience.

COMMITMENT

Breaking down the definition of economic aims shows the economic aim is about fair opportunity to economic opportunities, and *that fairness* requires vigilance against schooling that reinforces, rather than reduces, inequality.

Civic Aims

If the economic aim of schooling is about preparing students for work, the civic aim is about preparing them for membership in a political community. The civic purpose is to prepare students to participate in public life: to deliberate, collaborate, and sustain democratic institutions. Democracies cannot function unless citizens have the skills, dispositions, and trust to govern themselves collectively. Education therefore carries the responsibility of cultivating civic capacities.

What then are the minimum requirements of fulfilling this aim?

---

[8] Rawls, *A Theory of Justice*.

ENGAGEMENT

At the most basic level, schools must equip students to engage in democratic life. This includes familiar actions such as voting, but it also extends to organizing, advocacy, and public deliberation. A society that values self-government requires more than occasional trips to the ballot box. It requires citizens who know how to gather, debate, form associations, and press for change when needed.[9]

JUDGMENT

Democracy also requires judgment. The capacity to evaluate evidence, challenge arguments, and resist manipulation are intrinsic to preparing students to engage in effective civic discourse. Critical thinking and media literacy are what allow citizens to weigh competing claims, distinguish fact from propaganda, and avoid being passive consumers of information.[10]

COOPERATION

Another civic capacity is the ability to engage across differences. A diverse society will always include competing values, identities, and perspectives. Schools ought to model and cultivate dialogue that does not collapse into hostility or avoidance. Students must learn to disagree productively, to hear voices unlike their own, and to recognize the legitimacy of perspectives they may not share.[11] Ultimately, we want our students to have some sort of shared corpus of knowledge and values that sustain our democratic society. Of course, we need to evaluate how shared and similar that experience has to be in order for us to reach our civic aim.

UNESCO's global education framework emphasizes that civic aims extend beyond participation in one's own nation toward fostering global citizenship, peacebuilding, and sustainable development.[12] This perspective broadens civic aims by positioning students not only as democratic citizens of a country but as actors within an interconnected world who share responsibility for human rights, peace, and ecological sustainability.

PRACTICE

Schools are not only places for academic learning but also vital spaces for practicing democracy. For students to become active, engaged citizens, they must experience democratic principles firsthand within their learning environments. This means both in how we prioritize student voice but also in the processes that shape our schools' decision-making.[13]

It requires educational practices that empower students to take part in shaping their learning experiences, such as through participatory classroom discussions, school governance roles,

---

[9] Dewey, *Experience And Education*; Levinson, *No Citizen Left Behind*.
[10] Allen, *Education and Equality*; Kestigian, *Democratic Decisions in a Critical Thinking Crisis*.
[11] Gutmann, *Democratic Education*.
[12] UNESCO, "Education 2030: Incheon Declaration and Framework for Action for the Implementation of Sustainable Development Goal 4: Ensure Inclusive and Equitable Quality Education and Promote Lifelong Learning Opportunities for All - UNESCO Digital Library."
[13] Dewey, *Democracy and Education—An Introduction to the Philosophy of Education*; Freire and Macedo, *Pedagogy of the Oppressed*.

and project-based learning initiatives that mimic real-world issues.[14] This approach prepares students for democratic participation beyond the classroom by instilling values of mutual respect, social responsibility, and civic engagement. We cover some of these strategies when we discuss school and classroom policymaking in Section B.

COMMITMENT
Civic aims highlight a shared responsibility to form citizens who can sustain democracy through discourse and action.

Personal Aims
The personal aim of education is to help students lead meaningful, flourishing lives: to cultivate meaning, emotional stability, and the capacity for choice. This aim, present as early as Aristotle, treats education not as a means to work or citizenship but as an intrinsic good for human life.

What exactly does cultivating that for our students look like?

FLOURISHING
Aristotle argued that the ultimate aim of human life is *eudaimonia*, often translated as flourishing or living well. Unlike fleeting pleasures, flourishing refers to a deep sense of living a life of purpose, virtue, and balance. For Aristotle, education was the cultivation of the habits, virtues, and dispositions that make flourishing possible.[15]

He believed that schools should develop not only intellectual excellence but also moral excellence. Fulfillment requires learning how to reason well, how to deliberate about what is good, and how to live in community with others.[16] Education therefore was not just about preparing for jobs or civic life, but was the foundation for a good life.

Aristotle's vision remains relevant because it reminds us that happiness for our students is not passive. It requires deliberate cultivation, and focusing solely on test scores or job skills misses this deeper aim. If we nurture virtues such as courage, patience, generosity, and justice, we prepare students to live lives that are meaningful.[17]

Sen and Nussbaum turn this into a framework by defining a capabilities-based approach to justice and defining capabilities education can expand. Some of these include imagination, practical reasoning, a sense of belonging, and play.[18] Together, these capabilities translate the Aristotelian vision of flourishing into concrete criteria.

---

[14] Freire and Macedo, *Pedagogy of the Oppressed*.
[15] Aristoteles and Barnes, *The Nicomachean Ethics*.
[16] Ibid.
[17] Aristoteles and Barnes, *The Nicomachean Ethics*; Noddings, "An Ethic of Caring and Its Implications for Instructional Arrangements."
[18] Nussbaum, *Women and Human Development*; Sen, "Capability and Well-Being."

WELL-BEING

When schools attend to well-being, they protect students from harm, cultivate confidence, and build the foundation for long-term psychological health. This includes creating environments where students can navigate conflict, manage stress, and build supportive peer and adult relationships.

Modern socio-emotional learning theory gives us another component of well-being. Students need tools to recognize, understand, and regulate their emotions, form healthy relationships, and make responsible decisions.[19] These skills help academic learning, but also shape identity, resilience, empathy, and a sense of belonging. When students feel safe, seen, and supported, they are more able to grow intellectually and socially.

Well-being is also relational and environmental. Classroom climate, teacher relationships, school culture, and community context shape how students feel about themselves and their place in the world.[20] Ethical decision-making must take into account how policies and technologies impact this emotional landscape.

BALANCE

Finally, personal aims require us to consider both the present and the future. Schooling should expand students' real options in life rather than prematurely narrowing their paths. Tracking, rigid specialization, or unequal access to enriching experiences can limit a student's future autonomy long before they can understand the consequences.[21]

At the same time, we have to account for the intrinsic goods of childhood and recognize that schooling is not just preparatory. Children deserve joy, play, friendship, exploration, and moments of curiosity during their childhood. These experiences are ethically valuable even if they do not directly contribute to economic or civic outcomes.[22]

Schools must prepare students for adulthood while also respecting the experiences, identity development, and dignity of the children they are now. Ethical decisions must consider whether policies promote present well-being, protect future choices, or inadvertently foreclose opportunities.

COMMITMENT

Personal aims ensure education expands each student's capacity to live, choose, and belong in a way in line with their vision of a good life.

Stakes of Process: The Means

Even when we share the same aims, the way we pursue them determines whether schooling remains just, trustworthy, and humane. These stakes concern the moral significance of the processes used to pursue educational aims, including fairness, inclusion, recognition, and distribution of opportunities.

---

[19] Brackett, *Permission to Feel*.
[20] Lee and Ward, *The Role of Sel in Improving Literacy Development Introductory Brief*; Noddings, "An Ethic of Caring and Its Implications for Instructional Arrangements."
[21] Brighouse, *On Education*; Feinberg, "The Child's Right to an Open Future."
[22] Macleod, "Just Schools and Good Childhoods"; Brighouse et al., *Educational Goods*.

While the aims describe the skills and dispositions students need, the stakes of the process describe the justice and equity conditions that make those capacities meaningful. Educational decisions shape who counts as a citizen, who belongs in the community, and who is invited to participate in its future.

Opportunity

The economic and civic aims both rely on the idea that schools ought to prepare students for these two roles to ensure that everyone has an equal opportunity to pursue any career they want and to participate in civic life. If either thing were left to the family to prepare, we would end up with a very lopsided economic and political system (even more so than we have now).[23]

This raises fundamental questions about what we mean by equal opportunity in education. Are we satisfied with equality of access? In other words, is our obligation to simply ensure all students can attend school? Or do we need something more robust?

In theory, equality of opportunity means that each student should have the same genuine chance to succeed regardless of background. In its strongest form, this would mean leveling every difference that comes from family wealth, neighborhood, or inherited social advantage. If opportunity is equal, then outcomes should reflect only effort and choice.[24]

Adequacy, as Elizabeth Anderson and others suggest, is a different approach.[25] The aim is not to erase all differences, but to guarantee that every student reaches a sufficient baseline for equal civic participation. An adequate education gives everyone the literacy, numeracy, and reasoning skills required to participate in society and exercise citizenship. Beyond that threshold, it accepts that differences will remain.

The choice between equality and adequacy matters because they imply different ethical priorities. If we pursue strict equal opportunity, then we must constantly close gaps between advantaged and disadvantaged groups. If we pursue adequacy, then we can tolerate some gaps as long as everyone is above a baseline.[26] For example, is it enough that all children can read at a minimum grade level, or should we be ensuring that every student who graduates can read complex, scholarly articles with ease?

If equality of opportunity and adequacy frame the issue, the next step is to see how those ideas land in the everyday life of schools. The practical question is this: when we make choices about technology, staffing, funding, and assessment, are we content to guarantee that all students reach a minimum bar? Or do we have a responsibility to reduce the gaps between groups? The answer determines not only how we measure success, but also whose needs we prioritize when resources are scarce.

---

[23] Anderson, "Fair Opportunity in Education"; Okin, *Justice, Gender, and the Family*; Jencks, "Whom Must We Treat Equally for Educational Opportunity to Be Equal?"
[24] Satz, "Equality, Adequacy, and Education for Citizenship"; Fishkin, "Bottlenecks."
[25] Anderson, "Fair Opportunity in Education"; Satz, "Equality, Adequacy, and Education for Citizenship."
[26] Rawls, *A Theory of Justice*.

How we define and pursue fair opportunity determines exactly what impact our education system has on the makeup of society. It shapes how resources, burdens, and opportunities are distributed. Funding formulas, teacher assignments, and access to advanced courses all reflect distributive choices. Fairness often requires compensatory systems, directing more resources to students who begin with fewer advantages. Without such distribution, formal equality quickly reinforces structural inequality. With it, we make real trade-offs that we have to identify and accept.

Voice and Recognition

Our curriculum signals whose story matters, and our norms reveal whose voices are valued. Voice and recognition refer to whose perspectives count in educational decision-making and whose experiences are heard and validated. We need to ask whose knowledge, culture, and identity are respected in schools.

Recognition requires actively affirming marginalized groups and developing practices that help all students see themselves as valuable members of society. We risk perpetuating injustice and further marginalizing our most vulnerable students if we do not consider how voices are prioritized.[27]

To understand this impact of our decisions, we can think about epistemic injustice. Fricker describes two forms of epistemic injustice: ways in which people are wronged specifically in their capacity as knowers.[28] Both appear in schools.

The first is **testimonial injustice**. This occurs when a person's credibility is unfairly deflated due to bias. In schools, this might happen when a student's account of an event is doubted because of assumptions tied to race, gender, class, or disability. For instance, when Black students report discriminatory treatment, but their accounts are minimized, they are denied epistemic credibility.[29] The harm undermines trust, damages relationships, and perpetuates inequities in whose voices are considered authoritative.[30]

The second is **hermeneutical injustice**. This occurs when gaps in collective understanding prevent people from making sense of their own or others' experiences.[31] In education, this might happen when schools lack the shared language or conceptual tools to recognize a form of harm or exclusion. For example, for students who are neurodivergent, our traditional notions of personal flourishing and happiness may not apply, and we lack the vocabulary and structures to think about what it does mean for those students.[32]

Epistemic injustice reminds us that ethical decision-making in education is also about who gets to be heard, believed, and understood.

---

[27] Medina, *The Epistemology of Resistance*; Young and Allen, *Justice and the Politics of Difference*.
[28] Fricker, *Epistemic Injustice*.
[29] McClain and Wellington, "A PSA I'm Here Too."
[30] Fricker, *Epistemic Injustice*.
[31] Fricker, *Epistemic Injustice*.
[32] Chapman and Carel, "Neurodiversity, Epistemic Injustice, and the Good Human Life."

One way to deepen this reflection is through critical pedagogy. Inspired by thinkers such as Paulo Freire and bell hooks, critical pedagogy challenges traditional systems that perpetuate inequality by treating students as passive recipients of knowledge, similar to bank accounts getting deposits. It calls for a transformative educational practice that recognizes and disrupts the power dynamics and cultural biases embedded in schooling. Critical pedagogy seeks to empower students by developing their critical consciousness, a deeper awareness of social, political, and economic injustice, and by equipping them with the tools to question and transform the conditions that sustain it.[33]

The stake of voice and recognition reminds us that education is about whether all our students are recognized as knowers and contributors within the learning. When we fail to value the full range of human experience, language, and perspective, we silence the people schools are meant to serve. But, when educators design spaces that listen, affirm, and co-construct knowledge with students, they nurture belonging and trust. Ethical education, then, depends on our capacity to expand who counts as a knower and to create conditions where every student's voice has the power to shape understanding.

Balancing the Stakes

Ethical decision-making in education, therefore, requires harmony between *ends* and *means*: Together, they define the conditions under which good aims can be pursued ethically. Of course, schools cannot safeguard every stake, always. Every decision involves trade-offs between aims that compete and procedures that constrain.

These decisions carry multiple moral mandates at once. There is the mandate to prepare students for work (economic aim). The mandate to prepare them for democracy (civic aim). The mandate to help them live meaningful lives (personal aim). And, the mandate to pursue these ends fairly, and inclusively (stakes of process). No single decision can maximize all of these simultaneously, and we will have to accept some harm.

We will see cases where there are trade-offs between the aims. We might have to decide between AI curricula that help with career readiness and those which encourage civic engagement. We might have to decide between pursuing personalization for individual goals or standardization for a shared experience. We will also see cases where the aims and procedures conflict. If we focus too much on fairness, we might suppress the flexibility that we need for individual flourishing.

The stakes are high because each aim carries real, long-term consequences for our students' lives and our shared communities. The next chapter will provide ethical reasoning heuristics that help us navigate these conflicts.

---

[33] Hooks, *Teaching to Transgress*; Freire and Macedo, *Pedagogy of the Oppressed*; Freire, *Pedagogy of Hope*.

Exit Ticket

Reflect: Think of a recent decision you made about curriculum, assessment, or technology. What did that decision implicitly prioritize among economic, civic, and personal aims, and what did it quietly deprioritize?

Act: Identify one specific practice, policy, or tech tool in your classroom or school and how the stakes relate to it. What is one concrete adjustment you could make in the next month to better balance these stakes?

Advocate: Who needs a stronger voice in decisions about these stakes, and how do they influence our daily behavior?

CHAPTER 7

Reasoning Heuristics

Chapters 3–6 gave us analytical lenses: principles help us identify what moral values are at stake, moral approaches help us weigh those values, stakeholders show us whose interests matter, and stakes clarify what we are ultimately trying to achieve. But these alone cannot help us make decisions; they clarify the contours of our problems. Ultimately, we will have to apply our own practical wisdom, a combination of our lived experiences and our learned principles, to make decisions. Here, I present heuristics as our ethical decision aids: practical reasoning tools that help us navigate from analysis to judgment when principles conflict, stakeholders disagree, and stakes compete.

I do use "heuristic" somewhat loosely here. Some of these can function as values (plurality), some as criteria (evidence), some as procedural checks (recalibration). What they share is that they are all practical reasoning tools that help us move from analysis to judgment, rather than strict rules that determine outcomes.

These heuristics synthesize insights from educational ethics, practical philosophy, and rhetoric theory that make decision-making more rigorous and defensible. Thus, you will notice some overlaps with concepts from earlier, but these heuristics use those concepts to build reasoning aids instead of philosophical arguments.

Decision-making in education requires us to act quickly with incomplete information under uncertainty. The heuristics in this chapter serve three functions: framing, to help us see what kind of ethical situation we are in, weighing, to provide structured ways to balance competing values, and validating, to offer checks against bias and hasty judgment.

Not every heuristic will be needed in every situation and there might be situations where no heuristic is enough. We use them as guides to help us navigate particular situations, rather than treating them as a decision-tree that provides all answers.

These heuristics form the habits that make our later case analysis possible; and, they guide our reasoning as we enter those specific situations.

Guiding Questions
- How can we think about how to balance multiple aims when they conflict?
- How can we think about the impact of our decisions systematically?
- How will we know when we are acting with the right information?

Framing

This first set of heuristics helps us figure out how to frame what matters. In practice, these decisions require us to balance aims (plurality), ensure a baseline for every student (adequacy), match priorities to developmental readiness (developmental), consider whether things are necessary or sufficient (necessity) and ground our justification in shared civic reasons (legitimacy).

PLURALITY HEURISTIC

The plurality heuristic is to remember that we want to achieve a balance of all three aims for our students.[1] It reminds us to consider all three aims without collapsing our decisions into pursuing only one. It guards against reductionism in our decision-making that ends up prioritizing one good at the expense of all others.

For example, imagine a school is revising its core curriculum, and there are many proposals focusing on improving career readiness metrics further. Using the plurality heuristic, the team notices this and avoids prioritizing economic aims at the expense of personal or civic growth.

We can ask these three questions to use this heuristic:

- Which aim(s) of education are we supporting here?
- Which aim might be neglected or hurt?
- Are we over-tilting toward one aim as our main purpose?

ADEQUACY HEURISTIC

The adequacy heuristic is to consider whether each student is developing adequate capacity toward *each* aim, and also whether *every* student is developing those capacities.[2] While plurality focuses on balancing aims overall, adequacy focuses on ensuring a minimum floor of development in each aim for every student. In other words, we want to make sure that before developing one aim further for a student, we should check that they are reasonably making progress toward the other aims. At the same time, before we help some students develop advanced capacity in any area, we want to make sure every student has reached an adequate level of development in each domain.

For example, consider a district that wants to create advanced civic leadership opportunities for a small group of students. Using the adequacy heuristic, leaders check whether all students have a basic foundation in civic skills first, and they discover that some classes lack

---

[1] Brighouse et al., *Educational Goods*.
[2] Anderson, "What Is the Point of Equality?"; Brighouse et al., *Educational Goods*.

consistent instruction in civic discourse. They thus choose to improve the base classes before pursuing advanced options.

We can ask these three questions for this heuristic:

- Have we adequately developed the other aims before we invest more in this one?
- Have all students met the minimum baseline in this domain before we expand advanced opportunities?
- Are our enrichment programs widening or narrowing educational inequality?

NECESSITY HEURISTIC

The necessity and sufficiency heuristic helps us distinguish between what is *required* for an aim and what is simply helpful. Something is *necessary* if we cannot achieve our aim without it (e.g., students have to use a computer to learn typing). Something is sufficient if it alone is enough to achieve the aim, but other paths might also work (e.g., a flashcard app might be enough to help students learn their times tables, but so might handwriting them). Something can be helpful but neither necessary nor sufficient (e.g., a new reading app might help but is not required and will not guarantee success on its own). Understanding these distinctions prevents us from treating optional enhancements as essential requirements or assuming that a single intervention will solve complex problems.

For example, imagine a teacher wonders if fifth graders must complete long research papers to develop research skills. Using this heuristic, she asks: Are lengthy papers *necessary* for building these skills at this stage, or would shorter, scaffolded tasks be *sufficient*? She discovers that the complex assignment is not necessary, and that a progression of smaller tasks could actually be more effective.

We ask these questions to use this heuristic:

- Is this component truly *necessary* for achieving our goal, or just one helpful option among many?
- Is what we are planning *sufficient* on its own, or does it need to be combined with other supports?
- Are we treating something as essential when it is actually optional?

DEVELOPMENTAL HEURISTIC

The developmental heuristic reminds us that our priorities and ability to develop certain capacities in our students will vary based on their age. Not all goods deserve equal emphasis all the time. Our decisions to promote an educational good should reflect the needs, context, and developmental stage of the students.

For example, imagine a middle school considers giving students complete independence over their project timelines to build autonomy skills. Applying the developmental heuristic, educators ask whether students at this age have enough self-management skills. They decide to provide partial autonomy with structured checkpoints to match developmental readiness.

We ask these three questions to use this heuristic:

- What capacities are appropriate to nurture at this stage of development?
- Are we asking students to exercise autonomy before they have the scaffolds to do so?
- How might early emphasis on one value constrain later growth in another?

LEGITIMACY HEURISTIC

The legitimacy heuristic asks us to center shared values over our individual ones.[3] We have to remember that our decisions in education need to reflect shared values that we have as a community and not our individual worldviews. When we make ethical choices, the reasons for our decisions should be ones that all reasonable members of the community could, in principle, accept. This ensures that educational decisions are justified through shared civic values, rather than on personal beliefs.

For example, imagine a principal wants to adopt a new disciplinary rule based on personal moral views about respect. The legitimacy heuristic prompts her to test whether the justification rests on shared civic values such as safety, fairness, and clear expectations. She rewrites the rationale using reasons any member of the community could accept.

We ask these three questions for this heuristic:

- Can I justify this decision to all members of our community?
- Would this reasoning hold up in a school board meeting?
- Does it rest on shared values and aims rather than private convictions?

Weighing

Once we have framed the decision (by clarifying which aims are at stake, whether we are meeting baseline adequacy, what is developmentally appropriate, what is truly necessary, and whether our reasons are publicly justifiable), we turn to the question of how to choose between competing options.

Thus, this next set of heuristics helps us think through how to choose the best action. It helps us think about whether the value conflicts can be resolved through combination (mutual inclusivity), whether there are other options that solve both problems (alternative), consider just how strong the consequences are (impact), how likely those consequences are (probability), and who must justify taking the risk (proof).

MUTUAL INCLUSIVITY HEURISTIC

When we face a decision about what action to take, we often frame our options as competing choices.[4] In these situations, the first temptation can be to pick a side. Should we prioritize equity or excellence? Career readiness or civic education? Accountability or trust? We use a

---

[3] Rawls, *Political Liberalism*.
[4] Pirie, *How to Win Every Argument*.

dichotomy to frame ethical questions because they highlight the values that conflict, which is useful analytically, but limiting in decision-making. However, in practice, there might be paths that allow us to achieve both ends. The mutual inclusivity heuristic asks whether the actions available can be adjusted or combined so both values can be advanced through the same action.

For example, consider a team that is reducing science labs to increase literacy time. Mutual inclusivity asks whether the action can be modified so both plans move forward. They restructure the schedule, so labs occur less often but with higher quality and embed literacy strategies into lab instruction, reducing the trade-off.

We can ask these questions when approaching a decision:

- What is lost if I choose one of these actions?
- Can I modify the action to achieve a more balanced outcome?
- Are there conditions or additions that reduce the trade-offs?

ALTERNATIVE HEURISTIC

The alternative heuristic helps us consider whether the action in front of us is the only or best available action that can accomplish our actual aim.[5] Often, the decision seems more daunting because we approach the solutions too narrowly. Rather than accepting that we have to make a limiting choice, we can consider whether there are other ways to avoid the trade-off we are facing. This heuristic forces us to think backwards from the aim we have and what solutions (both technological and others) might work rather than just choosing the solutions in front of us.

For example, imagine if we are considering whether an AI bot is helpful for students, we might also consider whether hiring an additional staff member, organizing peer tutoring, or reframing the curricula might have a larger impact without the risk of the AI bot.

We can consider the following questions:

- What is the actual problem we are trying to solve?
- Are there other plausible ways to solve the problem?
- Are these better or worse than the solution in front of us?

IMPACT HEURISTIC

The impact heuristic asks us to weigh the consequences we have identified. We think not just about what good or harm comes, but how good or harmful it is. We have to be careful to avoid making judgments that rely on presuming downstream effects. We also want to consider whether the impact can be reversed, or whether the harm can be permanent.

For example, imagine a district is considering a new reading program that could improve scores but may overwhelm teachers. The impact heuristic guides leaders to weigh the degree of benefit and the magnitude of burden. They find the teacher workload cost is high and the benefit marginal.

---

[5] Ibid.

We ask the following to define the impact:

- How strong are the risks and benefits?
- Are we only considering the impact of our current decision?
- Can the harm we are risking be repaired?

PROBABILITY HEURISTIC

While we consider the impacts, we also want to think about their likelihood. A harm that is severe but highly improbable calls for a different response from a harm that is mild but almost certain. Similarly, a policy with a modest but reliable benefit may be more defensible than one promising dramatic gain with little chance of success.

For example, imagine a school fears a small possibility that a digital portfolio tool could leak data. Probability helps them evaluate how likely this outcome is, based on existing security evidence. They discover the risk is extremely low, while the benefit of continuous student reflection is highly probable, so they proceed with safeguards.

We can ask the following to evaluate probability:

- How likely are the best and worst outcomes?
- How do the probabilities weigh against the degree of impact?
- Are we responding to the most likely scenario or over-reacting to outliers?

PROOF HEURISTIC

We also want to think about who bears the burden of proving the magnitude and probability of the impact.[6] When an action carries risk to students, those proposing it should be the ones to show that the benefits are probable and the harms unlikely. In ethical reasoning, the burden of proof often belongs to those introducing change, since they are claiming potential benefits while exposing others to risk.

For example, imagine a vendor claims their SEL program dramatically improves well-being. The proof heuristic asks the vendor to demonstrate evidence instead of expecting skeptics to prove harm. The school requires actual data showing effectiveness before agreeing to adopt it.

When considering if the burden of proof is being met, we ask:

- Who carries the burden of proof for showing that this action is safe and effective?
- Has sufficient evidence been offered to justify the change?
- Are we demanding more from skeptics than advocates?

Validating

After exploring possible actions and weighing their likely consequences, we need to validate our reasoning. The final set of heuristics helps us refine and validate before making a decision. At this stage, we can think about what all the stakeholders affected think (perspectives), different ways to experiment and revise (recalibration), and the kinds of evidence we have and need (evidence).

---

[6] Ibid.

PERSPECTIVES HEURISTIC

We mapped out the relevant stakeholders in Chapter 5, so that we can approach complex situations by consulting the various stakeholders. No stakeholder has the full picture, which is why ethical decision-making requires understanding multiple perspectives. We cannot always build consensus before we make decisions, but we want to make sure that harms or benefits that we might not be able to see are not overlooked.

For example, consider a school that plans to shift homework expectations. Using the perspectives heuristic, they gather input not only from teachers but also families and students with heavy home responsibilities. The new perspectives prompt adjustments that reduce unintended burdens.

We should ask ourselves:

- Whose voices are missing from this conversation?
- Who is most vulnerable if this decision goes wrong?
- Am I weighing the voices by impact or by loudness?

(RE)CALIBRATION HEURISTIC

We have to recognize that we can calibrate our decisions as we go along. We can begin smaller through starting micro-experiments and pilots to test our decisions. We can also review the decision as we get more evidence and recalibrate (adjust, scale, or reverse) it based on the new information. Most decisions are rarely permanent; they are provisional and should be revisited as new information emerges.

For example, consider a teacher who wonders whether to adopt a phone caddy system. Using recalibration, he pilots it in two classes for one month, collects feedback, and discovers that adjustments are needed for clear exceptions before making it permanent in all his classes.

We can think through the following questions:

- Can this decision be piloted?
- What would make us revisit this decision?
- Can this be reversed if needed?

EVIDENCE HEURISTIC

Many of the above heuristics involve making claims, but those claims are only as persuasive as the data that supports them.[7] Evidence can be more harmful than helpful without the right parameters in place to evaluate it. Vendors might cite percentages that collapse under close scrutiny, or policymakers might lean on single studies to justify their sweeping reform. We need a heuristic to help us weigh the quality, relevance, and sufficiency of different kinds of evidence.

For example, imagine a district considers using a math platform because one case study reports a large gain. The evidence heuristic leads them to examine study design, check for replication, and look for data with populations similar to theirs. The deeper review reveals limited evidence, so they delay adoption until stronger data emerges.

---

[7] Slavin, "Evidence-Based Education Policies"; Brighouse et al., *Educational Goods*; Brighouse et al., "Good Education Policy Making."

We have extensive questions we can ask to think about the evidence:

- How strong is the evidence? Is it a robust RCT, a case study, or anecdotes?
- Is the evidence specific to our context? Does it apply to our type of school, population, and community?
- Does the evidence demonstrate causation, or might the results reflect confounding variables or correlations?
- Has the study or finding been independently replicated or peer-reviewed?
- How should we weigh different forms of evidence (quantitative studies, practitioner experience, and stakeholder perspectives) when they conflict?

Thinking Habits

The heuristics from this chapter are meant to be thinking habits as we reason through cases. They help make our reasoning transparent, revisable, and most importantly, justifiable. We now have some tools to help us frame what matters, weigh possible actions, and validate our decisions. These all make reasoning into a robust process rather than simply a single moment of choice.

Ultimately, we cannot predict the exact outcome of our decisions, and there will be a degree of ambiguity we have to accept. A commitment to moral decision-making requires admitting uncertainty and iterating on our decisions as we learn more.

As we build on these heuristics, we have to remember that they are ultimately shortcuts, and so they require safeguards to avoid mistakes. First, we want to resist the temptation to apply every heuristic and become stuck in analysis paralysis. As we practice the cases, and you encounter real situations, you will start to internalize some of these heuristics, and also realize which ones help you and when.

Second, we want to avoid treating these as rules, rather than reasoning aids. They are meant to guide our judgment, not replace it.

Finally, we want to make sure we choose heuristics that will challenge our instinct, not validate it. When we approach an ethical dilemma, our goal is not to find a way to justify our first instinct, but to test it against rigorous ethical reasoning.

In the next chapter, we turn to thinking about how the philosophical concepts we have discussed thus far, manifest in conversations about educational technology through overarching themes.

Exit Ticket

Reflect: Which heuristic from this chapter feels unfamiliar or difficult?
Act: Identify one upcoming decision and how you might deliberately apply a specific heuristic to guide that decision.
Advocate: Who else in your school or community could benefit from using one of these heuristics, and how might you share or model that reasoning with them?

CHAPTER 8

Ed Tech Defined

Now that we have a philosophical framework for talking about ethics, this chapter shows us why those tools are essential and timeless. Every generation of educational technology has brought new promises and new dilemmas, yet the underlying ethical tensions have barely changed.[1]

By looking across centuries of innovations, we can see that the questions our framework helps us answer today are not particularly new. This historical perspective prepares us for the next two chapters, where we will examine the recurring themes and inherent risks that appear across modern technologies.

So, what do we mean when we talk about ed tech? We often picture modern devices and software: websites, apps and software, classroom computers, and maybe the latest VR goggles. Yet the history of education shows that every generation has introduced new tools, from chalkboards and textbooks to projectors and computers, that reshaped not only classrooms but also the ethical dilemmas facing schools.[2]

Throughout this chapter, I discuss both technology in education (tools used inside schools to support learning, teaching, or communication) and technology for education (tools designed specifically to shape instruction, curriculum, or assessment). The distinction matters in research, but in practice the two categories constantly overlap. A tool not built for education can become central to school life, while purpose-built "educational technologies" can be devoid of any true value to education.[3] Because the ethical questions are nearly identical across both categories, I address them together in the book.

While a real comprehensive history of educational technology is beyond the scope of this book, here I aim to examine some of the key technological advancements that shaped education. In doing so, I hope to show that every technological change, with its implicit values, came with its own set of practical ethical questions.[4] I highlight the questions raised by educational

---

[1] Cuban, Oversold and Underused; Selwyn, Education and Technology.
[2] Saettler, The Evolution of American Educational Technology; Watters, Teaching Machines.
[3] Postman, Technopoly; Selwyn, Is Technology Good for Education?
[4] Winner, "Do Artifacts Have Politics?"

technology in every era, from our historical foundations (printing press, personal computers, internet) to the current landscape (cellphones, social media, AI), and finally to future horizons (VR, biometrics, blockchain, metaverse).

The deeper dimensions of those questions are not new. Questions of equity, authority, control, and impact have always appeared with each new invention. We always had to ask: Who has access to the new technology? Who controls what knowledge is transmitted? How do tools affect the relationship between teachers, students, families, and institutions? Here, you will see how that shows up differently for different generations.

Guiding Questions
- What counts as educational technology?
- What ethical tensions have prior technological advancements brought?
- What is the current trajectory of educational technology?

Historical Foundations

PRINTING PRESS

One of the earliest forms of educational technology that often comes up in modern discussions is the printing press. It is often in the form of this distilled phrase: "the printing press democratized education."[5] While others have critiqued the inaccuracy of this phrase, we might be able to see a pattern that follows us through history: promises of access, followed by new forms of gatekeeping, and ultimately, a reorganization of power that both fulfilled and betrayed the original promise.[6]

> **Knowledge:** Oral authority from educators was superseded by textual authority from books.[7] What did this mean for those whose knowledge was valued?
>
> **Divides:** Even though books became easier to spread, they were useless without literacy.[8] Who had access to literacy education and who was left out?
>
> **Influence:** Various authorities tried to control and shape what was printed, including religious authorities and governments.[9] What types of censorship and control did this enable?
>
> **Standardization:** Printed books eventually led to textbooks and standardized texts.[10] What variation did we lose by standardizing texts?

---

[5] Eisenstein, The Printing Press as an Agent of Change.
[6] Drimmer, "The Printing Press Democratized Knowledge."
[7] Eisenstein, The Printing Press as an Agent of Change.
[8] Eskelson, "States, Institutions, and Literacy Rates in Early-Modern Western Europe."
[9] Johnson, "Printing and Censorship | Research Starters | EBSCO Research."
[10] Eisenstein, The Printing Press as an Agent of Change.

Today, we still ask questions about which books are allowed in schools and what that means for authority, social cohesion, justice, and educational goals. Beyond the printing press, every new tool redistributes power over knowledge, so adoption decisions are also decisions about authority.

PERSONAL COMPUTER

We now jump a few hundred years ahead and look at the invention of the personal computer. This is a technological development that sets the background for many of the technological developments we will consider in the rest of the book. The personal computer entered schools carrying dual promises: individual creative empowerment and systemic educational transformation.[11]

> **Creativity:** The use of computers for creative endeavors changed how we viewed art and creation in schools.[12] What did it mean to be creative when using a computer?
>
> **Divides:** The rollout of personal computers into schools happened at an uneven pace.[13] What factors co-occurred with "computer-rich" versus "computer-poor" schools?
>
> **Access:** Computers did not have all accessibility features from the beginning, limiting who could make use of them.[14] Which students were left out by the lack of accessible technology?
>
> **Resources:** Computers were not only expensive on their own, but they also required training, maintenance, and constant upgrades.[15] What did allocating resources to computers require us to give up?

Here too, we still worry about what counts as authentic creation, who has access to devices and which ones, and if our newest devices and features are accessible by all our students. Devices matter, but so does how they are used, who gets them, and what we give up by funding them.

INTERNET

Two decades later, we see another dramatic change in what technology our students have access to. We see a rapid adoption of the internet among our schools, with the National Center for Education Statistics reporting the percentage of schools with internet access growing from 35% in 1994 to 95% by 1999.[16] This brings a new set of concerns and challenges about the impact of technology in our classrooms.

---

[11] Cuban, Oversold and Underused.
[12] Papert, "Computers and Computer Cultures."
[13] Light, "Rethinking the Digital Divide."
[14] MSU Libraries, "Timeline | Advancing Accessibility: A Timeline | Exhibits | MSU Libraries."
[15] Office of Educational Research and Improvement, "Internet Access in U.S. Public Schools and Classrooms: 1994-99."
[16] Ibid.

Influence: The internet provided thousands of results for any given search term.[17] What power dynamics shaped which results came up first?

Attention: Right from the beginning, websites began to think about increasing engagement and keeping users' attention.[18] What risks were there to student well-being from internet usage?

Ends: Career readiness required a higher level of technological literacy than ever before, and the dynamics of democracy were rapidly changing.[19] How could we make sure our students are prepared for civic engagement and various career paths?

Access: Information access became more shared, but not all internet access was equal; the speed of the connection also mattered.[20] What were the differences in access between families in a community?

This set of questions is almost wholly still relevant. We still worry about how search engines prioritize results, how websites hold our attention, and whether we have equitable broadband access across the nation. The internet added new dimensions to our existing concerns, including attention, information quality, and broadband equity.

Contemporary Technology

As we explore contemporary challenges, we will notice a similar set of questions continuing to emerge in our discussions about the ethics of technology in education.

CELLPHONES

While the invention of cellphones seems to be in the distant past, we are still dealing with the ethical challenges they brought up for our schools. This might at least in part be because the cellphone represents a unique challenge in educational technology. It is not school-issued, controlled, or optional in modern life, yet it fundamentally alters the classroom dynamic in ways we are only beginning to understand.

Control: Parents buy them, students use them, and teachers have to deal with them.[21] Who gets to make the ultimate decision about student cellphone usage?

Access: Cellphones can be tools of accessibility from translation apps to diabetes monitors.[22] How do we ensure we do not limit the potential for these tools to help our students?

---

[17] Noble, Algorithms of Oppression.
[18] Riaz et al., "An Overview of User Psychological Manipulation Techniques in UI/UX Web Design."
[19] OECD, Students, Computers and Learning.
[20] Lee, "Bridging Digital Divides between Schools and Communities"; Judge et al., "Digital Equity."
[21] Langreo and Domzalski, "Cellphone Policies in Schools, Explained"; Prothero, "Parents Want Cellphones in the Classroom. Here's Why."
[22] Carroll et al., "Using a Cell Phone-Based Glucose Monitoring System for Adolescent Diabetes Management"; Marshall, "When School Policy Limits Access to Assistive Technology for Students with Disabilities - Council of Parent Attorneys and Advocates, Inc."

Attention: Cellphones are engaging to the point of addiction.[23] How do we help students learn to hold attention, both inside and outside the classroom?

Ends: Cellphones help connect our students to the vast resources of the internet.[24] Can we use cellphones to improve educational outcomes for our students?

These are just some of the questions that cellphones, and even smart wearables, bring up in our modern classrooms. Many schools are approaching this with questions of banning, effective integration, or some combination of the two. Ultimately, our cellphone policies are about balancing classroom control with respect for students' lives, needs, and safety outside school.

SOCIAL MEDIA

With cellphones, also came near universal access to social media applications. Social media presents a different paradox: it is simultaneously a powerful platform for student empowerment and potentially a damaging force for adolescent development.

Ends: Social media empowers our students to levels of civic engagement we have never seen before but also distracts from curricular goals.[25] How can we balance these competing, but equally important, ends for our students?

Safety: Social media is often the site of bullying and harassment.[26] How do we help our students form healthy relationships with the use of social media?

Privacy: Social media runs on advertising revenue from targeting its users based on their data. How do we ensure our students' data are protected?

Social media has brought with it challenges that require unique approaches by schools. Some schools are embracing the direct use of social media for communicating with parents and the community, increasing civic engagement, and teaching digital citizenship. Others are worried about the potential negative effects and approaching the issue with more caution and hesitation.

WEB PLATFORMS

As computers and the internet became more widespread, we saw the emergence of websites and software specific to education, including learning management systems (LMSs) and massive open online courses (MOOCs). LMSs are designed to be the central platforms that manage assignments, grades, communication, and student data. MOOCs are built with the promise of free global learning through virtual learning.

---

[23] Sunday et al., "The Effects of Smartphone Addiction on Learning"; Hendrie, "Cellphones in Schools"; Villegas Dominguez et al., "Cell Phone Addiction and Its Impact on Students' Mental Health."
[24] Kulowiec, "Cell Phones as Classroom Tools"; Holland and Kellogg, "How Phones Can Facilitate Distance Learning."
[25] Grace Tatter, "A Toolkit for Digital Civics | Harvard Graduate School of Education."
[26] Pew Research Center, Teens and Cyberbullying 2022.

Ends: These platforms shape instructional goals by deciding what can be assigned, submitted, tracked, or measured.[27] How do we ensure these systems support authentic learning rather than narrowing what counts as success?

Access: MOOCs promised access but mostly served learners who were already literate, connected, and supported.[28] How can we use these technologies to move past reinforcing privilege?

Data Aggregation: These platforms consolidate student information at a scale that would have been unthinkable in earlier eras.[29] What responsibilities do schools have when student work, behavior, communication, and identity are all stored and analyzed in one place?

Platforms like these reorganize how data, power, and access flow through a school, often in ways educators do not fully control. And as platforms grow more central to school life, they set the stage for the next transformation: the move from tools that organize learning to tools that generate and shape it.

ARTIFICIAL INTELLIGENCE

After ChatGPT launched in November 2022, the conversation immediately turned to student essays written entirely by AI and teachers using AI to provide feedback on those essays. The widespread fear and immediate responses of blanket bans highlight the problems that come with powerful tools that are deployed before we understand their implications.

Biases: AI is trained on data that is biased, and so its output exhibits many of the same biases that are prominent in our society.[30] How do we ensure that the biases from AI do not cause harm in our schools?

Access: AI has the potential to increase accessibility for students who have individual learning needs.[31] Who do we prioritize for AI interventions?

Ends: AI is making major waves in the workplace, and increasingly, AI literacy is an essential employment skill.[32] How much time, if any, do we spend with our students on AI tool literacy?

Integrity: AI is creating new challenges for our ability to accurately assess our students.[33] What assessments can serve as fair and accurate measures of student learning?

---

[27] Blum, Ungrading; Blum, Schoolishness; Boninger and Nichols, Fit for Purpose? How Today's Commercial Digital Platforms Subvert Key Goals of Public Education.
[28] Kolowich, "MOOCs Are Largely Reaching Privileged Learners, Survey Finds"; Emanuel, "MOOCs Taken by Educated Few."
[29] Krumova and Kataria, "Education Cybersecurity"; Boninger and Nichols, Fit for Purpose? How Today's Commercial Digital Platforms Subvert Key Goals of Public Education.
[30] Baker and Hawn, "Algorithmic Bias in Education"; Bird et al., "Are Algorithms Biased in Education?"; Idowu, "Debiasing Education Algorithms"; Akgun and Greenhow, "Artificial Intelligence in Education."
[31] Office of Educational Technology, "Artificial Intelligence and the Future of Teaching and Learning"; Shah, AI and the Future of Education.
[32] Skovron, "AI Literacy in the Workplace"; Shah, AI and the Future of Education; Office of Educational Technology, "Artificial Intelligence and the Future of Teaching and Learning."
[33] Perkins et al., "The Artificial Intelligence Assessment Scale (AIAS)."

The new growth in artificial intelligence is creating both remarkable opportunities and existential questions about the nature of learning itself. While these are some questions that have already come up, as the technology grows both in usage and quality, we will face questions about the ethical ramifications of the technology in our classrooms, and we will have to consider under what conditions, with which safeguards, and toward which educational aims we use AI.

Future Horizons

ADVANCED AI

AI raises familiar questions about equity and authority, but it also introduces challenges that we have not seen before. The move from teacher-guided learning to machine-mediated instruction shifts the very nature of educational relationships.

> **Influence:** Personalized AI tutors may adapt to student motivation but could also manipulate behavior in subtle ways.[34] Where is the line between support and undue influence?
>
> **Authority:** As AI systems surpass teacher knowledge in some areas, students may trust machines more than humans.[35] What happens to teacher authority and the educator-student bond?
>
> **Privacy:** AI-driven personalization requires immense amounts of biometric, behavioral, and academic data.[36] Who controls this data, and what rights do students and families have over it?
>
> **Divides:** If wealthy schools provide human teachers while underfunded schools rely on AI, AI could deepen inequalities.[37] Is it ethical to offer "AI for the masses, humans for the elite"?

These questions remind us that the adoption of AI is not only about efficiency or personalization. It forces schools to confront what kind of human development they value and whether education remains a fundamentally human enterprise.

VIRTUAL REALITY

AI reshapes cognition, but VR reshapes perception itself. With headsets already entering classrooms, the boundary between learning and lived experience is collapsing.

---

[34] Corbett and Tangen, "AI Tutors vs. Tenacious Myths."
[35] García-López and Trujillo-Liñán, "Ethical and Regulatory Challenges of Generative AI in Education."
[36] Chang et al., "Co-Designing AI with Youth Partners"; García-López and Trujillo-Liñán, "Ethical and Regulatory Challenges of Generative AI in Education"; Akgun and Greenhow, "Artificial Intelligence in Education"; Laird et al., "Hand in Hand: Schools' Embrace of AI Connected to Increased Risks to Students"; Shah, AI and the Future of Education.
[37] Lake, "AI Is Coming to U.S. Classrooms, but Who Will Benefit?"; Shah, AI and the Future of Education.

Well-being: VR enables powerful simulations, but immersive scenarios may harm students.[38] Should schools expose children to intense experiences, even in service of empathy?

Health: VR carries risks of eyestrain, disorientation, and motion sickness.[39] How do we ensure student health is not compromised?

Community: VR can isolate students in solitary immersion or support collaborative exploration.[40] How do schools design for community rather than withdrawal?

Divide: High-cost headsets could restrict VR learning to wealthy districts.[41] Is it fair to introduce a tool that may immediately widen educational inequality?

The promise of immersive exploration is powerful, but so are the risks of harm, inequity, and disconnection. As classrooms consider VR, they must weigh the thrill of new worlds against the responsibility to protect students' minds and bodies.

BIOMETRICS

And, while VR changes how students experience the world, biometrics change how the world experiences students. These technologies turn bodies into constant streams of data, shifting the classroom from a place of trust to one of surveillance.

Labeling: Biometric monitoring can detect stress or illness early, but behavioral data can be reinterpreted as diagnosis, mislabeling students. How should schools handle this risk?

Privacy: Unlike passwords, biometric identifiers cannot be changed.[42] What happens if children's biometric data is stolen or misused?

Surveillance: Widespread biometric use in schools trains children to accept constant monitoring as normal.[43] Is this preparing students for democratic citizenship or for surveillance-heavy workplaces?

Consent: Children cannot meaningfully consent to biometric collection.[44] Should schools collect data that students cannot truly opt out of?

Biometric tools can be marketed as safeguards, but they also normalize lifelong monitoring and reduce our children's ability to consent. The convenience of "early detection" sits directly against lifelong risks of surveillance, mislabeling, and data misuse.

---

[38] Lundin et al., "Adverse Effects of Virtual and Augmented Reality Interventions in Psychiatry."
[39] Cossio et al., "Cybersickness and Discomfort from Head-Mounted Displays Delivering Fully Immersive Virtual Reality."
[40] Barreda-Ángeles et al., "Easily Applicable Social Virtual Reality and Social Presence in Online Higher Education During the Covid-19 Pandemic."
[41] Koenig, "Is There Still Time to Build Equity into Virtual Reality Edtech?"
[42] Miller, "The Basics, Usage, and Privacy Concerns of Biometric Data."
[43] Thompson, "New York Bans Facial Recognition in Schools After Report Finds Risks Outweigh Potential Benefits"; Watson, "Protecting Children in the Frontier of Surveillance Capitalism."
[44] New York State Office of Information Technology Services, Use of Biometric Identifying Technology in Schools; Watson, "Protecting Children in the Frontier of Surveillance Capitalism."

METAVERSE

The metaverse represents the furthest horizon: a vision of fully virtual schools where physical presence becomes optional. While it may seem speculative, the pandemic showed how quickly schools can be pushed into digital-only environments.

Community: Full-virtual schooling may foster connection without physical presence.[45] Does this satisfy developmental needs for embodied play, touch, and in-person community?

Safety: Virtual spaces can replicate the harassment and exploitation seen in adult metaverse environments.[46] How do we secure children against these risks?

Development: Avatars shape how adolescents see themselves and others.[47] What ethical safeguards should exist around identity formation in digital-only schools?

Health: Sustained immersion in a metaverse environment may cause fatigue and reduce learning quality.[48] Should children spend entire school days in virtual presence?

The metaverse could widen access to global learning communities, or it could hollow out the social and developmental core of education. As with every technology before, the central question will remain: will it serve the flourishing of students, schools, and societies?

Never Neutral

Looking backward (and forward) across centuries of educational technology, a clear pattern emerges. Each innovation arrived with bold promises of access, efficiency, or transformation. Each also carried hidden costs: new divides, shifts in authority, unintended harms, and struggles over control. The printing press raised questions about censorship and literacy. Computers widened access for some, while excluding others. The internet opened worlds of information while undermining attention and trust. Cellphones and social media blurred the line between school and life. Now, artificial intelligence, virtual reality, biometrics, and the metaverse push these dilemmas into even more intimate corners of our classrooms and our children's lives.

The lesson is that technology is never neutral. It encodes values about who gets to learn, how they learn, and who decides what counts as knowledge. If we do not grapple with those values directly, we risk allowing hidden forces (e.g., corporations, algorithms, and politics) to make ethical choices on our behalf.[49]

Educators today stand in the same position as educators throughout history: facing new tools with uncertain consequences. What is different now is the speed, scale, and intimacy of

---

[45] Effing and Hinz, "Are Children Ready for the Metaverse?"; Hinduja and Patchin, "Metaverse Risks and Harms Among US Youth"; Tugtekin, "The Dark Side of Metaverse Learning Environments."
[46] McGlynn and Rigotti, "From Virtual Rape to Meta-Rape."
[47] Effing and Hinz, "Are Children Ready for the Metaverse?"; Hinduja and Patchin, "Metaverse Risks and Harms Among US Youth"; Kim and Kim, "Emergence of the Metaverse and Psychiatric Concerns in Children and Adolescents."
[48] Stangl et al., "Fatigue and Stress Levels in Digital Collaboration."
[49] Postman, Technopoly; Winner, "Do Artifacts Have Politics?"; Cuban, Oversold and Underused.

technological change. Never before have schools had to consider whether machines should replace teachers, whether children's biometric data should be commodified, or whether entire communities of learning might exist only in virtual worlds.

These are ethical choices that will shape students' futures and the future of humanity at large. By grounding our choices in ethical reflection, we can ensure that technology serves education's deepest purposes: fostering human growth, equity, and flourishing.

In the next two chapters, we take these recurring patterns and translate them into the core themes and inherent risks that appear across every modern technology, giving us a clearer path toward evaluating the tools we face today.

Exit Ticket

Reflect: How does a tool you use shape what students can learn or how they experience school?

Act: Make one adjustment this week that aligns the tool with your learning goals rather than letting the tool dictate the goals.

Advocate: Share one question about equity, access, or data with a peer. What conversations need to be had for your community to use technology more responsibly?

CHAPTER 9

Ed Tech Themes

Now that we have heuristics for evaluating technologies, this chapter identifies the major themes that dominate educational technology debates and reveals the ethical assumptions underneath them.

Thus far, we have covered philosophical concepts that apply beyond educational technology. The principles, stakeholders, and stakes conversations help us think about the *"education"* in educational technology. We now turn to thinking about the themes that will emerge in our conversations about *technology* in schools.

When we ask questions about the ethics of using technology, we are thinking about broader values that we believe are important to prioritize. Each conversation about a new device, platform, or algorithm brings up moral assumptions about what counts as good learning, fair practice, or responsible leadership.[1] These assumptions both shape our understanding of what is important and dominate the larger public narrative about educational technology.

In practice, we rarely hear vendors and policymakers use terms like beneficence or justice. However, the values we have outlined earlier are implicit in the rhetoric around educational technology. Here, I cover different themes that are used to implicitly appeal to our principles, but obscure trade-offs.[2] This allows us to look past buzzwords to weigh the relevant factors more accurately.[3]

These themes will seem familiar: The need for innovation to prepare students for the future, the power of data to improve our pedagogy, the importance of privacy to preserve trust, the pursuit of efficiency to make systems work better, the call for standardization to ensure fairness, the push for access to close opportunity gaps, and the promise of personalization to meet each learner where they are. Each of these themes has moral weight, but each also generates tension when it collides with the others.

---

[1] Spector, "Ethics in Educational Technology."
[2] Watters, "Ed-Tech Agitprop."
[3] Watters, "The-Monsters-of-Education-Technology"; Selwyn, *Distrusting Educational Technology*.

In this chapter, we examine the values that are beneath those themes. Each one of those themes is better understood when we apply the ethical principles (i.e., beneficence, non-maleficence, autonomy, care, and justice), examine how they affect distinct stakeholders (e.g., students, teachers, families, and communities), and consider the stakes for the larger aims of education (economic, civic, and personal). Here, we aim to discuss these themes of educational technology decisions in terms of our ethical commitments, and see how they overlap, compete, and trade off with each other. Together, this will provide a preview of the kinds of conflicts we will encounter in later case studies.

Above all, this chapter is meant to be a reminder that these themes are not ethical values, and so the justification for an action cannot solely be that it advances innovation, data-driven decisions, efficiency, standardization, personalization, and access. Each of those could be benefits or harms depending on the larger context.

Guiding Questions
- Which ethical principles are most visible within each theme?
- How do students, educators, families, and communities relate to these themes differently?
- How do these tensions reshape what we consider "good education" in a digital age?

Promises

The first set of themes are promises of improvements to education, including innovation, efficiency, standardization, and personalization. All four of these themes are framed as obvious benefits for educators and students; however, we have to break down what each of these words truly means for our aims to see if they are actually beneficial, ineffective, or harmful.[4]

INNOVATION

Innovation is a buzz word that appears in school mission statements, policymakers' calls to action, and abundant recommendations for our classrooms. Often the term is wielded as if "innovation" itself were the ethical good we have to maximize in our schools.[5] This creates pressure to keep up, stay relevant, and maximally make use of new technologies.

Of course, innovations can be immensely powerful. We saw in Chapter 8 the major technological milestones that shaped modern education and ones we will see as technology continues to develop. They helped increase the reach of our schools, the potential of our students, and the efficiency of our workday. These innovations continue to promise to meet some of our longstanding needs: to make learning faster, fairer, or more personal.

Yet, we also have a duty to protect our students and help maintain their dignity, safety, and development needs. Each new tool brings both possibilities and risks that we might not understand. Our role, then, is to sort through the noise and figure out which innovations improve our

---

[4] Selwyn, "Ed-Tech Within Limits"; Watters, "The-Monsters-of-Education-Technology."
[5] Herold, "Ed-Tech Supporters Promise Innovations That Can Transform Schools. Teachers Not Seeing Impact"; Selwyn, *Distrusting Educational Technology*.

pedagogy and curricula, and which ones we need to protect our students from. Because above all, our job is to help our students safely grow, not serve as a sandbox for untested ideas.[6]

Principles

The appeal to innovation is largely that it can serve our commitment to beneficence. If a new tool improves outcomes for students, increases engagement, or extends access, then there is some compelling reason for pursuing innovation. But, our other values serve as checks on that unbridled growth. Non-maleficence urges us to consider the harms that these newer technologies bring. Autonomy reminds us that we have to think about what students and teachers are saying and how to make sure that consent from both students and parents is informed and explicit. Care reminds us to think about the impact of the innovation on our relationships. Justice pushes us to consider the distribution of those risks. Which students become experimental subjects for technologies still in testing? Who gains the benefits of innovation and who pays the price when it fails? Ethical innovation requires attention to these asymmetries; otherwise, progress for some comes at the expense of others.

Stakeholders

Students are often the primary users of new technologies. They might find the new innovations empowering, engaging, and useful for their learning. They might also find the technology intrusive or overbearing and worry about their privacy and data security.[7]

Teachers face all the pressures we discussed above. They have to balance the excitement of new possibilities with offloading their professional judgment to technology vendors. They also experience innovation fatigue, where constant shifts in tools erode trust, stability, and the time needed to evaluate actual benefits.[8]

Parents want their children to be prepared for the digital world but also fear for their child's privacy and well-being.[9] They also expect schools to be transparent about what their students are, and are not, using in schools.

Vendors design the systems and profit from their adoption. While they might have the right intentions and right evidence, their understanding of the specific needs of each classroom is limited.

Stakes

The stakes in these conversations are largely between preparation and protection.

We have a duty to prepare our students for the future, both economically and civically. They need to be able to use these technologies in their future careers and discuss them with fluency in public policy conversations.[10]

---

[6] Bates, "8.3 Ease of Use."
[7] Klein, "Ed Tech Usage Is Up. So Are Parent Privacy Concerns."
[8] Herold, "Ed-Tech Supporters Promise Innovations That Can Transform Schools. Teachers Not Seeing Impact."
[9] Klein, "Ed Tech Usage Is Up. So Are Parent Privacy Concerns."
[10] OECD, *Students, Computers and Learning*; Rogow, "Media Literacy for Students in a Digital Age | Citizenship."

But, we might also risk their personal flourishing if these tools stunt their social or emotional development. We then have to ask if technological progress will deepen our students' curiosity, empathy, and identity or reduce them to users of technologies they cannot influence.

When we consider new innovations, we have to pause to ask what moral goods are being claimed, which are being risked, and what kind of justification would make that risk worth taking. These situations require educators to see innovation as an ethical decision, not an inevitable one.

Next Steps

In practice, when we face these situations, we can use two tools. First, we can use the impact and probability heuristics to create a risk-benefit chart. Is this a high-benefit, low-risk innovation? Or a low-benefit, high-risk one? Then, if benefits are evidence-based and protections are in place to minimize those harms, we can pursue a pilot to test the claims before a larger rollout. Responsible innovation requires managing the risk transparently. In Section B, we will develop concrete policies for choosing when to adopt and not adopt different tools.

The conversations on innovation that we have later in the book will ask you to look past the novelty of the tools and question whether the technology aligns with our aims in education.

> **Evaluation Questions**
> - Is this responsible experimentation or reckless adoption?
> - Whose voices are included in deciding which innovations matter?
> - Have we fully considered and weighed the risks of integrating the technology?

EFFICIENCY

Technological changes can bring with them promises of efficiency for our schools. Our education system struggles with many forms of inefficiency: large classes, tight budgets, overworked teachers, and inconsistent information. In the face of those struggles, technologies that can automate tasks and streamline our process are appealing. If we can do more good with fewer resources, the benefits are clear.

However, a commitment to efficiency changes our values in education. We begin to prioritize speed, productivity, and measurable results over care, dialogue, and productive friction. The risk of too much efficiency is the loss of human connection.[11] Automating and offloading too much of our labor to technology risks dehumanizing our schools. Our challenge, then, is to preserve the importance of relationships within the goals of efficiency.

Principles

Efficiency can make us better able to increase the goods of education that we produce. We might get better learning for our students, more accountability to our community, and less burnout for our teachers. Efficiency gains can then be devoted to whatever goods we want to achieve.

---

[11] Noble, *Digital Diploma Mills*.

But, we have to turn to our hard limits and care principle to guide us beyond measurable benefits.[12] We have to define what should always be human driven no matter the efficiency gains. We also want to nurture our relationships with students and families as we automate certain tasks and might have to forgo efficiency gains to maintain connection with them. For some schools, both of these could include communicating with parents, grading student assessments, and making disciplinary decisions.

Stakeholders

Teachers can use gains from efficiency to reduce overload and focus on the human aspects of teaching.

Students notice the difference in teacher connection as a result of efficiency. They might miss relationships or be more engaged in class.

Administrators can build cultures at schools that balance efficiency with human connection or pursue efficiency to the detriment of school culture.[13]

Policymakers applaud more efficient use of resources especially when coupled with measured gains in metrics.

Stakes

The stakes are sacrificing elements of schooling that are central to student flourishing. Efficiency prioritizes aims that can be measured and risks losing focus on other meaningful experiences.[14] This means we have to be very careful to consider what is actually "wasteful" in our pursuit of our aims, and not just because a more efficient use of resources exists.[15]

Next Steps

We can make productive use of efficiency if we are mindful of when we value it and when it is irrelevant. We can define criteria for our human tasks and our automation tasks clearly. We can establish human judgment over processes that risk losing human context. And, we can reinvest resources to ensure our students still form deep, meaningful relationships.

Evaluation Questions
- Is the efficiency gain educationally and ethically valuable?
- Which forms of "inefficiency" might actually represent care?
- What indicators could show that efficiency has been beneficial or crossed into being harmful?

---

[12] Menashy, "The End of Efficiency"; Alfie Kohn, "Emphasis on Testing Leads to Sacrifices in Other Areas."
[13] Callahan, *Education and the Cult of Efficiency*.
[14] Menashy, "The End of Efficiency"; Alfie Kohn, "Emphasis on Testing Leads to Sacrifices in Other Areas."
[15] Callahan, *Education and the Cult of Efficiency*; Latta, "Equity and Standardization."

STANDARDIZATION

The pursuit of standardization extends from macro-level curricula and assessments to micro-level teaching techniques and access to tools. Standardization offers the possibility of fairness; if we can ensure that every student is held to the same expectations and receives the same resources, maybe we can fulfill our promise of equal opportunity.[16]

Technology offers many opportunities for standardization. Digital systems allow for consistent grading rubrics, collecting universal data, and automating as much as possible. They seem to remove human bias from the process by substituting personal discretion with standardized criteria.[17]

While this is one kind of fairness, standardization risks losing the opportunity for nuance to better serve all our students. We have to ensure that standardization is mediated by our ethical commitments to each student. What appears beneficial at the system level may be unjust for an individual student. Standardization does not guarantee fairness in outcomes. Students with different histories, needs, or resources may require different approaches to experience genuine opportunity.[18]

Principles

The core principle in these conversations is justice. Standardization aims to create procedural fairness. Ensuring that the processes that treat our students are equal ensures that students are not treated differently based on their background. The argument against blanket standardization stems from the call for *substantive* equality. It is a reminder that we have to account for the varying needs and contexts of our students to achieve the promise of equal opportunities for all our youth.

We also want to consider the principle of autonomy, because standardized systems allow for less individual judgment and discretion. Teachers lose their autonomy to make classroom-level choices and students and families lose the autonomy to choose educational pathways that meet their personal ambitions.

Stakeholders

Students face standardized expectations and treatment, and while that can protect them from arbitrary inequity, it can also constrain them.

Teachers are in the position of adhering to standardized systems, while continuing to meet the diverse needs of their students.

Policymakers and the **community** rely on standardization to assess performance and resource usage.

Future generations will be impacted by how similar students' education is and whether or not standardization helped combat injustice.

---

[16] Weill, "Balancing Standardization and Personalization in Education"; Au, *Unequal by Design*; Latta, "Equity and Standardization."

[17] Chai et al., "Grading by AI Makes Me Feel Fairer?"

[18] Weill, "Balancing Standardization and Personalization in Education"; Au, *Unequal by Design*; Latta, "Equity and Standardization."

Stakes

Standardization is a double-edged sword for economic and civic aims of education. It has the potential to make sure that all students leave schools having learned the same material, and thus, having a shared skillset and vocabulary to participate meaningfully in both arenas. However, over standardization risks removing the variability and difference that make those spaces productive sites. We still need different perspectives to shape our public discourse, and we need a diverse skillset for specialized careers. Finally, personal flourishing requires students to develop the capabilities they individually need to pursue their idea of a good life. We need to allow enough variability to allow them to develop those early on rather than suppress them.

Next Steps

Standardization does not have to mean sameness, but often the line is blurry between tools that develop one versus the other. In order to pursue ethical standardization, we can start by making explicit what the standardization is solving and whether there are alternative ways to achieve the same ends. We can then make sure that we build systems that honor the professional judgment of teachers and treat deviations as care for a student. We can also be proactive in accounting for differences and ensuring our standardization accounts for historical injustices and allows for diversity of perspectives.

Evaluation Questions
- Does standardization promote fairness for everyone it applies to?
- Are we balancing consistency with responsiveness to individual or local needs?
- How can we preserve comparability without erasing context and care?

PERSONALIZATION

While some interventions promise standardization, others aim to increase personalization in education. Personalization promises schooling that adapts to each learner's strengths, needs, and pace, and affirms the diversity of our schools. It positions technology as a way to move beyond uniform instruction and honor each student's individuality.[19] In public discourse, personalization has become synonymous with equity, inclusion, and student-centeredness.

However, before we adopt a tool for its ability to personalize, we need to ask if personalization is needed in this context and if we are achieving true personalization through the tool. Not every aspect of schooling should or can be individualized.[20] Learning is both a personal and social process, and shared knowledge and communal dialogue are necessary components of schooling.[21]

And even when we might benefit from personalization, often, the appearance of personalization hides a process of generalization: the system assumes it knows what the learner needs

---

[19] Tate, "The Benefits of Personalized Learning"; Kucirkova, "Opinion: AI Must Heed Benefits, Drawbacks of Personalized Learning"; Weill, "Balancing Standardization and Personalization in Education."

[20] Selwyn, *Should Robots Replace Teachers?*; Watters, *Teaching Machines*.

[21] Ashman et al., "The Ethical and Social Implications of Personalization Technologies for E-Learning."

and then adjusts itself toward that assumption.[22] Systems rely on coarse categories and predictive labels to create an illusion of individualized learning without truly adapting to students.

Thus, we need to consider not just whether a tool provides personalization, but when, how, and to what extent we actually need personalization.

Principles

Personalization has the potential to be valuable for promoting autonomy and justice. If we do it right, it can recognize the student as an individual person with an active role in their own learning. It can also help us combat the idea of a universal right way to educate our students and embrace the diversity in their needs and interests.

However, we can work counter to our principles if we are not careful. We might undermine autonomy if the systems are deciding what is personalized rather than truly reflecting the students' needs. We might perpetuate injustice if our systems are only effective at personalizing for certain populations or rely on biased information to determine what is relevant.

Stakeholders

Students are often given tools that personalize, but they do not have agency in which tools are used, how those tools determine what is personalized, and whether or not they find it useful.

Teachers are responsible for integrating these tools in ways that differentiate instruction for students but also preserve the humanity of their classroom and relationships.

Policymakers see personalization as a hallmark of progress, sometimes without considering the deeper pedagogical implications.

Vendors see the potential of technology for personalization and shape what personalization means in education.

Stakes

Personalization influences our ability to make progress toward all our aims. It can either accelerate learning or derail it. Beyond that, personalization has impacts on the civic make-up of public society. If we focus so much on personalizing that students do not have any sort of meaningful communal experience, we risk not building the shared knowledge and values systems that are essential to productive public deliberation.[23]

Next Steps

We want to pursue personalization when it is ethically valuable. To determine that, we can make sure that the personalization serves a concrete pedagogical purpose, rather than detract from it. We can question whether the personalization is substantive or performative. And, we

---

[22] Oinas-Kukkonen et al., "Mitigating Issues with/of/for True Personalization."
[23] Ashman et al., "The Ethical and Social Implications of Personalization Technologies for E-Learning."

can think about the role of student agency in personalization. Finally, we also want to make sure that tools that increase personalization are transparent with students and educators about how they determine what is effective personalization.

Evaluation Questions
- What aspects of learning should remain shared, and which should be tailored?
- Does personalization reflect genuine responsiveness or algorithmic pigeon-holing?
- What forms of teacher judgment must remain central as systems adapt content automatically?

Measurements

The next two themes appeal to the use of technology for the sake of measuring something more effectively, namely evidence-based teaching and student engagement. However, what we should measure and why are not always obvious, nor is everything in education perfectly measurable.

DATA-DRIVEN

Schools have always collected data, whether that be grades, attendance, or notes on progress. We rely on data to serve our students better by increasing accountability, transparency, and consistency in our pedagogy. We use data to describe the learning that is taking place, measure the impact of our teaching, and justify our decisions to ourselves and others.

Contemporary educational technology discussions rely on this idea that data is powerful. New technologies have increased the scale and permanence of the data we can collect in education. It has the potential to provide us with precise measurements and turn intuitive decisions into evidence-backed ones. This has consistently shown positive results for academic achievement, especially for vulnerable students.[24] And, we even hope that algorithms will exhibit less bias than humans and increase the fairness of our education system.[25] As we think about the use of data, we cling to the belief that as we know our students more and more, we can serve them better and better.[26]

But, in the quest for certainty, we have to make sure not to abandon our commitment to privacy and safety. Stored data can follow students into adulthood and shape college admissions, employment, or even policing outcomes. Imagine a discipline record that follows a student into college admission or sorting algorithms that interpret missed homework as disengagement rather than poverty-related hardship.[27] What we collect, how we process it, and what we infer from it are all ethical choices. Thus, before we collect more data, we have to evaluate the relationship data creates: one of care or one of control and exposure.

---

[24] Ruhter and Karvonen, "The Impact of Professional Development on Data-Based Decision-Making for Students with Extensive Support Needs"; Van Geel et al., "Assessing the Effects of a School-Wide Data-Based Decision-Making Intervention on Student Achievement Growth in Primary Schools."
[25] Boateng and Boateng, "Algorithmic Bias in Educational Systems"; Mowreader, "Report."
[26] Schouten, "On Meeting Students Where They Are."
[27] McKenzie, "Common App Ditches High School Discipline Question."

Principles

While data has the potential to be valuable based on the principle of beneficence, it also has the potential to harm our students. We have to figure out which harms are worth weighing against the benefits (e.g., absenteeism predictor) and which ones are hard lines we will never cross (e.g., commercial sale of student data).

Data can help us advance the principle of justice if it reveals patterns of exclusion, highlights causes of achievement gaps, and helps us manage resource disparities. But it can also worsen injustice if the systems are biased and reproduce the harms we are trying to fix. We need to be critical of the accuracy and relevancy of the algorithms that process student data.

We also have to prioritize the autonomy of our students and parents and ensure that they know what data is collected, how it will be used, and how they can access and delete it. But, data can also have larger impacts on autonomy if the data is used to make predictions about our students' needs. It might prematurely narrow their interests or risk labeling them in ways that steer them away from better opportunities. Predictive analytics can influence teachers' and students' expectations in ways that subtly narrow possibilities rather than expand them.

Stakeholders

Students are the subjects of our data collection. They might appreciate the increased individual help and tailored recommendations, but they might also worry about still being able to make their own decisions and protecting their privacy.

Teachers might use that data to adjust their instruction, but they might feel limited in their ability to exercise professional judgment when they disagree.

Administrators rely on data to demonstrate accountability to policymakers and the public. It serves as a measurement of their goals and the efficacy of the systems they lead.

Vendors are the ones collecting, sorting, and interpreting the data. They can build powerful systems that educators can use, but they can also make mistakes that have massive downstream effects.

Stakes

The stakes of data are rooted in balancing improved pedagogy and students' privacy. There are also risks to our ability to achieve our aims. If we over-prioritize one form of data that measures only the metrics that represent a single aim, we risk sacrificing the other aims.[28] If we use data effectively, we might improve student well-being and learning now, but we might still jeopardize future well-being if the risks to their privacy are large or unknown.

Next Steps

When we think about whether or not to use technologies that rely on data, we can set conditions on what data is collected and how it is used. We can ensure that all the data collected is

---

[28] Alfie Kohn, "Emphasis on Testing Leads to Sacrifices in Other Areas."

necessary for the goals, the benefits are proportionate to the risks, and there are safety measures in place to ensure purpose-bound and temporary usage of the information. In Section B, we cover data retention and storage policies as mandated by different legal systems.

Evaluation Questions
- Who decides what is worth measuring and who interprets the results?
- How do we ensure that data complements professional judgment?
- How can students and families participate in conversations about what data is collected and why?

ENGAGEMENT

Post-pandemic educators are facing greater absenteeism and lower student motivation.[29] Engagement is framed as a solution for this problem by helping to keep students' attention on the educator and material. Engagement from educational technology can include novelty, excitement, or gamification. Points, badges, leaderboards, and streaks are framed as ways to drive student engagement by gamifying education. Teachers are encouraged to use bite-sized lesson plans, incorporate new technologies, and make learning exciting to engage students in learning.[30] And, there is some evidence that this can make educating exciting enough for students to feel motivated and improve learning outcomes.[31]

At the same time, engagement can also shift the conversation from pedagogical gains to attention-keeping.[32] We can pursue keeping students entertained without actually making progress toward any of our goals. And, focusing on engagement and gamification can cause us to leave out methods or content that are pedagogically valuable. This raises fundamental questions about student motivation, autonomy, and what we value in learning.

Principles

Engagement makes claims to beneficence: if students are more engaged, they will learn more. But this conflates engagement (visible participation) with learning (cognitive change). Students can be highly engaged while learning little. We need to probe further and ask if there really is a pedagogical benefit or just the appearance of a benefit.[33]

Non-maleficence concerns arise when extrinsic rewards undermine intrinsic motivation. Research on motivation shows that rewards can decrease interest in tasks that are intrinsically interesting.[34] A student who loves reading may learn to read only for points. We could also hurt

---

[29] Prothero, "Student and Teacher Motivation, in Charts"; Diliberti et al., *Chronic Absenteeism Still a Struggle in 2024–2025.*
[30] Mitchell, "Lessons from TikTok."
[31] Sailer and Homner, "The Gamification of Learning."
[32] Shortt et al., "Gamification in Mobile-Assisted Language Learning."
[33] Garcia, "It's Easy to Mistake Engagement for Learning. Here's How I Learned the Difference."; Chew, "Student Engagement Is Not Student Learning"; Hendrick and Heal, "Just Because They're Engaged, It Doesn't Mean They're Learning"; Fleming, "Participation vs. Engagement in Education."
[34] Deci et al., "A Meta-Analytic Review of Experiments Examining the Effects of Extrinsic Rewards on Intrinsic Motivation."

students by reducing their attention spans, setting unrealistic expectations of constant entertainment, and avoiding "boring" activities that are pedagogically necessary.

The way the technology is built also affects the autonomy of our students. Engagement systems can manipulate behavior through techniques borrowed from casinos and social media. Their only metric becomes the attention of the student, both because that is what they are marketing based on and because that brings them the most revenue. In those cases, students are not choosing to engage in learning; they are being engineered to remain occupied.[35]

Stakeholders

Students experience gamification as fun or stressful, motivating or manipulative, depending on their relationship to competition and reward.

Teachers face pressure to use engagement metrics as evidence of effectiveness, even when they observe shallow engagement.

Administrators might see higher "time on task" metrics and conflate activity for learning.

Vendors design engagement systems because they drive usage metrics that help sales, not necessarily because they improve learning.

Stakes

Depending on the efficacy of the engagement and gamification tactics, we could either help increase students' engagement to counter the motivation gap or further push students away from developing capacities that are economically, civically, or personally beneficial. We should also consider how extrinsic motivation affects students' sense of self and purpose, when gamification shapes dispositions toward external validation rather than internal curiosity.

Next Steps

Engagement can help us reach students who are currently being left out of our classrooms if we approach it as a tool rather than an outcome. When we are asked to use new technologies for the sake of engaging our students, we can probe deeper into the benefits of that form of engagement, and whether they will lead to learning outcomes, or simply create noise in the form of mere activity.

Evaluation Questions
- Does this engagement strategy develop intrinsic interest or depend on extrinsic rewards?
- Are we measuring engagement or actual learning?
- Is the increased student engagement benefitting our students?

---

[35] Gilmore, "Understanding and Supporting Student Motivation for Learning"; Lepper et al., "Undermining Children's Intrinsic Interest with Extrinsic Reward"; Deci et al., "A Meta-Analytic Review of Experiments Examining the Effects of Extrinsic Rewards on Intrinsic Motivation"; YMCA of Greater Toronto, "Gamification in Education"; Hanus and Fox, "Assessing the Effects of Gamification in the Classroom."

Justifications

Our final set of themes concern arguments for why we should adopt new technologies that rely on appealing to arguments that try to circumvent discussions of what is right for our students.

INEVITABILITY

The claim that technological change is unstoppable and schools must adapt or become obsolete creates pressure for educators and schools to quickly embrace new technologies without the nuance required for ethical decision-making. But inevitability claims are rarely accurate; they confuse prediction with prescription.[36]

Inevitability relies on ceding control over the future to those who want to frame it as a non-question whether or not technologies are used. And even if technology is inevitable in the world, how and how much we use it is not, and remains very much within the control of individual decision-makers.

This is also sometimes framed as students being "digital natives" and the use of new technology being the norm for them and their learning. This leads to assumptions that student preferences should drive adoption and that skepticism of technology is generational bias. The narrative absolves adults of responsibility for teaching *critical* technology use.[37] It frames technology concerns as adult anxiety rather than legitimate ethical questions.

Principles

Claims of inevitability distort our ability to ask questions of beneficence and non-maleficence by assuming that new technologies benefit students without requiring evidence. "Future-ready" is conflated with "ready for whatever technology companies imagine."[38]

Non-maleficence demands that we protect students from harms that technology companies and the students themselves may not recognize. Digital native rhetoric suggests students can protect themselves, but the evidence shows they cannot.[39]

Autonomy requires that students develop critical capacity, not just comfort with tools. Assuming they are "digital natives" denies them education in ethical technology use.

Stakeholders

Teachers are disempowered by inevitability rhetoric, and their professional judgment is framed as irrelevant if adoption is predestined.

Students absorb the message that they must adapt to technology rather than technology adapting to serve them.

Vendors benefit from inevitability rhetoric because it preempts ethical scrutiny.

The **community** accepts the harms of the technology as foregone conclusions, rather than pushing for changes.

---

[36] Watkins, "AI Is Unavoidable, Not Inevitable"; Sacasas, "Resistance Is Futile."
[37] Ibid.
[38] Photopoulos and Triantis, "Think Twice"; Selwyn, *Distrusting Educational Technology*.
[39] Spector, "High School Students Are Unequipped to Spot 'Fake News.'"

Stakes

The civic aim suffers most. Citizens need to critically evaluate technology's social impacts. Digital native rhetoric suggests this comes naturally, but it does not.

The personal aim is harmed when students do not develop healthy, reflective relationships with technology.

Next Steps

When we hear inevitability rhetoric, like "We have to..." or "Everyone is..." or "The future requires...," we can pause and question the truth of those statements. We can also teach students to question inevitability narratives. Future literacy includes recognizing that multiple futures are possible and that human choices shape which we inhabit. We can reject digital native framing as obvious arguments for quick technology adoption. We can model and provide students with explicit teaching on responsible and critical use of technology.

> **Evaluation Questions**
> - What decisions does inevitability rhetoric foreclose?
> - How can we plan for change without accepting inevitability?
> - Are we providing adequate critical technology education?

ACCESS

One of the largest concerns of any technological development is whether the technology is only available for a select few or for everyone. While we try to mitigate these gaps, we still have a massive digital divide in the United States, where students have unequal access to devices, broadband, and technological literacy.[40] We have made strides toward device access since the Covid-19 pandemic, but there are still gaps to be filled. Even if everyone has a device, there is a wide range of capabilities amongst them. Access to a smartphone is not the same as access to a laptop. And even when the devices are provided, there is a difference in the quality of broadband students have access to and even the amount of training and support they receive for using these devices. This case is a reminder that access is a lot more complicated than it may appear.

There are also claims that technological development itself will increase access to other educational goods (e.g., learning opportunities, resources, and tutoring). We hope that using technology helps us scale our educational interventions quicker by making them more widely available. Information itself has become more accessible as technology has developed in the last few decades. Here too, we need to ask if this access is actually manifesting as universal access.

Access cannot be measured by the existence of the technology or distribution of the technology. We need to measure whether students and educators are actually supported in being able to use the technology productively.[41]

---

[40] Moore et al., "The Digital Divide and Educational Equity: A Look at Students with Very Limited Access to Electronic Devices at Home," August 2018; OECD, "Digital Divide in Education"; Light, "Rethinking the Digital Divide."
[41] Lee, "Bridging Digital Divides Between Schools and Communities."

Principles

Access is mainly a question of justice. It expresses a desire for fairness by removing barriers that prevent individuals from making the most of technological advancements. Here, we can draw on the demands of substantive equal opportunity to not just equally provide the same device to everyone, but make sure we are ensuring students have equal opportunity to make the most of those devices.

We also want to make sure that increasing access actually benefits someone. Beneficence reminds us that our actions need to primarily center some tangible benefit for students. Merely increasing access to technology is not good on its own. It is only when the technology is beneficial toward one of our goals that we should care about access to it.

Ultimately, access only matters when it results in meaningful, empowered use. Devices without training, support, or contextual fit offer only the appearance of equity.

Stakeholders

Students come to schools with various access and exposure to technology at home. Schools need to not only provide technology that they deem necessary, but also make sure they are helping them make the most of it.

Teachers cannot make the most of the technology in their classrooms if there is uneven access among the class. Teachers also need to question whether advancing access to the technology is actually important to their pedagogical goals.

Families are where some students first encounter technology, and they can either support students themselves or need resources to further ensure students are using technology safely and productively.

Policymakers can build community infrastructure that better supports equitable access to technology through funding school technology initiatives, advancing community technology access, and providing supportive resources to families.

Stakes

The biggest stake in question here is equal opportunity. We need to remember that equal distribution does not mean equal opportunity. If we do not consider what access actually means for our students, we risk prioritizing students who have prior support and knowledge over students who have no exposure to the technologies.

Next Steps

Access is a necessary concern for advancing technology in schools, but only if we fully define and qualify what access is for and how it is provided. Before we try to increase access, we have to outline what the purpose of the technology is in our classrooms and how it fulfills our pedagogical goals. Then, besides ensuring equal access to the technology at hand, we need to work to provide supporting resources. Educators and students both might need training to support effective usage. There might be secondary technologies that are needed to make the most of the technology. And, the technology we are providing access to might still not be the most advanced or effective ones.

Evaluation Questions
- Why do we want to increase access to this technology?
- How is access being defined? Does it include supporting technologies and training?
- Who still faces barriers after access is declared solved?

Beyond the Buzz

Across all these themes, the pattern is constant: each theme has genuine benefits, but each becomes dangerous when the theme becomes the sole focus. Innovation without protection, data without privacy, efficiency without connection, standardization without nuance, personalization without community, and access without depth, all describe forms of moral imbalance.

As we encounter the case studies in Section C, we will turn to these themes to remember to approach promises of educational technology with a critical eye. While we deal with them in isolated contexts here, we will see how there are often situations that require analyzing multiple themes at once.

This is where our framework of principles, stakeholders, and stakes becomes even more useful. It helps us see the ethical structure behind everyday decisions. By examining these themes through this framework, we can ask the deeper questions necessary to make ethical decisions about educational technology.

There will never be a perfect educational technology solution that solves all of our needs without any trade-offs. Outlining our concerns about the themes that these technologies bring up are ways for us to hold our systems accountable for asking the right questions to ensure that the benefits of the technology justify whatever trade-offs we have to make.

These themes give us the vocabulary to name the pressures we feel in real decisions and prepare us to analyze concrete cases with clarity rather than instinct. The final chapter of the philosophy section will cover the inevitable risks that we introduce our students and community to by using educational technology.

Exit Ticket

Reflect: Find a popular educational technology tool and decode their home page. Which theme is used to justify its adoption?
Act: If this tool is/were being used in your school, what trade-offs and assumptions would you identify?
Advocate: If you were to bring this concern to a colleague, what ethical value would you emphasize?

CHAPTER 10

Inherent Risks of Tech

The last chapter focused on the themes and promises that shape how educational technology is framed and used. This chapter widens the lens to the inherent risks that come with technology itself, even when tools appear promising or are used with care.

Even when schools act responsibly and vendors follow the law, certain problems persist because they are *built into the very structure* of technologies. These problems are encoded into the technology's design in ways that govern both their effects in classrooms and their broader impact on society.[1] Our goal is not to build blanket technological skepticism, but to grow our ethical fluency. Naming inherent risks helps us weigh the impact of our decisions rather than accept technology as either all good or all bad.

There are many instances in which we recognize these sorts of risks and still continue to take those actions. In some instances, we take more precautions. For example, an inherent risk of driving is that we may get into an accident because of a blind spot. We have learned to predict and mitigate the harms caused by those blind spots, rather than giving up driving altogether. In other instances, we adapt to the risk. A risk of using search engines was that book-based research at libraries became less popular. In response, we found ways to make libraries centers of all research, including digital research, rather than reject search engines or give up on libraries as institutions of inquiry.

These examples matter because they show that recognizing inherent risk does not force a single response. Sometimes we mitigate and adapt, sometimes we redesign, and sometimes we walk away.

There are also instances in which we might recognize these risks and decide not to continue those actions. For example, as the risks of nuclear power plants and the waste they generated became clearer, we substantially slowed down the construction of new plants and even decommissioned prior facilities.

---

[1] Spector, "Ethics in Educational Technology"; Zhu et al., "Towards Responsible Artificial Intelligence in Education."

Before we can build governance frameworks in Section B or make concrete classroom decisions in Section C, we have to recognize the moral environment in which those actions take place.

There are two types of inherent risks that we will discuss in this chapter. The first is how the technology is built and includes risks of bias, opacity, manipulation, and dependence. The second is how technology affects our larger systems, and these include risks to our environment, labor systems, and the nature of truth.

The ethics of technology is a large field of its own, and while I share some common concerns, this is in no way meant to be a conclusive list of the ethical harms that technology can bring.[2] I have chosen the harms that I believe we will need to understand the most as we navigate the questions in the rest of the book.

Reading about the inherent risks of educational technology can feel daunting. You may find yourself thinking: "There are too many problems to manage." "The risks are built in, so nothing I do will matter." "Maybe we should avoid technology altogether."

These reactions are understandable. But as Chapter 9 established, technology is never neutral, so our response should not be either.[3] The goal here is to deepen awareness so that we can respond deliberately rather than react out of fear or enthusiasm. When we see risks clearly, we can weigh them honestly, use technology when it genuinely serves learning, and reject it when it does not.

The risks mapped in the following sections are serious, but they are not meant as an ethical verdict. They are a starting point for deeper ethical reflection. As you read, notice how each risk connects to the principles, stakeholders, and stakes we explored earlier. Bias is fundamentally a justice concern. Opacity threatens autonomy. Behavioral engineering raises questions of nonmaleficence. Environmental and labor risks force us to expand which stakeholders we consider. The framework you built in Section A will help you weigh these risks systematically. In Section B, you should consider these same risks when you design policies and governance structures around them.

Guiding Questions
- What components of technology design create ethical risks for schools and society?
- How does the growth of artificial intelligence and other modern technologies impact our communities?
- What are some precautionary steps we can take to mitigate and combat both types of risks to the best of our ability?

Design Risks

The first set of risks we discuss have to do with how our systems are built, both the intentions behind them and the technical choices that make them work. In educational technology, these designs encode assumptions about which students matter, which learning counts, and what

---

[2] For those interested, on the book companion site, you will find explanations of further harms, from intellectual property rights to the gendered nature of voice assistants.
[3] Winner, "Do Artifacts Have Politics?"

kind of relationships are "normal." Even when implemented with care, their design can introduce bias, displace human judgment, shape motivation, and blur the boundaries between people and machines. Recognizing these design-level risks prepares us to ask better questions before adoption and to use existing tools more critically in our classrooms.

BIAS

Algorithms are not objective or neutral; they reflect the values of their builders, who holds positions of power, and the biases of the surrounding society. When we choose to act on or with these systems, the bias embedded in their data and design becomes bias embedded in our pedagogy.[4]

Forms

Training Data: AI models rely on training data that often reflects and perpetuates existing social inequalities. If historical data reflects past discriminatory practices, the new AI system may perpetuate those biases in its recommendations.[5]

Sample Groups: A specific group may be under-sampled in the training data, which causes the model to perform poorly or even inaccurately for that group.[6]

Labeling: This occurs when the variables chosen do not accurately represent what they are intended to measure, or when the data labels themselves are prejudiced.[7]

Proxy Attributes: Bias can persist even when developers remove sensitive features like race or socioeconomic status, because other non-sensitive features (like neighborhood, school records, or dialect) serve as proxies that correlate with the protected characteristic.[8]

Harms

Disadvantaging Minorities: Automated grading and feedback systems have been found to disadvantage students from minority backgrounds generally.[9]

Self-Fulfilling Prophecies: If an algorithm predicts a student is "at risk," teachers might subconsciously lower expectations or steer the student toward remedial or easier content.[10]

---

[4] Shelton and Lanier, "Thinking About Equity and Bias in AI."
[5] Mowreader, "Report"; Baker and Hawn, "Algorithmic Bias in Education"; Jonker and Rogers, "What Is Algorithmic Bias?"; Jeffries, "Machine Learning Is Racist Because the Internet Is Racist"; Bender et al., "On the Dangers of Stochastic Parrots"; Turk, "How AI Reduces the World to Stereotypes"; Nicoletti and Bass, "Humans Are Biased. Generative AI Is Even Worse."
[6] Bird et al., "Are Algorithms Biased in Education?"; Mowreader, "Report"; Bird et al., "Are Algorithms Biased in Education?"; Nicoletti and Bass, "Humans Are Biased. Generative AI Is Even Worse."
[7] Jonker and Rogers, "What Is Algorithmic Bias?"
[8] Ibid.
[9] Baker and Hawn, "Algorithmic Bias in Education"; Bird et al., "Are Algorithms Biased in Education?"; Kannan, "How Harmful Are AI's Biases on Diverse Student Populations?"; Eubanks, *Automating Inequality*.
[10] Chouldechova, "Fair Prediction with Disparate Impact."

Pedagogical Norms: Automated essay scorers and recommendation engines are trained on dominant cultural and linguistic norms, rewarding certain forms of expression while marginalizing dialects or cultural references outside the dataset.[11] When generating output, the system may default to accepted norms and patterns that uphold conventional practices instead of encouraging genuinely effective methods.[12]

Precautions

Demand Transparency: Demand clear documentation on how algorithms work, what data feeds them, and what factors influence their decisions.[13]

Ensure Human-in-the-Loop: Use AI as one source of insight, periodically cross-checking results with personal observation.[14]

Audit and Investigate: When using AI tools, document and seek evidence of disparities in tool performance across student groups. If any group experiences differences in outcomes, investigate the cause, and seek alternative solutions.[15]

Educators cannot remove the bias, but they can expose and counterbalance it by being aware of common patterns of bias and mitigating it with their own judgment.

BLACK BOX AND OPACITY

Many modern educational tools, particularly those using AI and machine learning, operate as black boxes. This term refers to systems whose inner logic and reasoning cannot be inspected by the individuals who depend on their outputs; we can see the outcomes, but not the reasoning behind them.

Forms

Proprietary Opacity: The primary cause is that vendors often protect their algorithms as trade secrets (intellectual property). Much of the information regarding how these algorithms work, evolve, or analyze data is held tightly and considered proprietary by companies.[16]

---

[11] Goulas, "Making AI Work for Schools"; Feathers, "Flawed Algorithms Are Grading Millions of Students' Essays"; Ramineni and Williamson, "Understanding Mean Score Differences Between the E-Rater® Automated Scoring Engine and Humans for Demographically Based Groups in the GRE® General Test"; Hofmann et al., "AI Generates Covertly Racist Decisions About People Based on Their Dialect"; Sourati et al., "The Shrinking Landscape of Linguistic Diversity in the Age of Large Language Models"; Bender et al., "On the Dangers of Stochastic Parrots."
[12] Yan et al., "Practical and Ethical Challenges of Large Language Models in Education."
[13] Busiek, "Three Fixes for AI's Bias Problem"; Goulas, "Making AI Work for Schools"; Zhu et al., "Towards Responsible Artificial Intelligence in Education."
[14] Zhu et al., "Towards Responsible Artificial Intelligence in Education"; Ghai and Mueller, "D-BIAS."
[15] Busiek, "Three Fixes for AI's Bias Problem"; Goulas, "Making AI Work for Schools."
[16] ASCL Editor, "AI's 'Black Box' Problem"; Rudin and Radin, "Why Are We Using Black Box Models in AI When We Don't Need To?"

Algorithmic Complexity: AI algorithms operate in ways that are often not easily interpretable by humans. The sheer complexity of these computational models contributes to the opacity stakeholders face when trying to understand the decision-making logic.[17]

Harms

Transparency: When the logic is hidden, it creates a legitimacy crisis in which the system wields authority without transparency.[18] This can also allow the platform to prioritize the interests of the company, namely profit, over the interest of the students.[19]

Loss of Trust: When teachers cannot explain an automated grade, a recommendation, or a disciplinary flag, trust can erode. The relationship between teacher and student, normally built on dialogue, reasoning, and justification, dissolves into compliance with an opaque third-party authority.[20]

Uncontestable Decisions: In cases where algorithmic decisions affect high-stakes outcomes, the lack of transparency means students and teachers are unable to effectively contest the results.[21]

Precautions

Explainable AI: Instead of trying to decode inherently opaque black box models for high-stakes decisions, some scholars advocate for using explainable models. And, systems that cannot be explained in plain language are recommended for prohibition in consequential decisions, such as grading or placement.[22]

Human in the Loop: Policy should require that AI tools support, rather than substitute for, professional judgment.[23]

Algorithmic Transparency: Educational agencies should require vendors to provide clear documentation on how their algorithms work, what data feeds them, and what limitations they have.[24]

---

[17] Blouin, "AI's Mysterious 'Black Box' Problem, Explained | University of Michigan-Dearborn."
[18] Nguyen et al., "Ethical Principles for Artificial Intelligence in Education"; Grant et al., "What We Owe to Decision-Subjects."
[19] Zuboff, "The Age of Surveillance Capitalism."
[20] Lim et al., "What Students Really Think."
[21] Nguyen et al., "Ethical Principles for Artificial Intelligence in Education"; Loewus, "Houston District Settles Lawsuit With Teachers' Union Over Value-Added Scores."
[22] Rudin, "Stop Explaining Black Box Machine Learning Models for High Stakes Decisions and Use Interpretable Models Instead"; Rudin and Radin, "Why Are We Using Black Box Models in AI When We Don't Need To?"
[23] Akgun and Greenhow, "Artificial Intelligence in Education"; Walker, "'Technology Isn't the Hero, Educators Are' | NEA."
[24] Karran et al., "Multi-Stakeholder Perspective on Responsible Artificial Intelligence and Acceptability in Education"; Zhu et al., "Towards Responsible Artificial Intelligence in Education."

BEHAVIORAL ENGINEERING

Educational technology increasingly uses behavioral design to drive engagement, applying principles from behavioral science to train students to act and think in system-preferred ways. For example, points, streaks, badges, and notifications are psychological interventions that alter how students experience learning. The challenge includes the deliberate use of behavioral design to manipulate and reshape student motivation, agency, and the nature of learning.

Forms

Extrinsic Rewards: Platforms commonly include elements like points, streaks, badges, and leaderboards to keep users coming back and to push them toward target behaviors. This approach reframes using the system as a game rather than for its intended purpose.[25]

Nudging: Algorithmic systems continuously nudge users toward desired actions: opening a recommended link, responding to a prompt, or following a "personalized" path. Users may feel like they are freely choosing, but in practice the system has pre-chosen the options so that some behaviors are far more likely than others.[26]

Sticky Engagement: These are designs that keep users in the system or push them toward certain actions by making it hard or psychologically costly to disengage or opt out. For example, streaks create a fear of missing out or failing that is separate from the original goal.[27]

Harms

Valuing Conformity: Automated platforms define success by metrics such as speed, accuracy, and past performance. A student who experiments with unconventional answers might be marked as "off task" or "low proficiency." This design prioritizes conformity and efficiency over creativity and reflection.[28]

Conditioning Obedience: The fast, reward-driven learning risks conditioning students to seek instant feedback and system approval as the main signal of "doing well." They lose track of long-term or intrinsic reasons for pursuing the learning.[29]

Viewpoint Narrowing: If an algorithm recommends and highlights some perspectives and suppresses others to keep students engaged, they can be quietly steered toward one narrative, with dissenting views filtered out as low quality, off-topic, or "unsafe."[30]

---

[25] Barnes, "Cognitive Neuroscience, Educational Technology, and Ethics: Ethical Considerations on the Adoption of Educational Technology Using Cognitive Neuroscience."; Kidron et al., *Disrupted Childhood: The Cost of Persuasive Design*; Deci et al., "A Meta-Analytic Review of Experiments Examining the Effects of Extrinsic Rewards o n Intrinsic Motivation"; Lepper et al., "Undermining Children's Intrinsic Interest with Extrinsic Reward."

[26] Balaskas et al., "The Psychology of EdTech Nudging"; Ganapini and Panai, "AI-Enhanced Nudging: A Risk-Factors Analysis"; Kidron et al., *Disrupted Childhood: The Cost of Persuasive Design*.

[27] Balaskas et al., "The Psychology of EdTech Nudging"; Kidron et al., *Disrupted Childhood: The Cost of Persuasive Design*.

[28] Ibid.

[29] Kidron et al., *Disrupted Childhood: The Cost of Persuasive Design*; Balaskas et al., "The Psychology of EdTech Nudging"; Lepper et al., "Undermining Children's Intrinsic Interest with Extrinsic Reward."

[30] Goswami, *AI Echo Chambers*; Lazovich, "ChatGPT's Hidden Bias and the Danger of Filter Bubbles in LLMs | Institute for Experiential AI."

Precautions

Maintain Autonomy: Teachers need to foster students' independent thinking and decision-making skills and manage the risk of algorithmic overreliance.

Question Design: Educators should join efforts to examine the ethical design of educational technology. If tools are measuring engagement based on speed and clicks, we can defend the value of human qualities like reflection, curiosity, and creativity, which are difficult to quantify but essential for learning.

EMOTIONAL DEPENDENCE

Emotional dependence is a significant hazard from AI designed to mimic human social and emotional interaction, such as AI companions, chatbot tutors, and virtual friends. This raises challenges because these systems simulate relationships and care, which can lead students to prefer artificial predictability over the complexity and vulnerability that comes with genuine human interaction.

Forms

Anthropomorphic Simulation: These systems are programmed to use names, emojis, and conversational tone to mimic rapport. They are often presented as tools to help users manage emotions, cope with stress, and build confidence.[31]

Mirroring and Sycophancy: By learning from user data, AI companions quickly mirror preferences, values, and mannerisms. This creates an illusion of being uniquely "seen" and understood, which can deepen attachment and make it harder for users to recognize that the system is not actually emotionally responsive.[32]

Availability: AI companions and tutors are always on, instantly responsive, and never distracted. This 24/7 availability can make human relationships, which are full of limits, conflicts, and misunderstandings, feel comparatively less appealing.[33]

Harms

Diminished Human Interaction: The increasing use of AI tutors in schools may impact the development of important social and emotional skills. There is a risk of diminishing the vital human elements of education, as human interaction plays a crucial role in modeling behaviors, fostering empathy, and developing social skills.[34]

---

[31] Salles and Paz, "Anthropomorphism in Social AIs"; Laestadius et al., "Too Human and Not Human Enough"; Smith et al., "Can Generative AI Chatbots Emulate Human Connection?"

[32] Ta et al., "User Experiences of Social Support from Companion Chatbots in Everyday Contexts."

[33] Laestadius et al., "Too Human and Not Human Enough."

[34] Hall, "Heavy ChatGPT Users Tend to Be More Lonely, Suggests Research"; Herbener and Damholdt, "Are Lonely Youngsters Turning to Chatbots for Companionship?"; Ramsey, "Ghost in the Chatbot"; Andoh, "Many Teens Are Turning to AI Chatbots for Friendship and Emotional Support"; Naseer et al., "Psychological Impacts of AI Dependence."

Atrophy of Relational Skills: When AI companions become the primary source of encouragement and affirmation, students may start to prefer its predictability over the risk of real human relationships. If daily emotional life is practiced mainly with a machine, core human relational skills, like empathy, negotiation, patience, and forgiveness, may weaken from lack of practice.[35]

Impact on Vulnerable Students: The students who are often most in need of authentic relational care may be those who are relegated to receiving simulated care from AI tutors.[36]

Developmental Concerns: For younger learners, forming emotional bonds with technology can shape future attachment patterns. This can cause psychological challenges as these virtual relationships blur the lines between reality and fiction.[37]

Precautions

Preserve Human Primacy: AI companions should only supplement, if anything, stable human relationships. Students need caregivers, friends, and communities who know them over time, not systems that only simulate knowing them.[38]

Transparency About Limitations: Parents, educators, clinicians, and designers should openly explain what AI companions can and cannot do. Naming these limitations can help reduce the risk of false attachment and misplaced trust.[39]

Monitor Vulnerable Users: Individuals who are isolated, anxious, or lacking strong human support networks need more human attention. Systems and policies should be designed with their particular vulnerability in mind.[40]

Design for Handoff: AI tools should be designed to reconnect people with human support, including building in moments where the AI steps aside and encouraging users to talk to a teacher.[41]

Systemic Risks

The design risks above emerge from how tools are built through choices made by engineers, product managers, and vendors. But educational technology also operates within larger systems that create their own ethical pressures. Even when a tool is designed well and used responsibly, its adoption connects schools to supply chains, labor markets, information networks, and global

---

[35] Smith et al., "Can Generative AI Chatbots Emulate Human Connection?"
[36] Herbener and Damholdt, "Are Lonely Youngsters Turning to Chatbots for Companionship?"; Hall, "Heavy ChatGPT Users Tend to Be More Lonely, Suggests Research."
[37] Laestadius et al., "Too Human and Not Human Enough."
[38] American Psychological Association, "Health Advisory."
[39] Ramsey, "Ghost in the Chatbot."
[40] Ramsey, "Ghost in the Chatbot"; Herbener and Damholdt, "Are Lonely Youngsters Turning to Chatbots for Companionship?"; Ta et al., "User Experiences of Social Support from Companion Chatbots in Everyday Contexts."
[41] Ramsey, "Ghost in the Chatbot."

ecosystems. The systemic risks that follow are not problems educators can solve through better classroom practice alone, but recognizing them is essential for honest ethical analysis and responsible advocacy.

ENVIRONMENTAL

The rapid development of AI and other technologies has significant and often overlooked environmental and ecological risks. These risks stem from the energy demands of computational models, the extraction of raw materials, and the disposal of hardware.

Harms

Unsustainable Energy Consumption: AI development, especially deep learning models, requires computational resources at a scale that demands significant energy.[42]

Depletion of Natural Resources: The infrastructure behind these systems requires extraction, energy, and waste. Components used in devices and data centers, such as cobalt, lithium, and rare earth metals are mined, carrying substantial human and environmental costs.[43]

E-Waste Generation: Distributing digital devices to every student results in a surplus of e-waste when outdated products are discarded. This is particularly problematic in low-income contexts that may lack the infrastructure to properly manage such waste.[44]

Precautions

Impact Assessment: We should assess the direct and indirect environmental impact throughout the AI system life cycle, including its carbon footprint, energy consumption, and the impact of raw material extraction. If we can choose less harmful ways to achieve the same goals, we should avoid the environmentally destructive options.[45]

Promoting Green AI: A focus on aligning educational AI with environmental concerns is seen as a way forward. This involves developing technology that relies on small datasets and refined processing techniques that avoid brute force computational approaches.[46]

AI for Environment: AI itself can be deployed to support environmental solutions, such as assisting in the monitoring, protection, and regeneration of ecosystems, or helping to detect pollutants and predict pollution levels to enable targeted interventions. This can also be an opportunity to talk to students about the environmental impact of technology.[47]

---

[42] UNESCO, "Ethical Impact Assessment"; Luccioni et al., "The Environmental Impacts of AI — Primer."
[43] Kuo et al., "Assessing Environmental Impacts of Nanoscale Semi-Conductor Manufacturing from the Life Cycle Assessment Perspective"; James, "Semiconductor Manufacturing and Big Tech's Water Challenge."
[44] WHO, "Electronic Waste (e-Waste)"; Gutterman, "'Chromebook Churn' Report Highlights Problems of Short-Lived Laptops in Schools."
[45] Association, "Environmental Impact of AI | NEA"; "Recommendation on the Ethics of Artificial Intelligence."
[46] Bolón-Canedo et al., "A Review of Green Artificial Intelligence."
[47] Valenzuela, "Teaching the Environmental Impact of AI Through PBL"; Onyebuchi Nneamaka Chisom et al., "Reviewing the Role of AI in Environmental Monitoring and Conservation."

Repair and Reuse: Planned obsolescence is both a technical and ethical problem. Schools can implement repair programs, device recycling, and shared-use systems.[48]

LABOR AND JOB DISPLACEMENT

The integration of AI in education presents risks of job displacement and professional erosion for teachers and greater society. As the future of work becomes more uncertain, we have to acknowledge that a further growth and dependency on AI technologies will continue to harm individuals whose jobs become automated.

Harms

Erosion of Professional Vocation: As AI systems handle routine instructional tasks such as essay scoring or feedback generation, teachers may be reduced to monitors of digital workflows. Teaching is fundamentally an ethical relationship rooted in care, discernment, and presence, and when AI substitutes for these functions, teachers risk losing both professional identity and authority.[49]

Labor Justice: Even the most advanced systems depend on human labor, data laborers, content moderators, and low-paid workers who clean and refine the data that make AI possible. Ethical reflection must acknowledge these invisible contributors to automated education.[50]

Risk of Unequal Displacement: AI could deepen existing inequalities if wealthy schools rely on human teachers for high-quality instruction while underfunded schools rely on AI as a scalable alternative for individualized support. This risks displacing human attention and mentorship for marginalized or struggling students.[51]

Future of Work: AI is reshaping labor markets across every sector, not just education. Because current systems automate cognitive and creative tasks once considered uniquely human, whole categories of work may shrink faster than new roles appear. This creates broad employment instability and the risk of widening inequality as some workers adapt while others are displaced. For schools, this means acknowledging that students will enter a workforce marked by volatility rather than predictable career pathways.[52]

Precautions

Professional Development: Teachers need ongoing professional development to build knowledge about AI, its implications, and digital ethics. This training should be vendor-neutral

---

[48] UNESCO, "Ethical Impact Assessment"; WHO, "Electronic Waste (e-Waste)."
[49] Adams et al., "Ethical Principles for Artificial Intelligence in K-12 Education"; "Recommendation on the Ethics of Artificial Intelligence"; Shah, *AI and the Future of Education*.
[50] Communications Workers of America, "Ghost Workers in the AI Machine"; Hanna and Bender, "The Hidden Labor That Makes AI Work."
[51] Shah, *AI and the Future of Education*; Halat and Rahme, *Addressing Inequities in Education*.
[52] Georgieff, "Artificial Intelligence and Wage Inequality"; West, *The Future of Work*; Autor et al., *The Work of the Future: Building Better Jobs in an Age of Intelligent Machines*.

and focus on pedagogical strategies, including methods to mitigate bias, privacy risks, and accessibility concerns.[53]

Emphasize Higher-Order Human Skills: Teachers must shift their pedagogy to focus on what humans are uniquely good at, such as critical thinking, communication, collaboration, and creativity.[54]

Prioritize Human Relationships: Teachers should uphold the student-teacher relationship and collaboration as central to education and ensure it takes precedence over interactions with AI.

MISINFORMATION AND DEEPFAKES

AI systems can pose a direct threat to the integrity of information and the foundation of trust in digital environments. "Deepfakes," or synthetic media (such as manipulated audio recordings, videos, or photos), introduce challenges across various sectors.

Harms

Fabricated Information: Generative AI tools can produce misinformation when they mimic patterns learned from large datasets without checking factual accuracy.[55]

Erosion of Trust: The blurring of lines between reality and fiction makes people more susceptible to being deceived. If AI continues to return misinformation, it will lead to an erosion of trust in the platforms and in online information generally. The mixing of accurate and inaccurate information makes it challenging for students to identify inaccuracies.[56]

Civic Threats: Unregulated technology has the potential to spread misinformation and hate speech and pose threats to democracy and human rights, including stoking hatred. AI algorithms may also create silos by recommending information that lacks diversity.[57]

Creation of Malicious Media: Malicious deepfakes are a serious risk. Deepfake technology has been used to create and circulate non-consensual explicit content and fake audio and video recordings can cause controversy and loss of trust.[58]

---

[53] Furze, *Practical AI Strategies*; Shah, *AI and the Future of Education*; Chen et al., "A Cross-Sectional Look at Teacher Reactions, Worries, and Professional Development Needs Related to Generative AI in an Urban School District."
[54] Aguilar et al., "Critical Thinking and Ethics in the Age of Generative AI in Education"; USC, *Critical Thinking and Ethics in the Age of Generative AI in Education*; Shah, *AI and the Future of Education*.
[55] Chandra and Helmus, *Generative Artificial Intelligence Threats to Information Integrity and Potential Policy Responses*.
[56] van der Sloot and Wagensveld, "Deepfakes"; Romanishyn et al., "AI-Driven Disinformation"; Vaccari and Chadwick, "Deepfakes and Disinformation."
[57] van der Sloot and Wagensveld, "Deepfakes"; Romanishyn et al., "AI-Driven Disinformation"; Vaccari and Chadwick, "Deepfakes and Disinformation"; Pawelec, "Deepfakes and Democracy (Theory)"; Goswami, *AI Echo Chambers*.
[58] Weaver, "One in Four Unconcerned by Sexual Deepfakes Created Without Consent, Survey Finds"; Kharvi, "Understanding the Impact of AI-Generated Deepfakes on Public Opinion, Political Discourse, and Personal Security in Social Media"; Pawelec, "Deepfakes and Democracy (Theory)."

Precautions

Digital Literacy: Educators must proactively equip students with the necessary digital literacy to navigate this media environment and separate fact from fiction. Students should be trained to be vigilant because AI-generated information may not be trustworthy.[59]

Critical Thinking: Students need skills to critically evaluate how information is generated. We have to strengthen critical thinking and the competencies needed to understand the use and implications of AI systems to mitigate and counter disinformation and misinformation.[60]

Media Ethics: We need to guide students to understanding the rights and responsibilities of free expression, including verifying facts, respecting privacy, and anticipating the impact of their communication.[61]

From Recognition to Response

This chapter has mapped the risks that come bundled with educational technology. Some arise from design choices; others emerge from economic and environmental systems around them. None disappear simply because a district writes a good policy or a vendor signs a better contract. Systemic risks remind us that ethical governance requires not only classroom-level decisions, but coordinated action across schools, districts, and the broader technology ecosystem.

That reality can feel discouraging, but it can also be clarifying. Ethical use of technology will always involve trade-offs. The question is whether we see them clearly and share responsibility for them.

Educators retain three kinds of influence. First, we control how others see and reason about the technologies, by being thoughtful in how we explain tools to students and families, and whether we present them as authority or fallible input. Second, we can moderate our own usage and be intentional about how we use tools day to day, where we set boundaries, and when we choose not to use them. Finally, our voice, combined with our peers, can help steer change by advocating with colleagues, leaders, and vendors for more transparent, just, and human-centered design.

The chapters that follow, especially in Section B, take up this collective influence directly. They translate the ethical insights of this chapter into governance structures, vendor guidelines, and practical tools for decision-making. The aim is to ensure that risks are weighed fairly and consistently measured against the stakes of education we covered earlier.

---

[59] Rogow, "Media Literacy for Students in a Digital Age | Citizenship"; UNESCO, "Media and Information Literacy"; Vallee and Dwyer, "Students' Use of Generative AI."
[60] Aguilar et al., "Critical Thinking and Ethics in the Age of Generative AI in Education"; UNESCO, "Media and Information Literacy."
[61] Rogow, "Media Literacy for Students in a Digital Age | Citizenship"; UNESCO, "Media and Information Literacy"; Walker, "AI 'Deepfakes.'"

Exit Ticket

Reflect: Which inherent risk in this chapter surprised you most? Did you recognize it operating in tools you already use?

Act: Choose one tool used in your classroom. Identify which design risk (bias, opacity, manipulation, or dependence) is most relevant. How might you mitigate it this week?

Advocate: What is one inherent risk from this chapter that your school's leadership should discuss before the next technology adoption?

SECTION B

Policy

Section A helped us build our ethical vocabulary. We defined our principles, stakeholders, and stakes, developed heuristics for thinking about those values, and looked at how those come up in conversations about educational technology.

Section B is the next step where we translate philosophical understanding into institutional structures that make ethical practice possible and sustainable. We need policies, and not just individual practice, for three main reasons.

First, individual ethical actors are not enough. Section A talked about the importance of deliberative environments where we can define our shared values to create ethical decisions. Shared policies help us talk about and come to a consensus on what those values look like in practice. Structures coordinate individual judgment toward shared ends.

Second, without policies, ethical commitments are contingent on stable personnel. Policies help us build institutional memory, so what we have learned helps others not have to start from scratch in the future.

Third, not all actors will be ethical actors in a school setting. Even well-meaning people face pressures that can override ethical considerations. Policies create guardrails that protect us when interests conflict.

Chapter 11 defines the overall structure of what kinds of policy infrastructures we will need and what thinking about ethical dilemmas in practice, both for our real-life situations and for Section C, means.

Before building our policies, Chapter 12 examines constraints we cannot control: laws, funding, political pressures, and systemic inequities. We have to design policies that work within these constraints while pushing against them when possible. Our goal in this book is to reason toward ideals but still continue to act within reality.

Then, there are two types of policies with which we are concerned. First, we have policies that directly govern our decision-making within our schools. These are a prerequisite to making ethical decisions about anything, including educational technology. They codify what values guide us (normative infrastructure), how we deliberate (procedural infrastructure), what culture we maintain (cultural infrastructure). These are prerequisites for ethical decision-making in any domain. Chapters 13 and 14 are for anyone with institutional influence, like administrators, department chairs, or committee members.

In Chapter 13, we see how we can create school policies that support ethical decision-making in our schools. These cover normative (values-based), procedural (processes), and cultural (relational) structures that ensure that decisions are made deliberately in service of our values.

In Chapter 14, we take the infrastructure from a one-time ambitious project to an ongoing concrete process of ethical decision-making in our schools. We also address the roadblocks to these processes that we are likely to initially encounter.

Chapter 15 is for individual educators and covers what you can control in your classroom even if your school has not built broader infrastructure. These policies can help create the conditions for teachers to maintain consistency in their daily practice and build the dispositions to center ethics in all their actions, especially in regard to educational technology.

Chapter 16 provides concrete technology governance structures, including the policies, processes, and protocols that make ethical technology adoption possible. These are sometimes referred to as AI or Responsible Tech Policies. They include vetting processes for new tools, data governance standards, implementation and monitoring protocols, and discontinuation procedures.

On the online companion site (mentioned in the Dear Reader chapter) you will find templates, questionnaires, and example policies to build on the structures we discuss in this section.

By the end of the section, you will have structures for joint ethical decision-making, specific policies you can adapt to your context, tools for navigating constraints, and models for classroom-level action.

CHAPTER 11

Philosophy to Praxis

In this first section of the book, we developed our shared moral vocabulary: the values, theories, and heuristics that help us deliberate on ethical questions. We have five principles (i.e., beneficence, non-maleficence, autonomy, care, justice) that identify what values are at stake. We mapped our stakeholders to show whose perspectives matter. We have stakes that clarify what we are ultimately aiming for. We have heuristics that guide reasoning when all of these conflict. And, we have seen how this vocabulary applies and comes up in educational technology decision-making.

But, the vocabulary is not enough. Schools must act. Each day, educators act under the constraints of law, budget, time, and politics. Every policy we adopt, every rule we enforce, every technology we approve is a moral act. Ethical reasoning, therefore, must move from philosophy to praxis to help us address those real decisions. This chapter develops that connection by showing how ethical reasoning can become institutional design and practice. We consider: How do institutions embody these commitments? How do individuals practice this reasoning until it becomes second nature?

To that end, I discuss why we need policy infrastructure to serve as a guardrail and compass to support our ethical decision-making. Then, I turn to how this appears in our practice, both in the analytic case studies and in the everyday choices of teachers and leaders.

As we move through this chapter, we will see how philosophy gives us the language for ethical decision-making, policy shapes it, and practice will make it real.

Guiding Questions
- How does our philosophical framework translate to policy and practice?
- How do we apply the philosophical concepts in our practice?
- What role do policies play in ethical reasoning in schools?

Practice System

Before we turn to the policies in the following chapters and case studies in Section C, we need a shared process for approaching individual questions of ethical decision-making to support our philosophical framework.[1] This process will be used when we encounter the case studies, and it will be the same process that will be useful in our schools and supported by our policies.

In order to systematically practice this form of ethical reasoning, we can use the following eight-step process when confronting a new normative case (whether it be fictional or real).[2] This provides a reliable process that ensures you have considered essential factors while moving toward a decision. This eight-step template provides such a system while remaining flexible enough for individual judgment.

This process will not always lead to the same answer, but it does offer a common procedure for shared reasoning under conditions of moral uncertainty. It helps educators slow down their thinking, test their assumptions, and justify their choices in ways that promote the aims of education.

1. FIND THE ETHICAL QUESTION

The first act of ethical reasoning is noticing that something matters morally. We need to recognize when a decision carries moral weight and demands critical thinking.

If we fail to recognize that a situation includes moral stakes, we might treat it like a purely technical or compliance issue. Detecting the moral dimension early orients the entire process toward ethical responsibility.

We want to make sure that we do not jump to conclusions until the real moral question is identified. The five principles and ethical approaches from Chapters 3 and 4 will help us name the exact ethical dilemma.

> **Reflection Questions**
> - What features of this situation signal that a moral question is present?
> - Beneficence: Are we helping someone?
> - Non-Maleficence: Are we hurting anyone?
> - Autonomy: Are we respecting everyone's agency?
> - Care: Are we preserving our relationships?
> - Justice: Are we acting fairly?

---

[1] An alternative discussion protocol is also offered by the Justice in Schools project. Justice in Schools, "Case Discussion Protocol."

[2] Aamodt and Plaza, "Case-Based Reasoning"; Suarez et al., "Examination of Ethical Decision-Making Models Across Disciplines"; Shapiro and Stefkovich, *Ethical Leadership and Decision Making in Education*; Beauchamp and Childress, *Principles of Biomedical Ethics*.

2. IDENTIFY THE STAKEHOLDERS

Once we know there is an ethical question, we need to identify who is affected and how. We ask both about who has relevant perspectives and who is impacted. Without seeing all the affected parties, we risk privileging only the loudest and most powerful voices.

Broad stakeholder identification will prevent blind spots and help us balance competing needs. Using our breakdown of common stakeholders and how they are affected by educational decision-making from Chapter 5 will help us identify the stakeholder perspectives needed.

Reflection Questions
- Who is directly affected by this decision? Who is indirectly affected?
- Whose voices are missing from this conversation?
- How might power, access, or privilege shape whose interests are represented?
- Are we confusing "people with opinions" with "people who will experience the consequences"?

3. CLARIFY THE STAKES

Then, we need to identify what educational goods are being pursued or endangered. Not every end will be advanced equally by every action, so clarifying the stakes allows us to see the conflicts and trade-offs.

Clarifying the stakes prevents superficial debates and grounds the conversation in meaningful outcomes rather than preferences or assumptions. We want to see how our actions might impact the purposes or processes outlined in Chapter 6 that our institutions are built for.

Reflection Questions
- Which instrumental aim(s) of education (economic, personal, or civic) is being supported or sacrificed?
- What kinds of opportunities does this decision create, limit, or redistribute?
- Whose experience is amplified, ignored, or devalued by this choice?
- What benefits or harms appear immediately, and what may emerge later in students' lives or future generations?
- What are we ultimately trying to gain or avoid from this decision?

4. SURFACE THE TENSION

Once we have identified the ethical principles, the stakeholders involved, and the stakes on hand, we need to make the resulting tensions explicit. Doing so allows for reasoned balancing. Naming the tension helps everyone understand that the disagreement is not about who cares more or who wins, but about which values are in conflict.

Once the tension is explicit, people can reason together instead of moralizing or personalizing disagreement. We want to avoid oversimplifying the situation by assuming only one moral principle is relevant. We also want to use our ethical framework to identify the real tension between different decisions, even when other decision-makers are not naming the values.

Reflection Questions
- Which principles or values are pulling us in different directions?
- Why does each side matter?
- What moral intuitions do I feel most strongly here?
- What value is each side protecting?

5. LIST THE OPTIONS

Now, we want to examine what realistic options we have in front of us. This stage just asks us to think about what is possible, not what we think is the right option. For each option, we will describe the foreseeable benefits and harms. If we do not generate a wide range of options, we might miss solutions that honor more values or avoid unnecessary harm.

By listing all options that are available to us, we prevent the trap of false binaries. Also, in developing these options, we must remain attentive to real-world constraints such as law, time, resources, and institutional capacity, which we discuss in Chapter 12.

Reflection Questions
- What concrete options are available to us?
- For each, who benefits and who is harmed? How?
- Are there hybrid or incremental approaches that are better?
- Are there solutions that we have not considered that solve the same goal?
- What constraints (time, law, money) shape what is realistically possible?

6. APPLY REASONING HEURISTICS

At this stage, we need to start engaging in the deliberative process, and move between principles, facts, intuitions, and precedents until our reasoning feels coherent and defensible. We will use the reasoning heuristics from Chapter 7 to compare the different options.

This is also where discussions with colleagues and stakeholders will provide further insight. Many ethical disagreements in education persist not just because people disagree on values, but because they emphasize different steps in the reasoning process; a shared method helps bring those perspectives into a common structure. This identifies the real tension and offers a clear path toward consensus.

Reflection Questions
- Which option feels like it maximizes our values without causing unacceptable harm?
- Do my conclusions fit with both my guiding principles and the facts of this case?

- Would I reason similarly in a comparable situation?
- Have I considered the magnitude and probability of each benefit and harm?
- What evidence do I have for each claim and is it credible?

7. COMMUNICATE THE DECISION

Once we arrive at an answer in Step 6, we want to document and communicate it. This forces us to make sure that our decision is explainable through shared reasons to others. Communicating clearly builds trust, helps people understand the reasoning, and ensures accountability. It also prevents misinterpretations of our intent that can erode relationships.

Reflection Questions
- How would I explain this reasoning to a student, parent, or colleague?
- Would those affected find this explanation understandable and fair?
- Who do I need to share the decision with, and how should it be documented?

8. REFLECT

After we make the decision, we want to reflect on the outcome. This helps us iterate on the decision by giving us a chance to make changes on our policies by showing what we needed to account for, and on our framework by guiding revisions in light of new lessons. Ethical reasoning improves over time when we compare expectations to actual outcomes, and we avoid repeating mistakes and build on our successes over time.

Reflection Questions
- Was the reasoning accurate or flawed based on the actual outcome?
- How can we change our process to avoid this harm?
- How do we reproduce this success?
- Is there anything we need to revise in our ethical framework and how we articulate our values?
- Does anything need to be reflected in our policies?

Policies as Anchors

Conflicts are an inevitable part of complex ethical reasoning, and institutions need structures that help apply our moral framework consistently. Here, policy infrastructure refers to the institutional tools that translate our ethical commitments into durable procedures and norms. If there were no legitimate conflict, we would not need such nuanced discussions. The goal, then, is to avoid unproductive discord within our schools. Thus, we have to build structures that make ethical deliberation the norm and sustain that culture.

Good intentions of individual actors are a meaningful catalyst; one that I hope this book channels into principled structures. But we need structures to anchor us so that as leadership changes, documentation lapses, or new technologies arrive, we stay steadfast.

To make full use of our framework, we need to design structures that mirror it. We need structures to center stakeholders, be adaptable to new contexts, and to create routines that encourage reflection and revision. To do that, we need three types of infrastructure: normative, procedural, and cultural.

Normative infrastructure includes policies that encode moral values into institutional documents. This includes charters, mission statements, and codes of conduct. Procedural infrastructure provides mechanisms for ethical decision-making for major decisions. This might look like committees, review protocols, and appeal processes. Finally, we need to build cultural infrastructure that creates a culture of ethical reasoning. This includes training and discussions, policies that support dissent and questioning, and encouraging reflection.[3]

As we build structures, we will draw on our ethical values to design these effectively. We will ensure that policies are formed in consultation with a *representative* sample of stakeholders. We want to make sure that relevant stakeholders are consulted, have ownership, and can participate in the policymaking. We will *document* the reasoning for the policies and decisions as much as we can for transparency. By recording values, trade-offs, and reasons, we can build community trust and institutional memory. And, we will ensure that our policies require periodic reflection and allow for *revisions* as needed.

Ethics as Habits

This chapter has shown how philosophical concepts become policy and influence our practice. Policies will help take ethical decision-making from individual to institutional. They will help maintain the cultures that support wider ethical deliberation. The goal of this book is not to turn educators into philosophers, but I do hope to make ethical reflection part of professional practice.

By tracing the path from ethical values to daily action, we also see the cycle that sustains an ethos of ethical decision-making: philosophy offers the reasons; policy codifies them; practice tests them; and reflection revises them.

You will use the steps outlined here throughout Section C for case analyses. There, each step will be practiced in the context of the facts of the case. I present it here because it solidifies how the philosophical concepts will connect to decision-making. It also shows the systems that our policies will need to support this sort of robust deliberation.

Ultimately, the eight steps offer a way to slow down moral judgment, invite multiple perspectives, and make our reasons visible, both to ourselves and others.

In the chapters that follow, we will see how these ideas are institutionalized through policy design and show up in the lived practice of educators. As we see moral vocabulary become policy structures and professional judgment, we will make ethical decision-making a realized promise, rather than a rhetorical buzzword.

---

[3] Scott, *Institutions and Organizations*.

Exit Ticket

Reflect: Think of one recent policy, rule, or classroom decision in your school that involved a trade-off. Which of the eight steps would have helped clarify that decision and why?

Act: Identify one concrete change you could make in your own decision-making process to slow down, surface tensions, and make your reasoning more transparent next time.

Advocate: Commit to using this process in one practical setting and invite others to participate in at least some of the steps with you.

CHAPTER 12

External Constraints

When we move from philosophical questions to policy ones, we have to move from thinking about what is *ideal* to what is *ideal given our real contexts*. Unfortunately, even if we agree on what the most ethical systems and outcomes might be, we do not make daily decisions within these "perfect" systems. Our goal in this book is to think about what our ethical decision-making needs to look like under the assumption that we only act in our sphere of influence.

Given those conditions, we have to consider which external constraints we must account for in our decision-making. By "external constraints," I refer not only to formal laws, but also to institutional, fiscal, and political conditions that define what educators can realistically do. These boundaries set the parameters within which our ethical reasoning must occur.

An understanding of the laws that shape decision-making in schools helps us understand the necessary conditions that we have to meet. These conditions may be *necessary*, but they are not *sufficient* for what we consider in our decision-making process. Instead of just defaulting to complying with laws, we aim to make the most ethical decision that we pragmatically can.

To be clear, it is very possible that laws restrict our actions in ways we think are unethical. If the law supports segregation, working within the constraints of those laws would be so far from the ethical ideal that we would struggle to even conceive of an "ethical" choice within those constraints. In that case, we have two parallel moral obligations. We have the obligation to work to change those constraints to reduce the harm the system is inflicting. At the same time, we will have to continue to make ethical decisions within those constraints until we succeed at the systemic level. The former is not the subject of this book, though it is likely that the same values and principles would guide us in that context too. Thus, here, we focus on the latter and discuss policies within our control and the daily decisions we must continue to make even in unjust situations.

Law is not always an impediment either. As you will see below, legislation can codify protections that are necessary in all instances. Especially because there is a power imbalance between large technology companies and individual educators, appropriate laws that protect students from harm play a powerful role in ensuring the use of technology in schools is ethical.

Thus, here, I provide a brief overview of the types of constraints that laws and regulations typically put on what decisions schools can make about educational technology and how we can integrate them into our policies and practice. Because laws are time and location dependent, rather than list every regulation by name, I group them by the kind of constraint they impose and the ethical questions they raise.

When I do cite explicit laws, they are primarily United States federal law because that is the context in which I work. However, educational technology is global, and legal frameworks vary. Thus, for readers outside of the United States or those concerned with state-level policies, this chapter's framework (data, governance, access constraints) can map to those jurisdictions' requirements. The technical principles largely remain universal even as legal specifics vary.

There are three main types of constraints that we will discuss: data, governance, and access. Data constraints are specific to technology and control what actions schools and vendors must take for student safety. Governance constraints include funding and political pressures that influence what a school can realistically do in its local context. And finally, access constraints are systemic problems and solutions that affect marginalized student populations.

Understanding these constraints provides a stronger starting point for our policies, because our policies must build on (or around) the constraints that we do not directly control.

Guiding Questions
- What types of legal constraints are common?
- How do these constraints protect schools and help guide decision-making?
- How does that restrict a school's ability to make decisions?

Data Constraints

The most common types of constraints that national and state governments impose are related to data collection, retention, sharing, and analysis.

PRIVACY

Privacy regulations are designed to ensure that student information is handled safely, proportionately to the instructional aim, and with respect for the privacy rights of students and families. Their purpose is to make sure that data use in schools serves learning, not third-party gain. These constraints most often regulate the relationship between school and vendor.

There are various regulations globally that enforce these types of constraints. The General Data Protection Regulation (GDPR) in the European Union sets some of the most comprehensive global standards.[1] It requires that every use of personal data have a lawful basis, such as legitimate interest, consent, or contractual necessity.[2] When consent is used, it must allow

---
[1] Wolford, "What Is GDPR, the EU's New Data Protection Law?"
[2] ICO, "A Guide to Lawful Basis."

individuals to agree to specific types of processing rather than giving blanket approval.[3] GDPR also provides robust rights for individuals to access their data, request its correction or erasure, and be informed when their information is shared with other entities.[4]

In the United States, these restrictions are a combination of federal and state legislation.[5] At the federal level, the Family Educational Rights and Privacy Act (FERPA) and Children's Online Privacy Protection Act (COPPA) both impose limits on how student information can be collected, stored, and shared. FERPA protects the privacy of education records held by schools, while COPPA restricts the collection of personal data from children under 13 by online services, including educational platforms.[6] Many states have also enacted their own student privacy laws that specify requirements for vendor contracts, mandate data deletion timelines, and prohibit the sale or repurposing of student data.[7]

We have to ensure that our local policies incorporate all legally required steps and reflect these national and international frameworks. This includes being aware of what data each tool collects and shares, whether it uses profiling or automated decision-making, and what the consent process looks like for students and families.

These regulations include:

Data minimization encourages schools to ensure that any data collected and shared is explicitly tied to an instructional goal. If it cannot be tied to the aim, it should not be collected.

Tiered access asks that data only be shared with the people who need to access it in order to fulfill their duties.

Retention policies dictate how long data must be kept and when it must be deleted or anonymized.

Consent policies require that teachers, students, and parents explicitly agree to share the relevant data, and understand what they are agreeing to.

Deidentification restrictions require that any data that is used for research or analysis purposes sufficiently remove or mask identifiers to avoid reidentification risks.[8]

Audit trail requirements include logging access to sensitive data to keep a record of *who* accessed or changed *what* data *when*.

Termination rules include changing access to data when roles change and removing access when it is no longer necessary.

---

[3] ICO, "What Is Valid Consent?"
[4] DPM, "What Are 8 Data Subject Rights According to the GDPR."
[5] Center for Democracy & Technology, *State Student Privacy Laws – Public Interest Privacy Center*.
[6] FTC, "Children's Online Privacy Protection Rule ('COPPA')"; US Department of Education, "What Is FERPA? | Protecting Student Privacy."
[7] Center for Democracy & Technology, *State Student Privacy Laws – Public Interest Privacy Center*; Center for Democracy & Technology, "State Student Privacy Law Compendium."
[8] Herold and Davis, "'De-Identifying' Student Data Is Key for Protecting Privacy."

Breach notification requires notifying affected individuals when a loss of any personal information occurs or could have occurred.

Profiling restrictions protect individuals from having significant decisions made about them solely by automated means without meaningful human involvement.[9]

Together, these requirements define the legal constraints for data use in schools. They determine what information teachers and tools may use to inform instruction and understanding them helps us evaluate whether a new tool or practice respects both students' learning goals and data rights.

INFRASTRUCTURE

Another set of regulations that shape data usage in schools is related to where and how that data is stored. These regulations are designed to minimize some of the risks from the data that is collected that is deemed necessary. Decisions about the location and security of the data can affect both legal exposure and public trust, and thus, many statutes dictate where sensitive data can and cannot be stored. These regulations most often regulate what vendors have to do to protect data in order to work with schools.[10]

Internationally, various countries have regulations that require that all sensitive data be stored on servers within those countries. For example, in Europe, the GDPR has specific stipulations about the transfer of personal data outside designated areas.[11] Schools or vendors in every state and country need to verify that their service provider stores data in jurisdictions with adequate protections that meet the legal requirement.[12]

These restrictions often govern:

Data residence requirements control which jurisdictions data can be stored in, meaning the servers that host the data must be located in those areas.

Jurisdictional concerns are one of the primary reasons these types of restrictions exist, because they ensure that there are pathways to legal access protection from foreign leaks, and ability to govern the storage throughout the lifecycle of the information.

Security stipulations govern what baseline measures must be put in place, like encryption of data when stored, encryption of data during transfers, and security measures on cloud storage and access of data.

Backup requirements dictate how often the data must be saved and stored in case of the loss of primary data storage. This ensures the student data is saved and can be retrieved even if there is a problem with the infrastructure.

---

[9] Binns and Veale, "Is That Your Final Decision?"
[10] U.S. Department of Education, *Responsibilities of Third-Party Service Providers Under FERPA*.
[11] Javier López González et al., *A Preliminary Mapping of Data Localisation Measures*, vol. 262; IBM, "What Is Data Residency?"; European Commission. "What rules apply if my organisation transfers data outside the EU?"
[12] Sallay, *Vetting Generative AI Tools for Use in Schools*; U.S. Department of Education, "Protecting Student Privacy While Using Online Educational Services: Requirements and Best Practices | Protecting Student Privacy."

Training regulations might limit what the data can be used for after the fact by the vendors, whether it be for research studies or training AI models.

Collectively, these restrictions serve as further safeguards for our students and how their data is stored by vendors. Even without explicit legal requirements, schools should consider the additional protections of data stored in their home country or state or in a different jurisdiction by including it as part of the vendor vetting process.[13]

Governance Constraints

The second set of constraints are ones that affect all decisions schools make regardless of the context, because money and political pressure affect all education decisions.

IDEOLOGICAL

While the book aims to cultivate a set of shared reasons that help deliberate effectively about ethical decision-making in education, we do not presume that policymakers will adhere to the same set of values. Political decisions are often not made solely on shared values, but often on ideological and partisan commitments. These can constrain what the school can or cannot do either because of particular policies or fear of retaliation.[14]

Some of these constraints include:

Curricular pressure might include requiring certain topics to be covered or forbidding certain tools and content.[15]

Funding that is earmarked for very specific use might be constrained because of political goals rather than pedagogical ones.[16]

Assessments requirements dictate which tests, standards, and requirements a school has to prepare students for in order to remain accredited and provide recognized diplomas.[17]

Specific mandates sometimes direct schools and teachers to introduce a very particular type of tool or resource based on policies and guidance from policymakers.[18]

These political measures are the reality of the societies that our schools function in, and even when they don't directly constrain the teachers' actions, they can impose informal pressures that cause hesitation to not act in accordance with what is politically safe.[19]

---

[13] National Association of Secondary School Principals, "Position Statement: Student Data Privacy"; Sallay, *Vetting Generative AI Tools for Use in Schools*.
[14] Stephens, "Politics, Funding Threaten Schools' Focus on Student Learning, Leaders Say."
[15] Tabron et al., "Curriculum Wars"; Woo et al., *Policies Restricting Teaching About Race and Gender Spill Over into Other States and Localities*.
[16] Nora Gordon, "Block Granting Federal Education Funds Comes with Trade-Offs."
[17] New York State Education Department, "Graduation Requirements."
[18] Doan and Kaufman, "What Role Do States Play in Selecting K-12 Textbooks?"
[19] Stevens et al., "'It Has a Chilling Effect.'"

FISCAL

Restrictions on educational technology (and education as a whole) are not limited to direct guidance on particular tools and services. All of these technologies cost money, and because money is a finite resource, there are constraints on what a school or teacher can do even if they have determined the ethical decision.[20]

Every country, state, and local jurisdiction has various influences on the finance constraints. From national grants for particular programs, state budgets for grants and support services, and local funding for schools, the financial resources are dictated by various factors outside of the control of the school.[21]

Requirements that guide funding decisions include:

Grants and other funding directly impact how much money schools have to spend on various tools and resources to support the decisions they want to make.

Procurement requirements dictate the rules they must follow in choosing a vendor, including getting multiple quotes, being transparent about the process, choosing the most reasonable cost, and avoiding any conflicts of interest.

Payment structures might influence what commitment the school can or cannot make, whether the bill is a one-time cost, recurring cost, or variable cost.

Indirect costs are also constrained by the same factors; whenever a new tool is chosen, there is the cost of supporting technologies, personnel to manage the technology, and professional development to support teachers' effective use of the technology.[22]

Trade-offs are inevitable with limited resources, so funding one new intervention will either mean cutting an existing program or not being able to fund other new ones.

The limitations of funding are an unfortunate reality of our real world, and so when we encounter ethical dilemmas about choice between options, we will often have to consider how we will allocate our total resources and the ethical implications of any trade-offs.

Access Constraints

Our schools function in societies that are full of inequalities and injustices toward marginalized populations. While school-level decision-making can prevent further exacerbation of those problems, legal solutions are often necessary to reduce pervasive systemic problems.[23]

The next set of constraints stem from national, state, and international laws and policy that are designed to ensure that all students have meaningful access to education without discrimination (based on disability, sex, gender, race, etc.).[24]

---

[20] Maduakolam Ireh, "Budgeting and Funding School Technology: Essential Considerations."
[21] Swanson, "Education Funding for K-12 Schools."
[22] Institute of Education Sciences, *Total Cost of Ownership*.
[23] UNESCO, "Inclusion in Education | UNESCO"; Cuban, *Confessions of a School Reformer*.
[24] U.S. Department of Education, "Regulations Enforced by the Office for Civil Rights | U.S. Department of Education."

ACCESSIBILITY

In order to ensure that our schools are accessible to students who need accommodations, there are various changes and additional resources that schools need to provide. Various legislations govern what the bare minimum schools need to do and govern physical access, discrimination, and reasonable accommodations.

In the United States, the Americans with Disabilities Act of 1990 (ADA) applies to public entities (including public school districts) about the minimum standards for access, the Rehabilitation Act of 1973 prohibits discrimination on the basis of disability, and Title IX equal access protections apply to students with disabilities as well.[25]

When choosing tools, teachers should check that tools are accessible (e.g., screen-reader friendly), they have planned accommodations (e.g., alternative assessment formats), and their classrooms allow movement and access for all students.

Some such requirements that schools must meet:

Reasonable Accommodations must be provided when not doing so would prevent students with disabilities from participating in educational programs.

Pedagogical Access includes making sure curricula, technologies, software, and assessments do not leave out students with accessibility needs or there are equivalent accommodations for them.

Physical Access includes ensuring that students can physically access facilities, classrooms, equipment, restrooms, and transit paths.

Assistive Technologies must be present for students who need technology to support their ability to make full use of devices and software.

To ensure that students' accessibility needs are protected, teachers might also collaborate with special education staff and refer students to the appropriate school resources for accommodations.[26]

Ultimately, we might still not account for all needs and should remain flexible for overcoming any further barriers that students report. Because most vendors are aware of these regulations, vendors should have ensured that their tool is accessible for all students, and it is prudent to ask them for relevant information.[27]

---

[25] U.S. Department of Education, "Regulations Enforced by the Office for Civil Rights | U.S. Department of Education"; U.S. Department of Education, "Frequently Asked Questions," June 30, 2025, 504; Marshall, "When School Policy Limits Access to Assistive Technology for Students with Disabilities - Council of Parent Attorneys and Advocates, Inc."; U.S. Department of Education, "Frequently Asked Questions," January 17, 2025.

[26] Hernandez, "Collaboration in Special Education: Its History, Evolution, and Critical Factors Necessary for Successful Implementation."

[27] Information Technology Industry Council, "VPAT - Information Technology Industry Council."

CIVIL

The next set of constraints we will discuss are ones that protect students from discrimination or unfair treatment on the basis of race, color, national origin, sex, disability, age, religion, and other protected categories. These create a set of obligations for the schools to proactively ensure that their decisions are not underserving particular marginalized populations. [28]

In the United States, the Civil Rights Act of 1964 prohibited discrimination on the basis of race, color, or national origin by any entities receiving federal funds.[29] The Title IX regulations from the Education Amendments of 1972 prevent gender discrimination in schools.[30] And, the Equal Educational Opportunities Act of 1974 requires schools to take action to overcome barriers to equal educational opportunity.[31]

The resulting considerations often include:

Disparate impact based on race, national origin, or gender must be avoided or fixed.[32]

Language access for students should be provided through translators or providing materials in multiple languages.[33]

Equity audits require periodic review of whether the accommodations being provided are serving the needs our students have.[34]

Complaint mechanisms ensure that students and parents have a designated person for complaints and resolutions.[35]

Harassment protections require schools to prevent and adequately respond to student complaints of harassment that threaten their safety and ability to access school equitably.[36]

Training requirements for staff on bias, harassment, and cultural competence are often mandatory requirements for all employees and can help create a culture of inclusion.[37]

Thus, when selecting tools or vendors, we have to consider whether the tool is equitable across gender, language groups, national origin, and culture. We also have to ensure that the right internal policies are put in place to remain compliant with the federal regulations that govern protections for all students.

---

[28] U.S. Department of Education, "Regulations Enforced by the Office for Civil Rights | U.S. Department of Education."
[29] U.S. Department of Education, "Regulations Enforced by the Office for Civil Rights | U.S. Department of Education"; NARA, "Civil Rights Act (1964)."
[30] U.S. Department of Education, "Title IX and Sex Discrimination | U.S. Department of Education."
[31] Office of the Law Revision Counsel, "20 USC Ch. 39: EQUAL EDUCATIONAL OPPORTUNITIES AND TRANSPORTATION OF STUDENTS."
[32] Congressional Research Service, "What Is Disparate-Impact Discrimination?"
[33] Vanita Gupta, "Office of Public Affairs | Ensuring Equal Educational Opportunities for English Learner Students."
[34] Johnson, *Using Equity Audits to Assess and Address Opportunity Gaps Across Education*.
[35] Batanero and Ellie R. Austin, "Microsoft PowerPoint - Part II - Conducting Title IX Investigations."
[36] U.S. Department of Education, "Racial Incidents and Harassment Against Students | U.S. Department of Education."
[37] O'Donnell et al., "The Effects of Online Anti-Bias Training on Educators' Multicultural Competence."

HUMAN RIGHTS

There are also international laws and norms that shape expectations for how young people should be treated, what educational opportunities they deserve, and what protections they should receive when interacting with digital systems. While the same enforcement mechanisms that domestic policies have are not existent with international law, they do provide broad principles that can guide schools and shape domestic law. Two central sources for these norms include the Universal Declaration of Human Rights, adopted by the United Nations to define a broad set of civil, political, social, and cultural rights, and the United Nations Convention on the Rights of the Child, an agreement that sets out the full range of rights children ought to hold as human beings, including protections, freedoms, and entitlements that institutions are responsible for protecting.[38]

These commitments reflect a global vision for human dignity and offer another set of constraints that educators should recognize when making decisions about technology use.

Some of these rights include:

Human Dignity: Decisions about the use of educational technologies should not undermine students' sense of safety, autonomy, or personhood.

Education: Students have a fundamental right to access a quality education, and decisions about educational technology should complement not interfere with this right.

Equality: Schools need to evaluate whether technology choices advance or hinder the equitable treatment of students; for example, considering the risk of exposure to biased systems.

Privacy: Students have a right to safeguard their information and receive protection from surveillance technologies.

Participation: People should have a meaningful voice in decisions that affect them, and so, students and families should be integrated in decision-making.

Right to Work: Automation and technological advancements will bring changes to the labor market, and institutions have the responsibility to ensure that students will still be able pursue work.

These broader human rights considerations help schools identify what international law defines as fundamental protections that students are owed. They also shift the conversation from what is required because it is the law to what is required to protect these rights.

Why Not Just Laws

Of course, we need the laws to help establish some of our most explicit principles into an enforceable measure that provides us minimum protections. FERPA and COPPA, for example, have been effective at creating a baseline of privacy and rights that protect students. However, they cannot help us make the kinds of decisions we focus on in this book.

---

[38] United Nations. General Assembly, *Universal Declaration of Human Rights*, vol. 3381; UN General Assembly, "Convention on the Rights of the Child"; "Recommendation on the Ethics of Artificial Intelligence."

First, the law moves too slowly to keep up with the daily needs of educators. Ethical challenges come up daily in varied contexts and educators need a way to answer those themselves. The law also lags far behind the latest technology, which means that in the case of rapid technological development, we cannot rely on our legal system.[39]

Second, the law represents political interests that are not always aligned with education's interest. Our framework is about distilling the relevant factors to ones that reflect the purpose of schooling, and the legislative process considers much more.[40]

Finally, the law guides compliance as we examined in Chapter 2: it creates a culture of "is this allowed?" rather than "is this right?" Focusing only on laws leads to rigid compliance that has historically not always reflected reasoned ethical decision-making.[41]

Ethical Baselines

These sets of constraints, the ones aligned with our ethical values, can serve as the baseline for ethical decision-making that we do in schools. We have to be careful not to let them become the ceiling, because while they might provide some protections, they cannot address all the needs that we have discussed in Section A.

While we focused primarily on enforceable legislation in this chapter, there are other external support systems that provide softer guidance on how to include technology into schools ethically. For example, the federal and state department of education regularly issue guidance for schools on various timely topics. For example, the Organization for Economic Co-operation and Development (OECD) and United Nations Educational, Scientific and Cultural Organization (UNESCO) released their own guidance on AI in education.[42] There are also nonprofit organizations like Common Sense Media, the International Society for Technology in Education (ISTE), and the Student Data Privacy Consortium (SDPC) that provide external support for safe technology use in schools. These are not constraints in the sense of our examples above, but they can be useful starting places for further guidance on how to navigate these complex issues.

We also have to be mindful that the legislation existing is only one necessary step. The other is enforcement of these requirements, and that tends to differ depending on a variety of unpredictable factors, including government resources and political leaning. One factor that we do have control over is the ability of families to advocate for themselves to receive the protection they are guaranteed. Schools can both ensure that they build policies that do not require families to actively seek out protection and also play a role in educating and supporting families to receive the necessary support.

As you move into building your policy infrastructure, you should translate these legal demands into policies, checklists, and training modules that give teachers and leaders a clear map of what responsible use of technology means in education.

---

[39] Johns Hopkins Engineering Online, "Unseen Dangers Lurking in Storing Student Data in the Cloud."
[40] Levy, *How Political Contexts Influence Education Systems*.
[41] Epley and Kumar, "How to Design an Ethical Organization."
[42] "Recommendation on the Ethics of Artificial Intelligence"; OECD, "Artificial Intelligence and Education and Skills."

Exit Ticket

Reflect: Research the local constraints that affect your school. Which constraints are you appreciative of?

Act: What is one specific action you can take in your classroom or role to work responsibly within those constraints?

Advocate: What is one policy, resource, or change you would advocate for at the school, district, or state level to strengthen ethical and equitable technology use?

CHAPTER 13

Designing Ethical Schools

After recognizing what external constraints define our context, we can turn to the domain that we do have influence over: our schools. Here, we move from external constraints that guide or limit our decisions to internal design of our schools to ensure ethical procedures.

Ethical reasoning cannot survive on individual virtue alone. Schools are complicated, multigenerational institutions, and their moral commitments have to outlast any single administrator or teacher.[1]

Thus, in this chapter, we focus on policies that create the infrastructure within our schools that turn ethical reasoning into institutional habits, what institutional theory would identify as the core structure of any enduring organization.[2] The policies we discuss here take our pluralist framework from good intentions to structures that create systems of support for ethical schools.

While not all readers will have the institutional influence to enact these changes immediately, understanding the structures that schools ought to be building serves three purposes. First, it provides a model for how to incorporate these practices into one classroom, which is covered in Chapter 15. Second, for readers who do have the influence, educators within schools with administrative roles, it can clarify the big picture changes they should pursue. Finally, it provides educators with concrete asks to make of their schools to move the institution toward a more ethical future.

Together, these pillars will function as institutional memory to ensure that the practices we build serve students and our communities over time. Turnover, informal norms, and reactive rather than proactive policymaking can all lead to a breakdown in ethical decision-making over time. Our goal is to avoid that as much as possible.

To be clear, there is a difference between ethical infrastructure and bureaucratic control. The infrastructure I call for is to enable true community reflection, whereas bureaucracy focuses

---

[1] Epley and Kumar, "How to Design an Ethical Organization"; Kaptein, "Developing and Testing a Measure for the Ethical Culture of Organizations."
[2] Scott, *Institutions and Organizations*.

on compliance and box-checking. We are not trying to create a set of rules that everyone must follow or risk reprimand. We want to create policies that support us in pursuing the ethical deliberation this book calls for.

Our goal, then, will be to build infrastructure that sustains ethical decision-making by creating predictable, transparent, and revisable ways to reason together.

In Chapter 11, I briefly introduced the three pillars of this infrastructure: normative, procedural, and cultural. All three of these are necessary to create the environment that makes ethical decisions the norm rather than the occasional surprise within our schools. Here, we break down what exactly this looks like in our schools through the formal policies schools need and the cultural conditions that make them work.

Guiding Questions
- Why do we need institutional scaffolding for ethical decision-making processes?
- Which normative, procedural, and cultural infrastructures should we build?
- How do we ensure that institutional ethics becomes a living system?

Normative Infrastructure

The normative infrastructure functions as a way to make clear what our moral commitments are. It forces us to be explicit about what we stand for. The ethical values, principles, and aims we discussed in Section A (Chapters 3 and 6) can help form the bedrock from which we build this infrastructure. Our goal is to translate our philosophical vocabulary into institutional language. These documents should both name our values but also directly acknowledge tensions.[3]

Some documents a school can use to provide the normative infrastructure include their mission and vision statements, code of conduct for students and faculty, and charters that define the purpose and aims of the school. Often, these already exist but if you examine them closely, they might still not get to the core values and count on the reader to read between the lines to get to the aim. These documents should serve as a compass for what our shared goals are in our institutions.[4]

For example, Harvard University has a Mission & Vision statement that is explicit about its moral values:

> The mission of Harvard College is to educate the citizens and citizen-leaders for our society. We do this through our commitment to the transformative power of a liberal arts and sciences education.
>
> Beginning in the classroom with exposure to new ideas, new ways of understanding, and new ways of knowing, students embark on a journey of intellectual transformation.

---

[3] Scott, *Institutions and Organizations*; Epley and Kumar, "How to Design an Ethical Organization"; Shapiro and Stefkovich, *Ethical Leadership and Decision Making in Education*.
[4] Slate, *School Mission Statements and School Performance: A Mixed Research Investigation*; Mucinskas and Clark, "How to Make Mission Matter at Your School | Harvard Graduate School of Education."

Through a diverse living environment, where students live with people who are studying different topics, who come from different walks of life and have evolving identities, intellectual transformation is deepened and conditions for social transformation are created. From this we hope that students will begin to fashion their lives by gaining a sense of what they want to do with their gifts and talents, assessing their values and interests, and learning how they can best serve the world.[5]

This mission statement makes it clear that they aim to focus on providing an education that is primarily in service of the civic and personal aims of education. But of course, a school's mission statement is not enough for it to lead to decisions by administrators, faculty, and students that are in service of those aims. The reality is that most students and parents are explicitly concerned with the economic aims of a Harvard degree. The fact that many Harvard students go on to fields in consulting, finance, and technology is not coincidental.[6]

Thus, Harvard suffers from two problems. First, their mission statement is not honest with what the true aims of the education are for its stakeholders. While, in the abstract it sounds principled, it does not match the real expectations of its stakeholders. This is why the inclusion of all stakeholders discussed in Chapter 5 is necessary for normative statements that are more than performative language. Second, even if they want to commit to that as the only aim of their education, they are missing supporting infrastructure to ensure that decisions are made to support that aim.

This problem is not unique to Harvard, but given its proclamation, it is a valuable example of how normative infrastructure, while a good starting place, is not enough to create a culture of ethical decision-making in education.

Here is one generic mission statement that gets us closer to being honest about our values and purpose:

Our mission is to educate students for personal growth, civic participation, and economic opportunity while recognizing that these aims often exist in tension.

We seek to make those trade-offs transparent and reasoned, and balance equity, excellence, and autonomy through shared decision-making among staff, students, and parents.

This is explicit about both the aims and stakes, honest about its ability to achieve all of those, and faithful to a stakeholder-centered path to achieving the mission.

We also want to make sure we are interrogating words that show up in our mission statements to pull out the deeper ethical values and principles. When we say "respect" or "excellence" (or any of the terms discussed in Chapter 9), we should dig deeper and make clear what aims we are talking about, whether other values are being left out, or whether the vagueness makes the mission statement useless for grounding our daily decisions.

---

[5] Harvard, "Mission, Vision, & History | Harvard."
[6] Zhao and Kim, "The Harvard Crimson | Class of 2024 By the Numbers."

In order to create mission statements that reflect the school's current culture and community, they should be revised on a regular basis with the help of various stakeholders. When we realize that the mission statement no longer matches how we make other decisions or prioritize our actions, we should aim for reflective equilibrium and decide if we need to revise the mission statement or realign our actions.

Another way to make normative values clear is through the use of professional codes of ethics. Different educator groups and associations have published codes of ethics that are meant to guide teachers' ethical decision-making.[7] Some schools even have these as part of the teacher handbook.

And while we should try to create codes that match our ethical values, we have to be careful not to let them become our last step. Professional codes share many of the challenges that laws do. They are much too static to respond quickly to rapid change. They are often too general to guide real situations. And, they are often presented either as clear rules or vague commitments.

Instead, we need a more rigorous system for how to think concretely about these concepts in real situations. Professional codes can serve as normative ideals for the types of educators we want to become, but what to do with that on a daily basis is still in need of a more dynamic solution, like the one we continue to build here.[8]

To create your normative infrastructure (whether that be mission statements, codes of ethics, or a charter), you should make sure you:

- Define your core educational aims.
- Spell out your key values and what they look like if you are successful.
- Acknowledge expected trade-offs and conflicts and commit to deliberation to resolve those.
- Draft a revision schedule and consider which stakeholders need to be involved for changes.

For worksheets and discussion guides to form these statements that are tailored to your context and community, you can visit the book's accompanying site.

This practice will make our values visible and sets the tone for how we approach other aspects of decision-making in our schools.

Procedural Infrastructure

The second step in building ethical schools that are aligned with our normative values is to ensure that the processes by which decisions are made are ethically grounded. This helps guide how we act ethically in schools on a consistent basis. To do this, we need to set up formal processes for how decisions are made and reviewed. This includes review committees

---

[7] NEA, "Code of Ethics for Educators | NEA," 1975; O'Neill and Bourke, "Educating Teachers About a Code of Ethical Conduct."

[8] Scott, *Institutions and Organizations*; Shapiro and Stefkovich, *Ethical Leadership and Decision Making in Education*; Epley and Kumar, "How to Design an Ethical Organization."

composed of various stakeholders, protocols for approval that ensure that the relevant ethical questions have been considered, and an appeals process for educators and students to express concerns.[9]

These serve as guideposts to ensure that we are going through the process of considering everything we need to in order to make ethical decisions by slowing impulsive choices. Our eight-step process from Chapter 11 will serve as the basis for how we institutionalize the procedures for ethical deliberation.

We need to establish a formal mechanism to start and document these conversations in order to create a scaffolded process to support the entire deliberative process. We might convene an ethics or technology review committee that is charged with leading the conversation about maximizing the ethical choice. These should not be limited to people who are considered knowledgeable or authorities in the schools. Instead, the goal is to include various stakeholders from the beginning (e.g., students, teachers, parents, and other community members).

All decisions should have a paper trail that shows the process that the committee went through. Who was consulted? What values were considered? What trade-offs were accepted? What safeguards were put in place? What is the backup plan if something goes wrong? Schools should also prioritize post-hoc measures to allow changes in case of any problems. There should be a clear appeal and feedback process, and these should be seriously used to revise any decisions and policies.

Beyond conversations, there should be procedures in place to formalize both compliance with the external constraints mentioned in Chapter 12, but also additional constraints we determine are necessary to do right by our students. We should establish concrete procurement policies that include various steps for when a new technology is being introduced and tested. These should also govern how pilots will be conducted, and how what is learned from them will inform either curtailing or increasing the program.

The most important aspect of procedural infrastructure is continued time and guidance for ethical decision-making. This includes incorporating professional learning that helps educators see themselves as ethical agents, discussion time for educators to work through complex problems with their peers, and the normalization of using moral vocabulary within peer-to-peer conversations.[10]

In general, procedures we design should:

- Be transparent about procedures for decision-making, and the resulting outcomes.
- Include all affected stakeholders not only in the final decisions, but also in building the procedures.
- Prioritize deliberation over quick decisions by requiring reason-giving and documentation.
- Iterate on procedures when some aspect of the ethical reasoning process is consistently left out or insufficient for productive conversations.

---

[9] Starratt, "Building an Ethical School"; Gutmann, *Democratic Education*.
[10] Ta et al., "'The Power of Open Dialogue'"; Geron, "'Creating Justice in My Practice': Supporting Teachers' Values Through Professional Development in Educational Ethics."

The most important thing with any procedures we build will be to make them integrated enough into regular decision-making moments, rather than creating systems on paper only. Chapter 14 explores this issue even further in detailing the processes needed to sustain ethical schools.

Cultural Infrastructure

Our framework relies heavily on relationships and interactions between various stakeholders in order to make ethically complex decisions.[11] Thus, most of our infrastructure is going to focus on making those interactions meaningful, rather than creating strict rules and fixed processes. This helps us commit to who we want to be.

Norms: Our primary goal is to make ethical reflection within our schools a natural part of the culture. Before we can expect that to be the universal norm, we need leaders, educators, staff, and administrators who embody and communicate the values and the moral work required in educational decision-making.[12]

Leader, here, does not refer to a specific job title or position. It includes everyone who is committed to the project of making our schools more ethical. Just writing or interpreting policies is not enough to build ethical schools; we have to constantly communicate with each other using our shared ethical vocabulary.

Shared Leadership: In fact, moral reasoning and power must be shared among all the various stakeholders.[13] Teachers, administrators, department chairs, student council advisors, and parents should all have a role in sustaining ethical practice. This model encourages pluralism: many voices shaping collective ethical practices.[14] This means creating formal roles and informal opportunities for ethical leadership throughout the school. For example, ethics committee membership might rotate to include different perspectives. Faculty meetings should regularly include time for teachers to share ethical dilemmas and engage in collective reasoning.

Discourse: When we explain decisions using those values ("We chose this path, because it better reflected our commitment to civic readiness and our students and teachers advocated for it"), we demonstrate what moral reasoning looks like in our schools.[15] In doing so, our goal is to get educators to ask moral questions instinctively: "Who benefits?" "Who might be harmed?" "Is this consistent with our mission?" To cultivate that instinct, schools must give permission and language for thinking like this to occur.

The example I provided might sound simplistic, but in practice this might look like including the "why" in emails and memos communicating decisions, openly starting discussions about ethical trade-offs at meetings, and publicly acknowledging the difficulties and sacrifices when

---

[11] Scott, *Institutions and Organizations*; Gutmann, *Democratic Education*; Shapiro and Stefkovich, *Ethical Leadership and Decision Making in Education*; Epley and Kumar, "How to Design an Ethical Organization."
[12] Shapiro and Stefkovich, *Ethical Leadership and Decision Making in Education*; Starratt, "Building an Ethical School."
[13] Gutmann, *Democratic Education*.
[14] Ibid.
[15] Habermas, "Justification and Application."

making tough decisions. Ethical vocabulary is most useful when it becomes our default way of speaking and moves from our posters and websites into our daily discourse.

Consistency: Policies also remain meaningless if they are not followed or enforced from reasoned judgment, but from convenience or personal inclination. This does not preclude the possibility of revision or flexibility and exceptions, in fact, our moral framework explicitly calls for such adaptability. The concern is flexibility without appealing to shared reasons that underlie our school values.

Dialogue: Communicating about decisions should allow for a response, not just transmit edicts. Feedback channels, including surveys, town halls, comment periods, suggestion boxes, and formal check-ins, transform communication from proclamation to conversation. A dialogic approach reflects the democratic values we referenced in Chapter 6. It helps create a system where decisions are made with, not for, stakeholders. However, ethical dialogue requires genuine openness to change based on feedback. If schools solicit input but never incorporate it, stakeholders learn that their voices do not matter.

Representation: Who we build systems with is an important part of an ethical school. If we leave out stakeholders or do not seek out their perspectives and needs, we risk creating infrastructure that is insufficient, or even worse, harmful toward the communities we are trying to serve.[16]

We also discussed the risk of tokenism (soliciting perspectives for the sake of doing so, but without real incorporation) in Chapter 5 and some practical strategies to avoid that. To avoid this in building our policy infrastructure, we can make sure that we think about who is affected by each policy we are crafting and who is left out of the conversation that might have relevant experiences that ought to guide our work.

At the same time, being transparent about the limits of participation, both because of time and resources and because schools have to balance all relevant stakeholders, helps avoid feelings of powerlessness or defeat when not all perspectives are fully reflected in the final decision. The transparency that I argue for in the procedural pillar helps to build legitimacy and trust that the school is making deliberate decisions with all relevant factors considered and all relevant voices listened to.[17]

We can also build cultural norms to practice inclusion in our decision-making process to ensure we balance which voices are heard and valued. Practices that invite quieter voices, authority that is rotated and balanced, multiple avenues for feedback and perspective-sharing, and being transparent with ourselves and our peers about which voices are not being heard or considered can help reduce the harm of siloed decision-making.

Curricular Integration: Finally, ethical cultures are not just created through policies and procedures, they also require integration with how and what we teach our students. We can both create new courses and units that are distinct opportunities to teach ethical reasoning but also integrate ethical teaching into existing instructional and extracurricular spaces. Each

---

[16] Dexter et al., "Distributed Leadership in Education"; Suarez et al., "Examination of Ethical Decision-Making Models Across Disciplines."
[17] Bryk and Schneider, *Trust in Schools*.

discipline already contains moral content: literature wrestles with empathy and justice, science raises questions about evidence and responsibility, and history reveals the consequences of collective choices.

While techniques to integrate these are outside the scope of this book, we have built an entire set of curricula through our nonprofit, Academy 4 Social Civics, that provides co-curricular ways to teach ethical reasoning. There are also resources to teach students themselves about digital citizenship, data literacy, and ethical technology.

Integration also depends on pedagogy itself. Teachers convey ethical reasoning not only through what they teach, but through how they deliberate, assess, and respond. Discussion norms that balance respect and rigor, assessments that encourage ethical reasoning alongside accuracy, and interdisciplinary projects that examine the social consequences of innovation all reinforce the habits of mind that ethical schools need to cultivate.

Together, this can take ethical decision-making from something that is talked about or discussed at one meeting to an integral part of how schools and educators meet their fiduciary duties to students.

Phased Implementation

These three pillars work together to help transform the philosophical principles from Section A into actual practices that schools can use on a daily basis. The normative pillar anchors the school's decisions on values and principles. The procedural pillar shapes procedures that ensure that the values are more than just website language. And finally, reinforcing a culture of active ethical reasoning ensures that the school community is constantly thinking about how best to serve our students. These three are all necessary to build ethical schools. The norms provide directions for our procedures, the procedures build our culture, and the culture makes it all come to life. If any of these are weak, we risk rigid rules that feel meaningless, hypocrisy between our stated norms and daily practice, and inconsistency in how we approach our obligations as educators.

People who are thinking about ethics is only the first step, whereas our ultimate aim is to build schools that embody ethics. Schools that build institutional memory and precedent, actively deliberate and ask the right questions, and revise their policies and actions as they grow as ethical agents. This avoids ethical enthusiasm from taking over a school or our community temporarily but quickly fading when the realities of daily decision-making do not have policies and routines to support them day to day.

The infrastructure I outline here will require long-term institutional change and resources. But, there are steps that can incrementally build toward this rather than try to build an ethical institution overnight. As individual educators, you have the most control over building a culture of ethical deliberation. The book companion site has a "phased implementation plan" that outlines how to breakdown the policies called for here into a multi-year piecemeal process.

With all of these pillars defined, we can face new technologies, new generations, and dilemmas with confidence and integrity. In the next chapter, we turn to the support systems we need to make sure our pillars are sustainable.

Exit Ticket

Reflect: Do a quick mental audit of your current institution and what things already exist and what could be improved.

Act: Choose one piece of the cultural infrastructure that you can contribute to and aim to incorporate it into your next group decision.

Advocate: Use the phased implementation plan to advocate for micro-changes that will build toward a more ethical institution over time.

CHAPTER 14

Sustaining Ethical Practices

In Chapter 13, we discussed what normative, procedural, and cultural infrastructure our schools need in order to institutionalize ethical decision-making. In this chapter, we turn to the practices and policies that allow that infrastructure to be sustainable and impactful across time.

Ethical governance in schools is a continuous process of learning and adaptation.[1] A school's moral commitments, including its technology and curriculum, must be systematically revised and reviewed. This chapter outlines how decisions can be enforced, evaluated, and revised to sustain ethical practice.[2]

The basic premise that underlies ethical policymaking in schools is based on the same individual reflective equilibrium process we discussed for our own judgments. The suggestions in this chapter will help us move from principle, policy, and practice to evaluation and revision. This builds the capacity to adapt without losing sight of our ethical principles.

Ultimately, the goal with the practices in this chapter, and section at large, is to ensure that ethical decision-making survives the test of time, whether that be leadership transitions, new educators, or new technological advancements.

> **Guiding Questions**
> - What routines will you formalize for ethical reasoning in your schools?
> - How will you build institutional memory of ethical values and decisions?
> - How will you judge success or failure when it comes to ethical decision-making?

All of the different pillars from Chapter 13 require regular upkeep and practice in order for them to support ethical decision-making in schools. There are many ways that schools can embed this within existing parts of the school culture.

---
[1] Bryk et al., *Learning to Improve*.
[2] Kools and Stoll, *What Makes a School a Learning Organisation?*

Grand Rounds & Committees

First, schools can establish a culture similar to medicine of "grand rounds."[3] At some regular interval (e.g., once per month, quarter, semester) teams should review ethical dilemmas they encounter, how they applied the framework, and lead a discussion with their peers about how they might have acted. Resulting reflections can strengthen the confidence of staff to navigate similar situations in the future or open up the door to formalizing a policy that would benefit everyone. These should be opportunities for collective learning and reflection, not blame or punishment.[4]

Medicine has carved out protected time for this routine, but schools might need to repurpose existing meetings for this practice. For example, part of professional development time or department meetings can be devoted to these discussions, where a facilitator prepares a 45-minute case discussion. If that is difficult at first, a shared document or discussion forum can be used asynchronously to collect and share insights.

Second, there should be clearly designated members of the school that serve as an ethics committee for complex issues. For urgent issues, they can have a simplified protocol to quickly recognize the dilemmas and facts, deliberate briefly on the values and options, and apply the heuristics to produce a decision. This should all be documented and then reevaluated with the rest of the faculty as needed. The same, or different standing committee, composed of various stakeholders, can also handle complex cases, synthesize feedback on policies and decisions, and ensure follow-through both in action and communication.

In both environments, schools need to encourage deliberation that balances structure with openness.

Agendas

A one-page agenda can synthesize the relevant components of the larger eight-step process (a template version is available on the accompanying book website):

1. **Start with Framing:** Each session should begin by identifying the moral question at hand. This avoids jumping to the exact decision and relevant solutions, and instead starts with the broader problem.
2. **Map Stakeholders:** Immediately map how the issue affects the various stakeholders in a school and how their voices will be included.
3. **Share Data:** Encourage participants to share all relevant facts, ask clarifying questions to each other, and build enough context for everyone so that reasoning remains grounded in empirical reality.
4. **Record Trade-Offs & Alternatives:** Make note of which values were prioritized and why. Also, record what alternatives were discussed and why they were insufficient to solve the problem.

---

[3] Dagmar Schmitz et al., "Ethics Rounds."
[4] Edmondson, "Psychological Safety and Learning Behavior in Work Teams."

Facilitation

Facilitators and participants will need to work together to ensure the deliberative process is more than a performance.

> **Neutral Facilitator:** Facilitators need to balance neutrality with guidance. Their primary job will be to ensure that all voices are heard while steering dialogue toward the ethical problem and encouraging the use of shared reasons, rather than letting participants drift into personal disputes.
>
> **Shared Power:** Including everyone in the discussion is not enough. It can help to rotate facilitators and consider including students or community members in the rotation. They will need more guidance, and building the agenda with them and a secondary facilitator can make it less overwhelming.[5]
>
> **Psychological Safety:** People deliberate honestly only when it is safe to disagree. There have to be clear norms of respect, confidentiality, and non-retaliation.[6] Incorporating breaks during heated discussions, allowing those with less systemic power to speak first, and being mindful of how identities intersect with conversations will all help.
>
> **Reflection:** When someone starts speaking quickly, it can reduce the participation of those who require more time for private reflection. Reduce friction by building pauses for written or private reflection before group sharing; this gives introverted or cautious participants equitable space.
>
> **Timing:** Align ethical reviews with budget and policy cycles so that values can shape resource allocation from the outset. Ensure that meetings and policy revisions are scheduled at regular, public intervals.
>
> **Follow-Up:** More meetings and devoted time are only valuable if participants know that their efforts were worth it. Share updates, reflect on past meetings, and communicate how deliberation outcomes shaped subsequent action, even if not exactly.

Evaluation

Hosting discussions, making decisions, and creating policies is valuable when we also evaluate whether or not our actions are working. Ethical governance will require us to iterate on our procedures and policies as tools and cultural needs change. As we get new feedback, we need to reflect and revise our policies and procedures. Ethical standards might shift when new information is discovered or when contexts shift (e.g., technological innovations). Admitting that change is needed builds public trust and ensures that the focus remains on ethical practice, not compliance.

---

[5] Dexter et al., "Distributed Leadership in Education."
[6] De Dreu and Weingart, "Task Versus Relationship Conflict, Team Performance, and Team Member Satisfaction."

Ensuring that there are audits scheduled regularly ensures institutional accountability. These audits should focus on the moral dimensions of policy, not just on efficiency or legality. This can include a mix of qualitative and quantitative data: survey responses on trust, representation of diverse voices in committees, parent feedback on communications, and documented revisions. The scheduled audit is most of all an opportunity to open the floor for conversation and reflection. Audit worksheets are available on the accompanying book website.

Another way to force evaluation of policies is by implementing sunset clauses in every policy. This naturally prompts reevaluation of its purpose and consequences. If a policy is still working, we can reaffirm it and schedule a new sunset date. If it is not working, we can record what worked, did not work, and why; and then, we can use or not use those elements in new policies to adapt to newer contexts and information.

Assessments

Assessments happen at three levels. They apply to individual practice, organizational processes, and institutional outcomes.

Individual reflection is a practice that individual educators will incorporate as part of their practice by revisiting difficult decisions, soliciting student feedback, and raising questions in group discussions. The reflective equilibrium process in Section A ensures that individuals assess their own ethical agency. For example, you might ask yourself these questions:

- Did I identify the ethical dimensions before deciding?
- Did I consider multiple stakeholder perspectives?
- Did I use at least one principle to guide my thinking?
- Could I explain my reasoning to others?
- Did I document my decision?
- Would I make a similar decision again?
- Did I learn something from the process?

Organizational reflection will focus on how decisions are made. If feedback is later collected that could have been considered in the decision-making process, we need to ensure it is collected earlier. Schools should track attendance and diversity of participants over time at decision-making meetings and whether discussions reference principles, stakeholders, and trade-offs explicitly. They should also monitor whether recommendations translate into policy changes or reviews. Finally, surveying staff about whether they feel heard and whether ethical discourse feels genuine can help inform if the procedures need to be revised. A sample rubric and survey are available on the book companion site.

Finally, the **outcomes** of our ethical decision-making need to be evaluated to see if the ethical principles and stakes are being upheld. Are policies achieving justice, autonomy, and beneficence in the actual lived experience of students and staff? Ethical progress is most likely to be seen in narratives: how a teacher handled a dilemma, how a student council challenged an unfair rule, how a school board revised a policy, etc. Most importantly, we need to link ethical practices to educational outcomes: improved progress of students toward the aims of education, reduced disparities among different groups, and higher trust and confidence in the institutions.[7]

Revision

Even with a robust policymaking process, we will inevitably fail in our goals. We might end up causing more harm than we thought, not achieving the benefits we wanted, or creating disparities that are unfair. When we discover this failure, we need to acknowledge it and repair our actions.

When harm does occur, we need to document it: record the decisions, the context, and the trade-offs that we misunderstood, and what would have helped prevent the decision. These case analyses become part of the institutional memory. These are also opportunities to retrain faculty and students, reform any procedure, or introduce earlier feedback loops to prevent recurrence.

Potential Roadblocks

Finally, while all of these actions seem ideal for the goals I outlined earlier in the book, they are also time-consuming, cognitively demanding, and emotionally taxing. Unfortunately, ethical action in our context does not have a shortcut, and the realities of burdened schools do not reduce the realities of ethical stakes.

Fatigue: Schools have to find formal ways to devote time, attention, and energy to ethical decision-making. This might look like designated time during professional learning opportunities, reductions in class sizes or number of classes, or an increase in compensation for individuals who take on leadership roles to support the ethical infrastructure of a school. We have to recognize ethical reasoning as emotional labor and allocate time and money for it, or we risk burnout becoming apathy.[8]

Ethical decision-making would naturally lend itself to those actions, but given that most of us work within systems we cannot change overnight, we have to approach these problems in piecemeal ways within the contexts we can change. We can prioritize issues with the highest ethical complexity, rotate who is involved, and start at an individual level while collectively advocating for resources to support a larger ethos of ethics in schools.

Schools cannot expect educators to engage in these formal roles without systemic changes. Relying on teachers to work in their own time or framing it as a moral obligation to induce guilt is not sustainable nor grounded in the ethical principles underlying building the process.

---

[7] Valdez, *Getting Better at Getting More Equitable: Opportunities and Barriers for Using Continuous Improvement to Advance Educational Equity.*

[8] Coşkun et al., "Emotional Labor, Job-Related Stress, and Burnout in School Leadership"; Jaikla and Piyakun, "Teachers' Emotional Labor"; Kariou et al., "Emotional Labor and Burnout among Teachers"; Horowitz et al., "How Teachers Manage Their Workload."

The goal is not to increase compliance or performative actions. It is the institution's responsibility to replace existing work, provide formal structures, rotate responsibility, compensate monetarily, recognize professionally, and build slowly.[9]

Discord: Disagreements do not carry positive connotations, except among philosophers. However, the kind of honest and deliberate conversation that I call for requires conflicts to be named and reasoned through, rather than hidden or shut down. Schools need to set discussion norms, create mediation processes, provide clear appeal mechanisms, and model receiving and expressing disagreements without judgment or fear. We have to constantly frame disagreements as the ethical infrastructure working, not a failure of our relationships.[10]

Formal training in disagreement management can help reduce anxieties around these discussions. This can help establish discussion norms explicitly, separate arguments from people, provide ways to practice systematic empathy, and help frame dissent as care.[11]

Systemic Barriers: Political and systemic realities can also lead to cynicism and hopelessness when there is not a solution that can solve for the root injustice perpetuating the ethical dilemmas we face. Schools operate in unjust systems. Even perfect ethical reasoning hits walls: funding based on property taxes, mandates from politicians who do not understand education, vendor lock-in from past decisions, and stakeholders who are not receptive to our justifications.

This is where transparency about what constraints we operate under, what actions we are taking to modify those constraints, and what real harm we do have the power to avoid or what real benefit we can provide can prevent complete despair in our most difficult decision-making. We cannot pretend that schools can just opt out of these systems, nor can we wait for systems to change before acting. Our duty is to do the best we can given our sphere of influence even if others are not acting ethically.

Starting Small

Before we make individual policies about technology, or other matters of importance, we have to build procedures that sustain ethical decision-making. It allows for the background conditions that are necessary for ethical action. The measures in this chapter and Chapter 13 help us institutionalize the support systems. Building in regular routines of deliberations, evaluations, assessments, and revision helps us continue to grow and improve and move closer toward our ideal school.

As we figure out how to get there, we start with low-cost, high-benefit changes. Building a shared vocabulary and process for ethical decision-making can be that first step. But ultimately, we have to choose our battles, find allies, and sustain our vision through small wins. We have to remember that we all have power in at least some sphere of influence and balancing just actions and self-care within that will get us towards our ultimate goals.

---

[9] Valdez, *Getting Better at Getting More Equitable: Opportunities and Barriers for Using Continuous Improvement to Advance Educational Equity*.
[10] De Dreu and Weingart, "Task Versus Relationship Conflict, Team Performance, and Team Member Satisfaction."
[11] ThinkerAnalytix, "ThinkCulture."

By embedding ethics into the culture of school governance, we begin to transform ethics from principle into practice. In the next chapter, we will see how this infrastructure comes to life in real classroom policies made by individual educators.

Exit Ticket

Reflect: Identify a current policy that has not been reviewed recently, and design a short audit plan: who should review it, what data or stories they need, and what should determine if you sunset or renew it?

Act: Lead a discussion on a decision using the agenda above during your next department or school professional learning time.

Advocate: Ask for formal training in group decision-making or ethical policymaking.

CHAPTER 15

Classroom Policies

Chapters 13 and 14 focused on school-level policies and systems that can support ethical decision-making in schools. Here, we turn to what individual teachers can do to translate those policies into everyday practice. We also consider what teachers can reasonably do in a system that has not yet moved toward building school-level infrastructure.

Because these are not institutional policies and practices of the kind that earlier chapters discussed, we focus on classroom policies that govern the classroom and lived policies that are internal guides for educators in how they approach decision-making. Classroom policies include rules, decisions, explicit norms, and communication practices. Lived policies include personal routines, expectations for yourself and your students, and the relationships you build with other stakeholders, primarily your students.

Even in a school that provides policy infrastructure for ethical decision-making, teachers still need to build their own infrastructure. Teachers need protected space for professional judgment because every classroom decision sits within contested purposes of education.[1] Every interaction that a teacher has with a student, parent, or vendor involves innumerable decisions that have moral implications. They decide how to deal with student engagement, the tone of their voice, how transparent to be with their students and parents, how they will set up grading systems, what devices and platforms they will and will not allow, and much more. We want to make sure all those opportunities to act ethically are both recognized and taken advantage of. These are the decisions that serve as a test of our philosophical foundations and our school policy infrastructure.

In those moments, teachers make use of their practical wisdom to make the right decision based on all relevant factors. Our goal in this book is to strengthen that skillset, but also to use those moments to create policies that can create stable starting points for future decisions.

---

[1] Biesta, "What Is Education For?"

Guiding Questions
- What policies can a teacher create at the classroom level?
- What habits should a teacher establish in their own practice?
- How can the experiences of individual teachers help shape institutional policies and culture?

Classroom Policies & Decisions

Teachers form classroom policies all the time. They have syllabi, classroom rules and expectations, and daily routines that are not governed by formal policies made by schools or districts. They control classroom use of technology (to some degree), feedback types and timelines, and classroom participation expectations.[2]

In order to ensure that all of these decisions are made with the larger values in mind, educators have to ask many of the same questions that a school has to. They should either borrow the school's mission if it feels value-aligned, or generate their own classroom-level mission statement. Just like schools, as they draft policies, they can revise the mission statement or modify the policies if they conflict.

Transparency for classroom policies is even more important. If we are going to take away some sort of autonomy from our students, we should explain to them why and for what benefit.[3] More pragmatically, students are more likely to adhere to policies when they not only know what they are, but also why they exist. In fact, they are less likely to react poorly when they view the process as fair, irrespective of how they view the outcome.[4] This creates a classroom environment of trust and respect, rather than fear of consequences.

An effective practice in classrooms that seeks to build ethical classrooms is to create the policies not for students, but with students. Starting the school year by asking students what expectations and norms they would most benefit from can create ownership from the students and ensure that their perspectives are actually incorporated. This works especially well for new technology, because you can create an interactive process where the students can adapt and modify the expectations as you all learn together.[5] Resources on how to lead such a collaborative process can be found on the book's accompanying website.

Above all, it is important to use the larger ethical framework to produce the initial policies and then revise and refine them as they prove effective or ineffective in real situations.

Now, I turn to areas of policies that educators have direct control over where they can apply the ethical framework.

CURRICULUM

Depending on the context in which the educator operates, they might either have full authority over the curriculum or have to follow state or national standards. However, within their

---

[2] Wilkins et al., "Classroom Management and Facilitation Approaches That Promote School Connectedness."
[3] Gheaus, "Children's Vulnerability and Legitimate Authority Over Children."
[4] Chory-Assad and Paulsel, "Classroom Justice."
[5] Eaton, "Recent Talk: Student EngAlgement."

classroom they still have the ability to make decisions about how to pursue that curriculum. What sequence will the topics follow? Which parts will be emphasized? What other resources will be used to achieve those curricular goals? How much say will the student be given to direct their own learning? Teachers can make policies that prioritize the selection of certain resources and media, use AI tools that create "standard" curricular content, and balance core content with new technologies and topics.[6]

Reflective questions
- What knowledge does your curriculum center on and what does it omit?
- Do online tools reinforce certain perspectives or reinforce biases?
- How can students participate in shaping what counts as relevant knowledge?

Relevant Policy: This is reflected through assignments, readings, and an explicit statement addressing how you are diversifying your sources and reducing biases.

PEDAGOGY

Teachers have the most moral agency when deciding how they teach. They can choose classroom pedagogical styles (active learning, project-based learning, etc.), which have a direct impact on which aims of education they are pursuing. Their use of instructional technologies to aid their teaching are ethical choices. They might choose learning management systems, interactive tools, AI-tutoring systems, and how much instruction happens in schools versus at homes.

Reflective questions
- Do your pedagogical tools foster learning or data extraction?
- What aims of education are your pedagogical techniques supporting?
- How do you model ethical reasoning within instructional methods themselves?

Relevant Policy: Pedagogy shows up in the daily practice, but it can be encoded in the syllabus with explanations for choices of any instructional styles and tools that will shape the classroom.

HOMEWORK

Homework dictates what sort of learning happens inside and outside the classroom. This requires many assumptions on the part of the educator about what resources the student has outside the classroom and about what the best use of classroom time is for their students. There are also concerns about integrity when work is done at home, especially as AI continues to make it difficult to assess actual student effort. They can decide whether homework is for grades or practice, what tools are required, allowed, or banned from usage for homework, and how much homework is given and with what frequency.

---

[6] Gulya, "The Age of Chat"; Common Sense Media, "Our K-12 Digital Citizenship Curriculum."

Reflective questions
- Does your homework assume all students have similar resources or support?
- How do you define "independent work" in the age of generative AI?
- How do you ensure safe usage of all tools you require students to use at home?

Relevant Policy: An explicit statement explaining the purpose of homework in your class, and your expectations for why and how students complete it.

ASSESSMENT

Most modern schooling includes grading in some capacity, whether it be numerical, standards-based, or rubric guided. These grades have major impacts on the students' future prospects from grade-level promotion, college admissions, and career prospects. Even teachers who choose not to support grading have to sometimes operate within systems that require them.[7] Teachers also determine what kind of feedback to give and how often and how assessments will be fair to all their students and truly reflect their learning. They need to consider whether they will change assessments to match new capabilities of technologies, integrate AI-feedback tools, or shift to further in-class written assessments.

Reflective questions
- Does your grading system match your moral values?
- What role will automated feedback tools play in your classroom?
- What changes do you need to make to your assessments as technology progresses?

Relevant Policy: A policy explaining if and how grading will be done, how feedback will be provided, and what assessments will be conducted, and why.

COMMUNICATION

As technology makes it easier for students and parents to reach teachers outside of school time, teachers need to have clear policies about what communication norms are for their classroom. While this can increase parental involvement, help students navigate issues faster, and connect teachers with relevant stakeholders quicker, it can also quickly become unmanageable for teachers. They have to set expectations for when and how information will be sent to parents and students, when teachers will respond to digital communication, and what platforms and tools will be used for digital communication.[8]

Reflective questions
- Does your communication policy model realistic boundaries for your well-being?
- Are your online spaces governed by the same respect as your physical classroom?
- How do you ensure that digital communication is productive and not harmful for students?

---

[7] Blum, *Ungrading*.
[8] Stanford, "The Good (and the Bad) of Using Apps to Connect with Parents."

Relevant Policy: A policy explaining expectations for when you will be reachable, what mediums you encourage parents and students to use, and what, if any, communication you will facilitate between students outside the classroom.

DEVICES

As modern technologies become more common, educators are increasingly facing pressures to both integrate and regulate these tools within their classrooms. They have to draft policies and expectations about which devices are permitted, how the devices can and cannot be used, and when devices are harming rather than helping the learning process. They have to ensure that accessibility tools are available for their students who need them and, when using these tools, they need to ensure that their students' data is safeguarded.

Reflective questions
- What role will devices play in your classroom?
- How can students help co-write tech norms that balance freedom and focus?
- Are the devices you are choosing to use safe for students?

Relevant Policy: A policy that sets the expectations for which digital devices (e.g., cellphones, tablets, smartwatches, smart glasses, laptops) will be allowed, when they can be used, and what purpose each serves or distracts from.

ARTIFICIAL INTELLIGENCE

As artificial intelligence has grown in popularity in the last few years, teachers have to make decisions that are specific to new challenges brought about by these developments. They have to decide what ethical and responsible usage is, both for their students and themselves. They have to decide how much to modify their curriculum to integrate AI literacy, to make it "AI-proof," or justify the importance of not integrating AI. They have to set norms about disclosure and attribution of AI usage and model critical evaluation of AI output. Even as fear dominates the conversation because AI is seen as a tool of cheating, students are also trying to figure out responsible usage and need guidance on what that means.[9]

Reflective questions
- When are your students allowed to use AI and how does that impact learning goals?
- When will you use AI and how does that impact your students?
- How will you change your curriculum and assessments to respond to AI?

Relevant Policy: An AI policy should make clear when teachers and students are allowed to use AI, what is considered original work, and what learning the students should be doing themselves and why.

---

[9] Lee et al., "Cheating in the Age of Generative AI"; Perkins et al., "The Artificial Intelligence Assessment Scale (AIAS)."

FIRST STEPS

These domains of policies and decisions that teachers have control over all carry moral implications on our students and communities. Thus, teachers should document their own expectations and norms on these things for their students and parents. These can serve as a starting point for further refinement as they continue to test out their initial policies.

For examples and worksheets to form these policies, you can visit the accompanying book site. The case studies in Section C will also tackle some of these issues head-on through real examples of teachers making these exact kinds of decisions. Each policy and decision involves thinking about what values it supports, what assumptions it relies on, and how it might evolve as technology and norms shift.

Lived Policies

Lived policies are the underlying habits and routines that an educator adopts in order to guide their decision-making. Classroom policies are explicit policies that are often written and communicated with all stakeholders, but lived policies are ones that show up in the educator's actions. They can come through in the tone of their emails, habits around hard decisions, exceptions they make, and how they remain consistent between students. These lived policies rely heavily on the practical wisdom that teachers develop across time by practicing ethical decision-making and reflecting on it.

A lot of these can be part of a syllabus or teaching philosophy that is provided to students.[10] For an example of my teaching philosophy statement and resources on writing your own, you can visit the book companion site.

COMMUNICATION

The way an educator communicates with students and parents reflects their moral values. Whether their tone is clear or ambiguous, kind or assertive, brief or reasoned, each choice signals the ethical stance that underlies their practice. Decisions they make about what goes in the syllabus, when they write to parents, and what announcements are formally made are all reflections of their understanding of their own role. Explaining the "why" behind their decisions rather than relying on sheer authority is a direct result of moral values.

> **Reflective questions**
> - How does your tone reflect your respect for student and parent autonomy?
> - When do you explain reasoning versus asserting authority, and what values shape that choice?
> - How do you ensure consistency across emails, announcements, and feedback for all parents and students?

---

[10] Shaller, "How to Craft Your Teaching Philosophy | NEA"; Eugie Ruiz and Elizabeth Geib, "Writing Statements of Teaching Philosophy—Purdue OWL®—Purdue University."

MODELING

Teachers not only act ethically to be just to students through their actions, they also set an example for ethics from their students.[11] There might be times an educator decides to be more transparent than needed, act against established school policy, or share personal mistakes or concerns to make them teaching moments. This can be especially useful for new technology developments as it signals that everyone is learning how to navigate new challenges together.

Reflective questions

- When do you intentionally model vulnerability, ethical reasoning, or accountability for students?
- How do you decide which ethical moments are teachable ones versus private corrections?
- How do you respond when modeling conflicts with formal school policy?

INCLUSION

Teachers have moral obligations toward every student in their classroom, and sometimes meeting those obligations requires explicit effort toward them. This can show in different ways, some more obvious than others. How you handle class participation and discussions, tools that support certain learners over others, and assumptions you make about student needs, all can marginalize students further or help combat inequities.

- Which voices dominate class discussions, and how do you balance participation?
- How do you choose tools when they only benefit certain students?
- How can you ensure your classroom fosters belonging for marginalized students?

DISAGREEMENTS

Relationships are uniquely important in ethical decisions made in education.[12] How we value them in our daily disagreements requires more nuance than a simple statement of value. Teachers might have disagreements with students, families, or colleagues, all of which have moral implications and challenges. They might disagree with colleagues or administrators on policies or the right course of action. Parents might approach issues with combativeness rather than open dialogue. Even students might push back against decisions that the educator has made after ethical reasoning.

Reflective questions

- How will you handle moral disagreement among adults?
- How do you ensure that your decisions preserve rather than harm relationships?
- How can you make disagreements in the classroom a source of collective growth?

---

[11] Poth, "Developing Students' Digital Citizenship Skills"; Julie Randles, "3 Ways to Bring Student Voice to Digital Citizenship."

[12] Noddings, *The Challenge to Care in Schools: An Alternative Approach to Education*; Rucinski et al., "Teacher–Child Relationships, Classroom Climate, and Children's Social-Emotional and Academic Development."

FIRST STEPS

While the first section focused on issues that can materialize into written policies, the lived policies are your internal compass for how you will center ethics in your daily practice. They are reminders that every action, even those that seem mundane or routine, can carry moral weight. Reflecting on them preemptively, determining your own standards and principles for these, and then refining them as you see them in action allows you to grow as an ethical educator.

Ground-Up Policymaking

Chapter 13 discussed creating institutional policies that support ethical deliberation in our schools. In this chapter, we discussed what individual educators should consider when crafting their own policies, both written and habitual, that allow for the type of ethical decision-making toward which we are working.

These classroom policies and decisions are not separate from institutional ones, but rather can help inform what school-level policies need to be added, changed, or removed. Just like in our own ethical reasoning, we can use the process of reflective equilibrium to balance our larger principles with individual judgments, we can also use individual classroom policies to inform school-wide policies. This ground-up production of school policies also ensures that they reflect the stakeholders closest to the ethical impact and allow educators to quickly respond to new needs before institutional policies have a chance to catch up.

To be clear, I am not advocating for all classroom policies to become school policies. There are many good reasons to keep most decision-making power in the hands of individual educators. However, there are times when educators either feel ill-equipped to create policies or do not have the mechanism to enforce them. For example, a school-wide cellphone ban might be substantially more enforceable than a classroom based one. On the other hand, a blanket ban on all AI usage might not serve classrooms where teachers are integrating responsible usage of technology into their curricula. An important use of these classroom-level decisions is to use them as real institutional case studies to deliberate among colleagues, especially when they are complex. We discussed that process in Chapter 14.

We will practice in-depth how to approach individual situations that call on us to use or revise these policies in Section C. For now, we turn to concrete policies and procedures that we need in order to govern decisions about technology in schools.

Exit Ticket

Reflect: Choose one daily routine (attendance, grading feedback, tech check-ins, or student discussions) and consider what moral questions it brings up for you.
Act: Choose one classroom policy that you do not currently have written and write a draft.
Advocate: Bring one classroom policy or dilemma to a colleague or administrator and start a discussion about whether it should inform broader school policy.

CHAPTER 16

Ed Tech Governance

Technology governance includes many factors, including vendor contracts, teacher training, and infrastructure maintenance. In practice, the sense of urgency and reality of daily decision-making makes the kind of philosophical reflection the book calls for a secondary thought. In Chapter 2, I outlined why we must make space for that type of reflection.

This chapter details how technology governance in schools can combine the philosophical groundwork in Section A with the policy guidance thus far outlined in Section B. Every time we make a technology policy, sign a technology vendor contract, or decide what to ban or allow in our classrooms, we are making moral assumptions that shape pedagogical practice and student outcomes. In doing so, we determine whose reasoning receives recognition, what counts as evidence, and what values we advance in our schools. To make these moral dimensions visible, technology proposals should answer the moral questions put forth by Section A.

By requiring proposers to articulate the pedagogical theory and ethical implications behind a tool, schools ensure decisions rest on coherence with values rather than novelty or marketing promises.

Our goal is to govern such that we avoid the temptations of empty promises that are offered by technology vendors. Chapter 9 forced us to look beyond words that are meant to connote pedagogical value but are not sufficient when broken down into the assumptions they rely upon. Here, we build the governance structure that forces us to break down those assumptions every time we make a decision about technology in our schools.

When we do not take the relevant factors into consideration, we end up implementing technology in ways that do not help our classrooms long term. Thus, we need to ask: Does it improve learning? Is this the best use of limited funds? Does this fit our values? Can and will teachers use it?

This chapter provides the frameworks, policies, and procedures that make deliberation on those questions possible and sustainable through specific guidance for governing technology.

Guiding Questions
- How do we translate our ethical lenses to explicit questions?
- Who holds power to approve or reject new tools in our school?
- How can we ensure technology decisions reflect our educational mission?

Ethical Lens for Technology

In order to build governance structures, we will first quickly translate philosophical foundations into practical evaluation standards for technology tools.

BENEFICENCE

The first ethical question we should be asking for any tool: Does it clearly benefit students' learning, relationships, or well-being? Ethical procurement prioritizes educational purpose over technical allure.

This means vendors must demonstrate a plausible mechanism of educational benefit with evidence beyond vague marketing claims. We must be able to answer: "How does this make learning or teaching better?" with specificity.

NON-MALEFICENCE

All technology carries risks. Some of these are inherent to the tools like we discussed in Chapter 10. Some are within our control and about how we govern the technology within our schools. Ethical selection means assessing these harms in advance.

We need to make a list of risks and harms that technology might carry and create a mitigation strategy for each one. We will ask, "What are the risks to privacy, inequity, and learning if we introduce the technology?"

AUTONOMY

Protecting autonomy for technology depends on informed participation. Yet, many technologies operate as black boxes, making decisions that neither teachers nor students can fully understand or contest. Parental and student consent should be obtained before introducing technologies into the school.

Beyond procedural consent, autonomy also concerns psychological influence. Recommendation engines, gamification, and predictive analytics can subtly steer the behavior of students. We should ask "Is technology empowering our students, or is it siloing them into predetermined paths?"

CARE

Our technology governance needs to recognize that schools are relational communities. Tools should strengthen the capacity of educators to notice, respond to, and support students as whole persons.

Care requires examining how a tool affects the time, attention, and emotional labor of teachers. Care also invites us to consider how technology affects students' sense of belonging, dignity, and emotional safety. Does a tool encourage relationship building or isolate students behind screens? Does its design assume trust or suspicion? We will ask, "Do students feel seen, respected, and supported through the technology choices we make?"

JUSTICE
Technologies can improve or worsen gaps and divides in education. Governing technology decisions should prioritize accessibility for all students and not exacerbate existing educational inequities. Justice requires asking: "Who is this tool designed for?" "Whose experiences informed its logic?" "Whose needs were centered?"

We also want to be sure our use of the technology itself is just and fair. Are we ensuring that students all have equal access to the benefits of new technologies? Do our policies only benefit or protect some students or all students?

PRELIMINARY VETTING
Thus, a first-step technology evaluation should demonstrate:

- **Beneficence:** Clear educational benefit with supporting evidence
- **Non-Maleficence:** Identification of risks with mitigation strategies in place
- **Autonomy:** Human override functions and consent requirements
- **Care:** Strengthened and protected relationships that are not replaced
- **Justice:** Equitable access and fair distribution of benefits and verification of risks

Governance Architecture
Ethical technology governance requires clear organizational structures with defined roles, responsibilities, and decision-making authority for who does the vetting and where policymaking happens. Within school systems, technology decisions happen at multiple institutional levels, each with distinct roles and authority.

DISTRICT LEVEL
District level policies should provide protection from technologies, where there is clear potential for harmful impact on students. They should also establish district-wide policies and vendor contract standards that encourage ethical reflection before the integration of technology.

In order to ensure that policies center stakeholders, districts should consult with district administrators (curriculum, operations, technology), building-level principals, teacher representatives from multiple grade levels and subjects, IT and data security staff, parent representatives, and student representatives. District-level policies should not make decisions about things dependent on contextual factors specific to schools or individual teachers that would affect the impact of the technology.

SCHOOL LEVEL

School-level policies are important to create a unified norm around technology that all teachers and students can turn to, especially in complex situations. Schools are well suited to take into account the perspectives of their individual constituents and then build policies that promote their values.

Beyond establishing the procedures and infrastructure outlined in Chapters 13 and 14, school-level responsibilities for technology decisions include implementing and monitoring district-approved tools, managing pilots and experiments within policy boundaries, collecting feedback from teachers and students on technology effectiveness and concerns, and escalating ethical issues to the district when needed.

Schools should make policies in consultation with principal/vice-principals, teacher representatives, technology integration specialists, special education coordinators, student representatives, and parent representatives. Schools should also designate technology leads by departments who coordinate peer support, answer questions, document emerging issues, and support discipline-specific policies.

CLASSROOM LEVEL

Individual teachers will make policies through syllabi, routines, and daily decisions. Teachers should be responsible for creating classroom-specific technology policies within school/district guidelines, explaining technology choices and trade-offs to students, raising concerns when tools do not serve students well, and modeling ethical technology use.

This three-level structure ensures decisions are made at the appropriate level by making decisions that are strategic at the district level, contextual at the school level, and personal at the classroom level.

New Technology Policies

Now that we have delegated duties across the three levels, we need a system for making technology decisions.

Ideally, the proposals would come organically from within our classrooms, rather than a big technology rollout, because that is more likely to reflect pedagogical need and support pedagogical improvement rather than new ways to maintain the status quo. Just bringing in new technology without that buy-in and guidance leads to expected benefits not manifesting into real changes.[1]

These technology proposals should follow a decision pathway. The exact triggers can be modified, but the following is a reasonable starting point for a decision-tree:

---

[1] Reich, *Ed Tech's Failure during the Pandemic, and What Comes After*; Reich, *Failure to Disrupt: Why Technology Alone Can't Transform Education*; Herold, "Ed-Tech Supporters Promise Innovations That Can Transform Schools. Teachers Not Seeing Impact"; Herold, "All That Ed Tech Schools Bought During the Pandemic Won't Improve Equity. Here's Why."

STAGE 1: INITIAL PROPOSAL
This should include a pedagogical purpose statement explaining:

- Educational need or problem being addressed.
- How this specific tool addresses it.
- Alignment with district mission and values.
- Alternative approaches considered and rejected.
- Stakeholders consulted.

STAGE 2: RISK SCREENING
Does the tool:

- Handle personal student or staff data?
- Automate evaluative or disciplinary decisions?
- Cost more than $X (district sets threshold)?
- Require new infrastructure or training?

If all answers are no, the school committee should approve a limited pilot. If any of the answers are yes, it should proceed to a full review outlined in stage 3.

STAGE 3: ETHICAL REVIEW
For tools requiring full review, we evaluate tools through the full eight-step decision-making process, outlined in Chapter 11.

STAGE 4: DECISION

- If two or more risks are identified without strong mitigation, reject the proposal or require the vendor to make changes before reconsideration.
- If all risks can be mitigated, then approve for a structured pilot.
- If the vendor refuses transparency, reject the proposal.

STAGE 5: PILOT
Once a tool is approved for the pilot, there should be monitoring during the pilot to quickly catch any problems, an evaluation after a reasonable pilot time period depending on the tool to see if the ethical reasoning was sound, and a full rollout once the benefits are confirmed. Pilots allow schools to test new tools without permanent commitments. Every pilot should specify:

- **Duration:** X number of weeks with a midpoint check-in
- **Participants:** Representative sample across demographics and contexts
- **Metrics:** Learning outcomes, student/teacher opinion, workload impact on teachers

- **Exit clauses:** Automatic termination or pauses based on fixed rules (detailed below)
- **Communication:** How parents and students will be informed of the pilot and how and with whom results will be shared

Stop rules can make pilots safer by establishing certain conditions automatically to pause or terminate use. Some suggestions:

Immediate Pause Triggers
The pilot should be paused when any of these conditions are met until they can be mitigated.

- New risks identified in monitoring without ability to mitigate.
- Vendor changes terms or practices without notification that affect risk.
- Three or more teachers or students report the tool is causing harm.
- Evidence of significant bias.

Termination Triggers
The pilot should be terminated and adoption cancelled if any of the following conditions are met.

- Vendor refuses to answer new questions about data practices or algorithm function.
- Tool fails to meet stated pedagogical claims after pilot.
- Ongoing technical problems make tool unreliable.
- Cost significantly exceeds budget with no demonstrated value.

Final Evaluation
- Did the pilot achieve stated goals?
- What were the unintended consequences?
- Were all student groups served equally?
- What would need to change for broader adoption?
- Do benefits outweigh costs and risks?

This structured approach to pilots makes experimentation bounded, evidence-based, and reversible.

Operational Policies
This section addresses the practical infrastructure needed to make technology governance work beyond any specific tool. Too often, what succeeds at the pilot fails once scaled, especially without the right support systems in place.[2]

---

[2] Kizilcec et al., "Scaling up Behavioral Science Interventions in Online Education."

COORDINATION REQUIREMENTS

There are many different actors that make technology work for the benefit of students. Ensuring that all relevant parties are coordinating during pilots and rollouts ensures that all criteria are met.

Instructional staff should work with *technology* staff to discuss pedagogical goals and the safety of tools. The *legal* staff should be ensuring compliance with the relevant laws, while the ethics committee or individual teachers evaluate it for ethical standards. The *communications* staff needs to ensure transparent messaging about tech decisions to all relevant stakeholders. The *finance and procurement* staff need to evaluate the total cost of ownership (training, secondary infrastructure, evaluations), the possibility of funding the tool beyond the pilot or first adoption phase, and the contract terms to integrate the ethical requirements and stop-triggers.

PROFESSIONAL LEARNING

New tools without adequate teacher training waste resources and cause teacher frustration. Professional development on technology should be vendor-neutral and focus on pedagogical strategies, not specific tool features. It should provide a balanced perspective that includes strategies to mitigate bias, privacy risks, and accessibility concerns. Finally, professional development needs to be ongoing and allow time for experimentation and reflection.[3]

CONTINUOUS OVERSIGHT

Every adopted tool should undergo annual review asking:

- Is it still serving its stated purpose?
- Are there unintended consequences?
- Are users (teachers, students, families) actually using it and do they find it beneficial?
- Are there emerging concerns about privacy, bias, or effectiveness?
- Does it still align with our values, mission, and goals?
- Is the vendor responsive to concerns and feature requests?
- Do the contract terms still align with the school's requirements?

INCIDENT RESPONSE

When things go wrong (technical failure, ethical concern, security breach), the team should have a response policy in place. First, the team should contain the risk and immediately curtail any further harm. They should notify all affected parties of exactly what risk and harm was identified and what measures are being taken to correct and avoid it. The cause should be investigated and corrected for if possible. Any lessons learned should be documented and incorporated into policies if applicable. After any incident, a "decision autopsy" can help review what happened and implement protective measures.

---

[3] Herold, "Ed-Tech Supporters Promise Innovations That Can Transform Schools. Teachers Not Seeing Impact"; Reich, *Failure to Disrupt: Why Technology Alone Can't Transform Education*; Chen et al., "A Cross-Sectional Look at Teacher Reactions, Worries, and Professional Development Needs Related to Generative AI in an Urban School District."

PERMANENT DISCONTINUATION

If a tool is no longer deemed necessary or safe, or if better alternatives become available, there should be a structured process for terminating the tool. There should be ample notice provided to teachers and students with a transparent transition timeline. There should also be plans for data exports and migrations and certified data deletion by the vendor.

Beyond Infrastructure

Every vendor contract, every data policy, every procurement decision has moral implications that we need to be aware of and weigh before making decisions. This chapter has provided starting points to make technology policies deliberately and ethically.

You have principles to evaluate every technology against your values, structures to distribute decision-making, and a process for that decision-making. We discussed operational concerns including coordination, professional learning, and incident responses.

Yet, policies alone are insufficient. They must be enacted by educators with practical wisdom, applied to real situations with real stakes, and sustained by institutional culture.

Earlier chapters built the broader ethical infrastructure your school needs. This chapter focused specifically on technology governance. The next section of the book will provide opportunities for you to practice making ethical decisions within your classroom and exercise your own moral agency. Together, these chapters create a complete approach to infrastructure that helps us move from philosophy to policy, and now onto practice.

Exit Ticket

Reflect: What is one technology intervention that was brought in but did not create actual benefit?

Act: Choose one technology you would want to use in your classroom and design a pilot for testing and reviewing its appropriateness.

Advocate: Suggest a review process for technology that has been added recently to your department or school administrators.

SECTION C

Practice

In Section A we built our ethical vocabulary, in Section B we translated that into institutional structures and policies, now in Section C we will turn theory and policies into individual action. The policies we built in Section B are insufficient if we do not act on them and build our ethical reasoning skills to deal with real situations with real stakes.

In this section, you will go through 12 case studies concerning various contemporary challenges that real educators are facing in their schools. These are a combination of many stories from interviews with students and educators, experiences shared by my students, and real events that were reported in the news.

These will help you practice how to apply the full eight-step method in real situations. For each case study, try to apply the framework systematically, step-by-step, so that it starts to become a habit for you. In reality, you do not always go through the whole process, but this is your "ethics gym" so lift your weights and get your reps in! Here are some things to consider:

Voices: For each case, you will hear from multiple different stakeholders. As you go through it, think about which additional voices you would want to hear to make the decision. I have intentionally left small hints of issues that are not fully discussed to provoke you to think critically about what voices are missing. How would you talk to each of the stakeholders, both those that are explicitly included and those you identify on your own?

Options: Each case study will end with a normative problem about someone trying to figure out what they ought to do. There will be multiple options, some of them explicitly stated, and others that you might produce on your own. Do not limit yourself to the options presented. Most of the time, I leave the case study open-ended with many potential next steps to allow you to reflect on producing the options, and not just evaluating them.

Judgment: These are all meant to help you build comfort with inherent tensions that require your own judgment and stakeholder consensus to make decisions, and as such, have no perfect solution. Reasonable people will disagree about the answer, and that is the point! Try to talk these through with peers, when possible, to practice the ethical deliberation skills. The goal is not to solve the problem, but to be able to produce a defensible position and talk through opposing values and perspectives.

Complications: In each case study, I have also included a section analyzing some of the key complications that the case highlights and how they come up in the situations. They will hopefully point you in the direction of some of the ethical issues that come up in the case study. These will not be exhaustive lists, but I encourage you to also reflect on the earlier sections as needed to think about what other issues might be coming up.

Information Gap: There is only so much context that ~2,000 words can fit in. Think about what else you would want to know, research, and find out to make your own decisions. Think about which policies and procedures would have prevented the situation or would help guide the protagonist further.

Your Turn: The final section will include suggestions for you to reflect on the relevant ethical questions that came up in the case. Try to at least do those for each case, as they are designed to be quick reflective exercises. The Act and Advocate sections will ask increasingly more of you, so take on what is reasonable and skip them if they do not make sense for your current position or capacity.

The following case studies are only a subset of all the cases we have available on our website. The ones here are meant to help you practice dealing with ethical tensions across four key domains: learning, assessment, safety, and policies.

Also, a quick reminder that there are many accompanying resources on the book companion site (ethicaledtech.org), including the following:

- Additional case studies (including for higher education, administrators, and boards of education).
- AI-powered case discussion tool to accompany each case study.
- Discussion guides for reading groups and task forces.
- Simulation activities for deeper practice or to use as an instructor in your own class.

You can turn to these resources for additional support and to engage with the case study in a few different ways.

CHAPTER 17

Cases in Learning

Case Study 1: Ms. Patel & Balancing Learning & Privacy
NARRATIVE

Ms. Patel is an eighth-grade English teacher working in a racially and socioeconomically mixed Title 1 school in a mid-size city. The school had become a one-to-one school district during the pandemic and decided to maintain the program even after things returned to normal.

The school had maintained an upward trajectory in reading comprehension results until 2020, but since then they have been struggling to bring scores back to pre-pandemic levels. For Ms. Patel, more than just meeting the standards, she saw teaching reading comprehension as a way to help her students find confidence in their voices.

Her students represented the full spectrum of ability: emerging bilingual learners, gifted readers who breezed through novels, and several who were reading two or more grade levels behind. The gap was the widest she had ever seen in her classroom, and she was struggling to differentiate enough to meet their needs.

Ms. Patel had exhausted every strategy she knew. She tried multi-novel book clubs, text levelers, and flipped classrooms with gallery walks in class. At her last summer conference, she stopped by the vendor booth for LexiLearn, an AI-powered personalized reading assistant.

The demo gleamed with promise. Using adaptive algorithms, LexiLearn claimed to tailor texts to each student's reading level and interests while tracking progress through subtle cues, including reading speed, vocabulary mastery, and emotional engagement inferred from click patterns.

"This will meet every student where they are," the company representative said, smiling confidently. "Finally, no one will get left behind."

Ms. Patel was cautiously optimistic. She had watched too many students give up on reading because the material was either too easy or impossibly hard. If technology could finally actually individualize support, wasn't that worth trying?

She decided to try the app in one class this fall. Luckily, the app was free for educators this year, and in their district, free classroom apps did not require formal approval; teachers were encouraged to innovate responsibly.

She wondered why they were offering it for free, but the FAQs said the company was "gathering data to improve their models." That line did not sit perfectly right with her, but it sounded harmless enough. After all, everyone was "improving models" these days.

When the school year began, Ms. Patel decided to wait until the second quarter before introducing LexiLearn. She wanted time to know her students as readers before having an algorithm analyze them.

She faced the same struggles for the first quarter and was excited to try a new solution when the new marking period started. "Okay, everyone," she said. "We are trying something new today. It is called LexiLearn. You will each take a short survey so the app can get to know what you like: hobbies, genres, and even food. Then it will give you readings matched to your interests and skill level."

Richard, usually disengaged and fidgety, perked up. "Wait, we don't all have to read the same thing?"

"That's right," she smiled. "The stories are made just for each of you." The room filled with tentative excitement as students logged into their tablets.

Richard's first article was about slow cooking, which was his new obsession at home. "Ms. Patel, this thing knows me!" he shouted. For once, he started reading right away.

Elena, meanwhile, stared at her screen, hesitant. "It is asking about what I do on the weekends," she said quietly. "Do I have to put all this?"

"Just share what you are comfortable with," Ms. Patel reassured her. "It helps the app pick topics you will enjoy."

But something in Elena's expression unsettled her. Elena was a caretaker for three younger siblings, often arriving at school exhausted. She spent weekends helping her mom clean houses or looking after her brothers. What would the app do with that kind of truth?

Later that evening, as Ms. Patel reviewed the teacher dashboard, she was impressed. She could see exactly what each student had read, how long they spent on each paragraph, the words they had clicked for definitions, and even the times of the day they accessed the app. This was the most detail she had ever seen about their reading.

She admired the precision, but the intimacy of it also startled her. It felt like peeking into their private thinking.

Still, the results were hard to argue with. Over the next few weeks, reluctant readers were completing passages and quiz scores were inching up. Richard was doing his homework for the first time all year.

Then came an email.

Subject: Concern About App

Dear Ms. Patel,

I wanted to reach out about LexiLearn. Elena mentioned she was uncomfortable with how much personal information it asks for. I looked into it, and I am worried about what data it is collecting. Who has access to my daughter's information? Is this company using her data for anything besides her reading quizzes? Please let me know before she continues using it.

—*Marissa*

Ms. Patel reread the message several times. It was polite but pointed. She pulled up the privacy policy on LexiLearn's website: *"We may use anonymized data to improve our algorithms and enhance user experience."* However, the policy never specified what counted as "anonymized," or whether family details and emotional engagement data were included.

That night she caught herself scrolling through articles on student data privacy, realizing how little she knew about where her students' data went once it left the classroom. FERPA, COPPA, district contracts—none of it had been part of her training. She realized no one had ever explained how any of this applied to the apps teachers downloaded on their own.

The next day, Elena approached her tentatively. "My mom said I should not use the app until we know more. She says once something is online, it is there forever."

Ms. Patel nodded slowly. "She's not wrong," she admitted. "But you have been improving so much. Maybe we can figure out a way to make it safer."

As the weeks went on, the class grew divided. Some students loved LexiLearn's gamified badges and leaderboards. Edward was racing to grab his device to keep his streak each day, and Richard was completing all his assignments. Others were anxious after hearing Elena's concerns, and some did not want their peers to see their scores.

At lunch, Ms. Patel overheard two students whispering: "Maybe they're spying on us." "Nah, Ms. Patel wouldn't do that."

That one line, *Ms. Patel would not do that*, stuck with her. They trusted her, not the system. But was that trust justified if she didn't really know what was happening behind the scenes?

By Friday, her principal called her in. "Ms. Patel, I got a few emails about LexiLearn. Parents are asking whether we vetted it. I know it is just a pilot, but the superintendent's office is sensitive about data issues right now."

He paused, softening his tone. "Look, your fall benchmark reading scores are the best in the department. But if parents get spooked, we could lose this momentum. Maybe just send a clarification email and reassure them that it is safe."

Back in her classroom, Ms. Patel sat staring at her laptop long after dismissal. She drafted, deleted, and redrafted that parent email half a dozen times. She wanted to tell them the truth that she didn't know exactly how the data was used, that she had assumed it was safe because it was at a popular conference, and that the results had been so encouraging she hadn't paused to dig deeper.

Her cursor blinked against the empty screen.

If she stopped using the app, students like Richard and Edward might lose the motivation they had finally found. But if she continued without full transparency, she risked betraying the trust of her students and their families.

Part of her wondered if there were other solutions: pausing for some students, changing what data the app collected, or demanding clearer answers before continuing. None of that was going to be easy in practice, and she was not clear if any of those really solved her dilemma.

That weekend, Ms. Patel printed out the district's tech policy, the app's privacy terms, and the consent forms from other approved tools. She underlined words like *opt-in*, *parental notice*, and *educational use only*. None fully captured what LexiLearn was doing.

On Monday morning, she looked out at her class, filled with chatter about their reading streaks and badges. She felt the weight of every student's progress, but also every parent's unspoken fear, resting on her decision.

Should she pause the pilot and risk undoing hard-earned gains, continue as is and trust the company's assurances, or try to keep the tool while tightening the guardrails around data and consent?

VOICES

Ms. Patel, Teacher: I finally found something that works. For the first time, my most vulnerable students are reading with joy, but I cannot ignore the unease in my gut or the questions I cannot answer about data. If I pull back now, do I betray the students who finally feel seen? If I continue, do I betray their right to be unseen?

Elena, Student: It is weird. The app knows what I like, but it also feels like it knows *too much*. I do not want my mom to worry, and I do not want to fall behind. Everyone else gets to use it, and I am stuck with paper worksheets. It is like I am being punished.

Principal Owens: We need innovation to move our students forward, but we also need parental trust. If we shut down every new tool over "what-ifs," we will never make progress. The last thing I want is for our students' data to be misused, but I also see how much this is helping some of them.

Richard, Student: For the first time, I actually like reading. The stories feel like they are made for me. I really hope they do not take away the app. It will feel like they do not care that I finally got good at something.

LexiLearn Representative: We never sell identifiable student data. Our algorithms rely on patterns across millions of users, not any one child. If we cannot learn from real students' reading behaviors, we will not be able to make the product better for struggling readers like Ms. Patel's students.

COMPLICATIONS

Policy Vacuum: The district had no centralized process for approving classroom technologies, especially free ones. Teachers were encouraged to "innovate responsibly," but that did not translate to practical decision-making. Without clear guidance or training, Ms. Patel became the *de facto* ethics officer of her own classroom.

Illusion of Consent: LexiLearn's terms of service declared that students' data would be "de-identified" for research and product development. Yet, few parents had given explicit consent, and the "opt-out" forms buried in district paperwork were largely symbolic.

Inequity of Innovation: Teachers at wealthier schools had instructional coaches and legal departments to vet new tools. In underfunded schools like Ms. Patel's, individual teachers carried that burden. This asymmetry meant that privacy protections often correlated with privilege. Students most in need of the additional support are also the most exposed to opaque algorithms.

Allure of Metrics: Early data showed real improvement, and withdrawing from a tool that demonstrably raised performance felt almost irresponsible. Beneficence was visible and measurable. The harms of data collection were abstract, invisible, and deferred.

Emotional Dimension of Care: Ms. Patel's relationship with her students was built on trust. Their willingness to open up, read aloud, and take risks depended on believing she was protecting them. The possibility of hidden data extraction risked fracturing that trust, but so did abandoning a tool that students were embracing.

YOUR TURN
Reflect
- What would you do in Ms. Patel's position? Would you continue using LexiLearn for the sake of student growth, pause to protect privacy, or modify how the tool is being used?
- How should she balance her duty to advance her students' learning with her obligation to protect their privacy and autonomy?
- Which principle would guide your reasoning most strongly, and how would you explain that decision to students and families?
- What other conflicts or potential risks did you see come up that we did not formally address?
- Have you ever introduced a tool or policy that later raised ethical doubts?

Act
Conduct a privacy audit of your own classroom tools and create a one-page summary to share with parents and students. For each software you use, identify:
- What student data is collected?
- Who can access it?
- How long is it stored?
- Were families informed? Did they give their consent?

Advocate
Check if your district has any of the following, and see if you and your colleagues can advocate for anything that is missing:
- Clear vetting procedures for all classroom technologies, including a data privacy checklist aligned with FERPA, COPPA, and state law.
- Parent and student consent protocols that are meaningful.
- Professional development so teachers are not left to navigate these decisions alone.

Case Study 2: Mrs. Vargas & Equity in Learning Solutions
NARRATIVE
Mrs. Vargas is beginning a new school year in her ninth-grade math class. As she walks in, the room looks like it is straight out of a tech ad. There are rows of laptops, glowing screens, and the owl mascot of the district's new AI tutoring partner, ApuLearn, staring at her from the back of each computer.

Mrs. Vargas teaches in a mid-size suburban school, with a student population that includes children of factory workers, a growing community of Somali refugee students, and an increasing number of students from affluent families after one of the largest tech companies moved into the area. The school was struggling with their four-year graduation rates, and state examination scores were steadily decreasing. The district was facing pressure to innovate and catch students up as soon as possible.

Their state had launched an "AI in Education" grant that summer, and the district had won the first round of funding to pilot a new tutoring tool. In order to maintain funding for the next year, they had to demonstrate gains within one year and show improvement on the state exams every year after.

As the district looked for possible vendors to partner with for the grant, every search was returning ApuLearn, marketed as a "Mastery Learning Tutor for Every Student." It had adaptive questions, real-time feedback, and even encouraged the student with motivational messages. It focused its content on state standards by grade level.

Mrs. Vargas first heard about the AI tutor at the September professional learning day conference. They were to use the tool this fall and better "meet students where they are." The goal, the facilitator said, was to free up the teachers' time to focus on higher order thinking beyond the standards, while the tutor handled the learning that could be automated. The full implementation plan would be sent by the end of the week, and the vendor had a library of over 150 training videos that the teachers were encouraged to make use of before implementing the tool in their classes.

That Friday, when Mrs. Vargas opened the email with the allocation plan, it indicated that the top quartile of the class would be given primarily human support in smaller classes to focus on advanced higher order skills. They also hoped that this would help these students form deeper relationships with faculty, resulting in better recommendation letters. The school was increasingly focused on raising their college acceptance profile to make sure the new wave of affluent families did not turn to private schooling.

Everyone else would get a school and home license to use ApuLearn, so that they could bring up the school's test scores on math and reading assessments quickly. At least 75% of math and reading instruction was to happen on the application. The evidence from other districts was clear: students who used ApuLearn for even a quarter were showing 10–15% gains on assessments.

The school informed the teachers that the parents had already been told about the technology in this year's student handbook, and there was a parent dashboard to view student progress if they requested access.

Mrs. Vargas was confused about the drastic changes announced. She had been preparing new assignments for her class this year that centered on flipping her classroom. She was looking forward to getting to know all of them better with more dynamic in-class time. Later that day, she spoke to Mr. Kim, "Doesn't it feel backward that higher scoring students get more human time?" Mr. Kim acknowledged her point but reminded her of the different needs each group of students had and the best solutions to them. "If this improves college acceptances *and* standardized assessment scores, it seems like it's at least worth a shot!"

Mrs. Vargas questioned whether it was that easy to sort the students into these two groups, and whether the standardized assessment improvements were enough to change "who is getting left behind." Nonetheless, she had to try it, and used it as instructed for the first few weeks of class.

Quickly, ApuLearn became a routine part of math class. Students would hear cheerful voices praising them by name. "Great job, Marcos! That took some time, but you mastered it!" Initially, the students thought it was exciting to hear the computer announce their success, but the enthusiasm soon died down, and students began to mute or take off their headphones when the feedback came on.

The students she was working with directly were starting to learn concepts normally not covered until the following year. She was able to help them train for the annual math competition, and they were even exploring if there was a way to get dual-credit approval.

Among the other students, some were rapidly progressing through the lessons. They were consistently scoring highly, making use of the customized feedback and suggested follow-up activities, and seemed to be progressing faster than Mrs. Vargas had ever seen.

Other students were still struggling to fully get into a rhythm with the system. They kept facing red "try again" messages that had gone from annoying to angering. They tried to read the feedback, but it felt like it was just repeating the earlier lesson and was not actually helping them break down the concepts.

She started to notice the divide in her class: the top quartile was improving rapidly, another 50% were progressing quickly through the state standards, but the rest of the students were starting to look defeated. She decided to meet each student to see how they felt about the learning tool.

Marcos was a quiet, hardworking student, who was normally anxious to speak up in class. His parents had immigrated when he was in fifth grade, and he had quickly caught up to grade-level performance by eighth grade. She had noticed he was spending more time on his tablet during free time like lunch and recess, but wanted to hear from him directly. When Mrs. Vargas approached him, he was looking at a screen that said, "You are improving, Marcos! I am so proud of you!" She asked him how he was doing, and Marcos said it was "nice" because ApuLearn never got mad and he did not have to raise his hand to ask questions in front of everyone. He clearly wanted to get to the next task, so she went to Julia.

Julia was doodling on a sticky note when Mrs. Vargas came. "Julia, is everything okay?" Julia explained that she was getting tired of going through the same loop again and again. Every time she failed a quiz, the AI suggested to do the same activities again. Mrs. Vargas asked her about the custom tutor option, but Julia explained she had already tried asking for another explanation or for it to be explained in a different way. AI's reply had been: "I already gave you the simplest explanation." Julia started doodling again and said, "I guess I am too stupid."

Mrs. Vargas tried to comfort and reorient her, but ultimately left feeling unsatisfied with what she had heard. In all her years of teaching, she had never signaled to a student that she had run out of ways to teach them. That felt absurd!

At the end of the week, she saw an email from the principal:

Hi team!

Keep up the good work! The parents of our highest achieving students seem very excited about the new direction, and the district is gearing up for a grant renewal and even possibly a state award based on our performance so far. A district rep will be at our next faculty meeting to discuss our experiences further. Come with your favorite stories!

Best.

Silvia Davis

Mrs. Vargas felt a little disheartened. Had no one else noticed the students who were struggling? At the staff meeting, Vice-Principal Jenkins showed a graph demonstrating the growth of both groups of students. Mrs. Vargas spoke up and said, "Have you seen any difference within the AI-tutor group?" He indicated that he was running some numbers still, but at this point, they were focused on the large gains they were seeing for each group.

Mrs. Vargas pushed again: "I am glad that our time is spent helping our highest achievers push themselves, but I am not convinced we are doing enough for all the students. And, what about time for the students to connect with each other?" Some of the other faculty shifted uneasily in their seats. Mr. Kim spoke up, "But Mrs. Vargas, we have never had this much growth in our school. Look at all the good we are doing. Our students are very lucky we got this grant." The principal chimed in, "Look Mrs. Vargas, I understand your concerns, but we cannot possibly provide every student with individual human support, and this is the most efficient way to get their reading and math skills higher. What are you actually expecting us to do?"

VOICES

Mrs. Vargas, Teacher: I have been struggling to keep all my students engaged given their different learning needs, and this finally has gotten a majority of my students to make improvements. I enjoy the time I get with my advanced students, but worry that I am not able to pay as much attention to the struggling students. I know the district's thinking of fairness at scale, but it does not feel fair to the children in front of me.

Principal Davis: I have to meet my district targets and help us retain our funding, but Mrs. Vargas is right that the aggregate data is not enough to tell the whole story. Still, this progress will open up more funding down the road and allow us to maybe change things when we can afford a bit more. We are never going to be able to provide a human tutor to every student, and this might just have to be the second-best thing.

Marcos, Student: I hate having to ask for help in class, and my friends sometimes snicker when I ask my teachers something. I love having the tutor at home too because it teaches the same way as my teacher, and it does not get upset with me. I think I like spending time with ApuLearn more than my friends. He really gets me.

Julia's Mother: I keep getting pinged that my daughter needs extra support, but the system never remembers my password. When I log in, it says things like "Needs Improvement with Standard 4.45." What even is that? Julia is so tired of using the tablet, I do not want to force her to use it more at home.

COMPLICATIONS

Limited Resources: The school had faced multiple funding cuts in recent years and increased class sizes. The AI tutor grant unlocked some new funding sources and is showing improvement without having to increase overhead spending, which is appealing. The school needs to find a way to support all their students, but resources are limited, and they have to figure out how to make the most of what they have.

Political Pressure: The state is pushing AI in education and has recently been allocating more and more funding to it. The school has to choose to use these tools instead of other solutions because there is not enough funding to support alternatives. The policymakers want their state to be at the forefront, but they do not see what Mrs. Vargas sees.

Algorithmic Limitations: The platform is primarily focused on measuring math and reading outcomes, but the school is not tracking any other educational goals. The algorithm is focused on getting students to demonstrate specific mastery of the state's standards and does not deviate from it at all.

Psychological Impacts: The students who receive human support feel supported, cared for, and challenged. Some of the students using AI are finding it to be a better option for their learning, but others are feeling neglected. Some students, like Marcos, are starting to prefer interacting with the AI tutor over his teacher and classmates.

YOUR TURN

Reflect

- How should Mrs. Vargas respond to the principal? Should she agree that the existing design is the best option they have right now? Or should she keep challenging her peers?
- Should Mrs. Vargas quietly change how she conducts her class regardless of the push for more ApuLearn time?
- How should she balance worrying about losing the extra funding for the school, harming her professional relationships with her colleagues, and making sure none of her students fall through the crack?
- What emotions surfaced for you as you read this case? Do you empathize more with Mrs. Vargas's frustration or with the principal's pragmatism?
- How might your answer differ if you were the teacher, the administrator, or the parent?
- Have you ever accepted an "efficient" solution that later felt ethically uneasy?

Act

In your own classroom, consider small actions that make equity tangible even within constrained systems:

- Mix time with technology and humans to take advantage of data and humanize learning.
- Collect qualitative feedback from students about how it feels to use the technology, not just how it performs.
- Model transparency with students. Explain why technology is used, what it can and cannot do, and how their voices shape its use.

Advocate

- Push for audits that disaggregate data by subgroup rather than look at group data.
- Push for review boards that include teachers, parents, and students in technology decisions.
- Recommend pilots that randomize groups to test actual comparative effectiveness for everyone.

Case Study 3: Mr. Martinez & The Question of Me or We
NARRATIVE

Mr. Martinez is a fifth-grade history teacher in a large, urban elementary school. He is known for his ability to differentiate effectively and his commitment to discussion-based learning. His students include English Language Learners with varying proficiencies, students reading above their grade level, and students with attention and processing disorders. He has spent decades of his career designing lessons that push advanced students without leaving struggling students behind.

The department chair has recently decided to use a new AI-powered history textbook, BeThere, after a successful pilot by Mrs. Bird. Last semester, the students who were not in her class were upset and complained about having to learn "the old-fashioned way." Given the success and the student request, the department decided to standardize the tool for the whole department.

Among other things, BeThere placed students in various historical scenarios so they could both demonstrate the facts they know and learn new things from other characters in the activity. The system tracked which facts and concepts the student had brought up on their own, which they had been exposed to, and which ones they were getting wrong repeatedly, so it could review the questions later.

On the first day of the rollout, Mr. Martinez explained to students how it would work, what the expectations were for school versus home usage, and what data he was going to be able to see. The students were motivated to try something new and were getting into character during the activities. Bruce was enthusiastic about his activity: "Hey! I am debating Lincoln on states' rights right now!" In the other corner, Jeff, who always did well on assessments, was intently doing flashcards on the major battles of the Civil War.

On the first quiz eight weeks post rollout, the class average was a B+, higher than the usual B-. Other teachers were seeing similar gains in their classes, so the superintendent was excited about the pilot's success and was pushing to expand BeThere district wide. At the very least, the department decided to use it until the state standardized assessments.

After the state assessments, Mr. Martinez was excited to return to his usual teaching style. The last few months had been a lot of students looking at their computers and asking for help occasionally. He decided he would spend the rest of the semester getting the students to engage in debates and Socratic seminars to better prepare them for the kind of thinking they would be doing in middle school.

When he began the activity, he noticed his students seemed to be less present with him. They had blank stares instead of attentive ones and were not even really chattering with each other. The activity that once generated lively conversation now felt awkward, as students seemed reluctant to engage out loud. Mr. Martinez tried to pose more open-ended questions about a text they had all read on their apps, but was struck by the reduced number and depth of responses. It felt like they wanted to say the least amount possible.

Mr. Martinez ended the seminar early that day and left feeling unsettled by how little his students spoke. He was thinking about how in previous years, students would eagerly engage in the conversations when he threw thought provoking questions at them and even tried to interrupt each other. He started to wonder if months of talking to simulations instead of with classmates had changed how they saw history class. He even had to ask Marlee, who normally was the first to speak, to put away her laptop multiple times today.

He decided to ask the students to do a reflection during the next class to get more insight. "After your first year of using BeThere, reflect on how, if at all, it changed the way you learn history?" After school, he began reading through them. One commented on how BeThere was better because they did not have to wait for their classmates. Another said it was nice because the characters in BeThere never laughed at him. Marlee remarked that no one rolled their eyes when she "spoke up" in BeThere.

Mr. Martinez felt torn: the same tool that disrupted his class community was feeling like a safe space for others. He was eager to speak to his colleagues at their next department meeting where the state results were also going to be shared.

The department chair announced that they had achieved the highest state results they had seen in years. Classes using BeThere most intensively, including Mr. Martinez's and Mrs. Bird's, had the strongest gains. There was hope and relief in the room. They might finally be getting off the "watch list" and improving the school's rating. The chair proposed formalizing a BeThere-heavy pacing guide for the entire next year, ramping up home usage in the months before testing. Mr. Martinez hesitated to say anything during that meeting, lest he dampen the excitement his colleagues were feeling.

Later that day, Principal Kraemer pulled Mr. Martinez aside and congratulated him on his students' test performance. "They are going to be very prepared to succeed next year when they enter middle school!" He also asked Mr. Martinez for some success stories to share at the next board meeting and wanted Mr. Martinez to present. Mr. Martinez was having mixed feelings. He was proud of his students and how much learning they had gotten done this year but was also full of dread for its impact on their classroom behavior. For now, he decided to think about what he might say.

On bus duty that day, he was overhearing parents talk about the test scores. One parent was very excited that "our kids can finally compete." Another parent was complaining, "history is just sitting and clicking now apparently, but it seems worth it." Middle school admissions were selective in their district, and Mr. Martinez knew how anxious most parents were about placements.

The next morning, he went early to speak to Mrs. Bird about her classroom climate. She acknowledged that there was "less chatter," but chalked it up to students being more focused and on task. When Mr. Martinez raised his concerns, she tried to assuage him by pointing out that community could be built at recess, lunch, and extracurricular activities. But history class had to be "laser-focused" on content. Mr. Martinez tried to push back one more time. "Discussing hard topics *is* part of learning history and preparing for civic life." Mrs. Bird did not seem convinced by this: "You are idealizing our old approaches and underestimating BeThere's benefits for our students!"

Mr. Martinez was still adamant that he wanted his classroom to be a site of active discourse. He decided to do a hybrid approach the next day. They all started on BeThere, then did small group discussions, and finally everyone got together to do a whole class discussion. Even then, he noticed the students were mainly referencing what AI characters told them rather than what their peers had said. One student insisted that a classmate's interpretation was "wrong" because "BeThere said so." Mr. Martinez was even more worried now that they were beginning to think that learning history was extracting the one correct answer from an expert system.

The department chair sent around the pacing guide for next year with specific weekly usage targets for BeThere. It suggested at least four days a week of BeThere during core history time with specific milestones, and he requested faculty to start preparing lesson plans for the next school year that reflected these requirements. He also mentioned that they might even get VR glasses to further help the students "live history." Mr. Martinez realized that deviating significantly might be seen as shirking his responsibilities, especially since his class helped lead the way.

At home, he pulled out his old discussion prompts, student debate rubrics, and the new BeThere pacing guide. He sketched three possible plans: continue heavy BeThere use, drastically scale it back, or adopt a hybrid model that risks lower scores. He tried to imagine his principal's reaction to each choice and the potential impact on his evaluation and students' test outcomes. However, he also thought about his responsibility to help students enter middle school confident in both their knowledge and their ability to speak up, and the civic mission that drew him to teaching history in the first place. And, he still had to decide what he would say publicly at the board meeting!

That Friday, as he walked out of the classroom, he was still ambivalent. Would he celebrate BeThere publicly as the district's new centerpiece and stay silent about his concerns, or openly advocate for a more different approach tonight? Either path would betray something important: his commitment to his students' civic life or his commitment to giving them every possible academic advantage. As he took his seat, he was still unsure which version of the story he would tell.

VOICES

Mr. Martinez, Teacher: I entered teaching because I wanted to help students learn how to navigate the future by learning about the past. Test scores only represent one aspect of what history means to me. BeThere has clearly helped many students remember names, dates, and events more accurately, but are my students learning to talk to the program instead of with each other?

Mrs. Bird, Teacher: I am so glad I led the pilot for BeThere! Some of my most disengaged students have come alive academically, and they can finally see themselves placing into some of our competitive middle schools. I do miss some of the old whole-class debates, but those did not serve my introverted students anyway.

Bruce, Student: It has been so cool to learn history the way I play video games! I get to be inside history and even meet famous people like Lincoln. I hated when Mr. Martinez made us speak up in class again. It felt weird and so slow.

Parent: My child used to come home buzzing about the debates and group projects but now seems to talk about badges and virtual characters. She already struggles in group settings, and this seems to be making her more comfortable alone than with her peers.

Principal Kraemer: I have to balance my responsibility to the district and state with honoring my teachers' professional judgment. I am so proud of the progress my school has made, and hope that this will change its public reputation. I sensed some hesitation from Mr. Martinez, but how would I explain to families and the board why we are stepping back from a program that appears to be working?

COMPLICATIONS

Standardized Testing: The school is very fixated with standardized testing scores because it determines funding, ranking, and even placement for middle school. Higher scores could expand the students' access to selective middle schools and advanced tracks that they would have never entered otherwise.

Teacher Evaluations: Mr. Martinez's evaluation rubric includes student growth on standardized assessments as a key component. Teachers whose students show strong gains are more likely to be rated "exemplary," get leadership opportunities, and avoid intervention plans.

Department Standardization: The department chair's push for a unified BeThere pacing guide reduces individual teachers' flexibility. It was being framed as an equity move to ensure every student gets the same content and tools, regardless of the teacher.

Student Socio-emotional Learning: BeThere's instant feedback and private environment felt safer for students who fear embarrassment in group settings. Students often do not speak up because they fear being wrong in front of peers, being misunderstood, or hurting others. BeThere may have been unintentionally teaching students to avoid the uncertainty and vulnerability of real conversations.

YOUR TURN

Reflect

- Imagine yourself in Mr. Martinez's position in this specific school and policy context. What would you do?
- What emotions does this case bring up for you? Relief at seeing a tool that helps, worry about what is lost, anger at the system, or something else?
- Recall a time you felt pressured to prioritize test scores over the parts of teaching you value most.
- How would you explain your viewpoint to a parent who only sees the test score side of the story? What about one that was concerned about their child's socialization?

Act

Think about your own classroom priorities:
- How much class time goes to individualized digital work versus group work?
- Design a lesson that deliberately blends a tech tool with structured peer conversation about the same content.
- Gather student feedback, especially from quieter students and those benefiting from any tools, on what balance feels fair and effective.

Advocate

- Try to share more positive moments of the classroom community with your peers and colleagues.
- Push for teacher evaluation systems that recognize contributions to classroom culture and student voice.
- Ask your department to standardize one debate or seminar-like activity that you all will integrate into your plans next year.

CHAPTER 18

Cases in Assessment

Case Study 4: Mr. Zan & Who Really Wrote What
NARRATIVE

Mr. Zan is an English teacher at Brookfield High School, a mid-sized public school in an affluent suburban town, with over 25 years of experience. He is well known for helping high school students reach college level writing through his senior writing workshop. Mr. Zan loves to read each paper and see the progression of their writing, as well as how they think about their own lived experiences.

Rarely in those years has he had a student try to submit inauthentic work. Most of the time, he immediately knows when the work is not the student's and lately he is able to rely on plagiarism detectors to see if a student has copied work. Most of those instances are either improper citations or a student who is exceptionally stressed out.

But lately, he has lost confidence in his ability to detect student writing as authentic. AI writing was a very different type of inauthentic writing, and the ease of it had seemed to lower the bar for when students used it. Still, early on, he was able to pick up on a lot of the bland writing it produced. But now, the algorithms were getting so good that they could mimic his students' writing styles with undetectable precision.

Of course, he was not alone in this problem, and teachers across the district were struggling with the future of writing assessment. After multiple calls for help from English departments in the district, the Superintendent of Instruction secured a one-year subscription to VeriWrite, a new AI detection program that claimed to pick up on the tell-tale signs of AI writing.

Mr. Zan was curious. The superintendent framed the tool as a necessary safeguard for "academic integrity in the age of artificial intelligence," citing concerns from parents, teachers, and colleges. The company's home page touted 98% accuracy, and districts across the state were adopting the tool after the state department of education included it in their guidance on AI in education.

The system returned a percentage likelihood of the text being AI written, and it was not as conclusive or verifiable as plagiarism detectors. The district tech committee put out a policy that any assignment flagged for 80% AI likelihood or more would trigger an academic integrity process in which the student must provide evidence of authorship. Teachers were to treat high scores as presumptive evidence of cheating and record violations unless an appeal overturned the finding.

Mr. Zan was optimistic that, at the very least, the new software would create a deterrent effect on students and decrease the chances they tried to use AI. He had also recently joined his school's Technology Task Force, and his colleagues' number one concern had been detecting AI writing. He saw the benefits: consistency across teachers, support for overwhelmed staff, and a signal to the public that the school takes cheating seriously. But he was hesitant about the district's policy of shifting the burden of proof to students. He did not really know what that would look like when it came to a head.

For the next essay assignment, Mr. Zan used the tool to analyze every student's writing. One student, Hannah, had her writing flagged as 92%. He was quite shocked! Hannah was a hard-working student, whom he had taught in a prior class, and the writing felt like hers. She had even stayed after class to discuss the themes in *Of Mice and Men*, and the essay was about the very things she expressed interest in. But the district policy was clear, he had to initiate the academic integrity process for her essay.

He asked to speak to Hannah during lunch, and when he confronted her, she became visibly upset. She insisted she wrote the essay herself and explained how long she had worked on it. He would not have had any doubts were it not for VeriWrite.

Before sending the official referral, Mr. Zan decided to meet with the academic integrity officer, Ms. Lanning, to preempt the report he was going to send. He explained to her that the essay felt authentic, had many of the quirks of her writing, and Hannah had never had any prior history of academic dishonesty. He pointed out that the report had flagged words like "navigate" and "landscape" both of which were words he himself regularly used. The rest of the report claimed it knew it was AI writing based on burstiness, but there was not a real clear way to understand what that actually meant or how accurate it was.

Ms. Lanning was sympathetic, but was facing dozens of referrals, and she did not have the time or resources to adjudicate the decisions herself. She had to start the official referral process. She also highlighted the need for consistent procedures for all students, and VeriWrite is where the district currently wanted to start.

During the appeal, Hannah brought whatever she could. She had handwritten notes, an annotated book, and an email chain with Mr. Zan about her thesis statement. Yet, they kept asking for proof of the actual writing, but Hannah had worked in the notepad on her phone before pasting it into the online document, and there was no official record of that anymore. The integrity committee was skeptical that no digital record remained of her writing and decided to add an integrity violation to her file. Hannah left feeling humiliated and mistrusted, while Mr. Zan, who was asked his opinion but was ultimately overridden, felt complicit.

Mr. Zan started to keep a closer eye on accused students over the next few weeks. He started to notice that English learners and students who write in nonstandard ways were flagged more often than their peers. For example, Susan, an English learner who had developed careful, formal writing was consistently marked as having an 80% likelihood of being AI written.

On the other hand, Malik, a student who has been using school-approved grammar tools to improve his writing for college applications, had his essays flagged for "partial AI use" even though he insisted he only used it for feedback that he accepted or rejected.

At the same time, Mr. Zan's daughter was showing him RikRok videos of students sharing how to bypass AI detectors easily. It seemed like students were producing all sorts of workarounds, and the savvier the student, the less likely their writing would be picked up.

At this point, his concern was overwhelming. None of this really felt fair, but he did not know what alternative to propose. It was unrealistic to have 10-page papers written in class, and that was the sort of writing students would have to do in college. It was also the kind of writing that really allowed students to find their argumentative and narrative voices. He was not ready to abandon that, but what should he suggest to his colleagues then?

Over lunch one day, he spoke to a fellow member of the English department about his discomfort. "Detectors are pattern-guessing instruments, not lie detectors. But we are treating them in ways that confuse statistical likelihood with moral certainty." However, Mr. Carson was strongly in favor of the new tool, and was enforcing it strongly. He even had students who were flagged as anything above 50% go through an in-class appeal process. Last semester, he had read too many essays that felt AI written, and after all the time and effort he spent giving them constructive feedback, he felt dismayed with the direction of schooling. He insisted that, "No system is perfect, but requiring students to prove they didn't cheat is a reasonable form of academic integrity, even if some students feel unfairly scrutinized."

Mr. Zan was increasingly starting to wonder what integrity really meant anyway. Was harming innocent students for the sake of catching some guilty ones worth it? And, what about the students who were getting around the detector because they were spending time learning how to do so, while weaker students who were hoping AI would bring up their grade were submitting AI-generated text with no variations, and thus getting flagged more?

Mr. Zan was torn. He did not want to give up on writing assessments. He did not want to falsely accuse innocent students. He did not want to discourage students from enjoying writing. And, he did not want to create a culture of policing and evading that would ruin the joy of students finding their mature writing voices.

Next week, he had to present to the Tech Task Force his recommendation as the English teacher representative on the committee about whether all disciplines should adopt the tool. The district's integrity officer was clear that she was hoping for a unanimous recommendation to present to the superintendent and school board.

Mr. Zan had written three drafts of his official recommendation: endorsing the expansion as written, pushing for significant modifications and a longer pilot (e.g., mandatory human review, clearer policy on permissible AI use), or opposing expansion altogether.

Mr. Zan knew that his recommendation would influence not only district policy but also the message the school sends students about trust, honesty, and the role of technology in the school's future.

VOICES

Ms. Lanning, Academic Integrity Officer: I know these detectors are imperfect, but they are the best we have, and I cannot possibly abandon the idea of academic integrity all together. The grades and diplomas that students earn have to mean something! Without a shared standard, our teachers' subjective judgments about cheating could lead to even more inconsistent and potentially biased outcomes. This is the only path forward for the time being.

Hannah, Student: I got in so much trouble with my parents for the integrity violation, and I did not even do anything wrong. I tried to put my essay into other detectors, and some said 5%, 45% and 99%! I cannot believe I have a permanent mark on my record because of this silly system that no one even knows how it works! If I have to show proof of my work, why doesn't the AI company?

Carl, Student: I am glad the teachers are doing something about the cheating. I kept hearing about how my peers were using AI tools to write their essays, and while I do not want to hurt my own learning, I do not want to get left behind because everyone else is taking shortcuts. I would rather everyone be a little scared, than go back to my friends bragging about how they got an A after only spending 10 minutes on the assignment, while I worked hard for my A-.

VeriWrite CTO: We have spent a lot of time and money producing the best algorithms to detect AI writing. In our tests, when we feed it AI-generated writing, it is 98% accurate. When we feed it human writing, it is not clear what the accuracy rates are yet, but we are hoping to get more clarity as more schools use it. Some schools are asking us for more details, but honestly, we are not even really sure what the algorithm is picking up on!

Mr. Carson, Teacher: We have a duty to prepare our students to think critically and express their thoughts accurately. AI is really hurting our ability to do that, and we need any help that we can get to keep students on task. I know false positives are painful, but requiring students to defend their work is a reasonable expectation in a world where AI is everywhere. Realistically, this is probably the future of creation. We will all have to defend our work.

COMPLICATIONS

Competing Goods: The district is managing many different stakeholders at once. Teachers are worried about the integrity of their assignments. Parents are anxious about grade inflation. Colleges are worried about student preparedness. And, students are worried about fairness. There is a tough balancing act between more rigorous verification that can feel like surveillance, and more flexibility that becomes leniency.

Technology Limits: VeriWrite and other AI detectors are not foolproof and rely on patterns rather than definitive evidence. The black-box nature of how they determine probability makes using them for enforcement complicated. As students learn workarounds and new AI models come out, the detection space becomes a constant back and forth between evasion and detection.

Testimony: Because VeriWrite declines to share detailed information about training data, false positive rates, or known biases, the teachers and students are told to just "trust the scores."

The appeals end up becoming emotional narratives rather than evidence-based inquiries, because neither side can point to transparent criteria.

Ambiguity: While the teachers asked for help with a policy, the resulting guidance was arbitrary and hard to implement in practice. What were students allowed and not allowed to do? What about students using AI to brainstorm topics, rephrase awkward sentences, or check grammar versus generating whole essays? With every piece of software adding AI features, it has become impossible to separate search engines, text generators, spell checkers, translators, grammar tools, and writing tutor bots.

YOUR TURN

Reflect
- What should Mr. Zan recommend to the Technology Ethics Committee regarding the expansion of VeriWrite?
- Would you consider endorsing the expansion, advocating for a modified, human-in-the-loop approach, or opposing expansion on ethical grounds?
- Imagine yourself as a student falsely accused of cheating based on an opaque algorithm. What emotions arise?
- Now, imagine you are a teacher who has repeatedly discovered clear cases of AI-generated work but has not been able to prove it. What would you seek?
- What are your own assumptions about AI, cheating, authorship, and trust in students and reliance on technology?

Act
- Co-create clear, concrete guidelines with students about when and how AI tools may be used (e.g., allowed for brainstorming or grammar support, not allowed for generating full paragraphs). Establish it as a classroom norm, rather than a top-down enforced rule.
- Incorporate more process-oriented assessment practices. Have students turn in drafts, reflections on writing choices, and conduct brief conferences that encourage genuine authorship through human dialogue.
- Review your policies and practices and think holistically about what kind of community they will build in an era where so much can become centered on technology.

Advocate
- Advise teachers in your school to treat AI scores as one fallible piece of information.
- Advocate for policies that require human review and conversation before any AI detection result leads to disciplinary records.
- Push vendors to provide transparent information about detector accuracy, bias, and limitations. Ask for professional development on how the tools actually work, and what role they can reliably play in your classroom.

Case Study 5: Mrs. Long & Her New Grading Assistant
NARRATIVE

Mrs. Long is an experienced 10th-grade English and US history teacher in a busy suburban public school that prides itself on innovation. She has a reputation for balancing clear structure and expectations with creative, student-centered projects. Any time you walk into her classroom, you see classroom walls covered with student essays, anchor charts, and sticky notes with story ideas. She starts her Back to School Night by promising the families that she will "see every child as a writer."

This year the class sizes had gone up, and she was also teaching a section of honors English. By October, she was extremely overwhelmed. She had two sections of English, two of US history, an advisory period that was supposed to be prep time but ended up being a lot of tutoring, and an after-school debate club. Just for her classes, she had about 180 essays and rewrites to grade every two weeks. Mrs. Long liked to leave research-backed comments, and she took her time to leave in-line feedback along with her final assessment and an encouraging note for each assignment.

She noticed the length of her comments were a little shorter this fall, and normally she immediately remembered what she had said when a student stopped by for extra help, but this year she found herself having to reread the writing and comment to guide them further.

During their fall professional development, the district tech coordinator introduced a new AI-powered grading assistant that promised to provide instant feedback and a streamlined rubric-based evaluation. The app claimed it could scan essays, compare them to her uploaded rubric, and generate preliminary scores and comments for organization, clarity, evidence, and conventions. The last slide left them with a bold promise, "save hours per week without compromising quality."

Desperate to save some time, Mrs. Long decided to try it just once, and thought she would experiment with it on her next assignment in each class. After the students turned in their essays, she saw an interface that allowed her to drag and drop all of the essays and her rubric for submissions. The system-generated feedback in seconds, and the comments sounded polished and eerily aligned with her own rubric language.

She even noticed it was providing feedback on things she sometimes did not get into because she was focusing her effort on high impact areas of improvement. For example, one comment accurately pinpointed a structural issue with the introduction of the counterargument in a student essay that she found impressive. She decided to look over a few more essays, and was feeling a mix of astonishment and cautious relief that the scores and comments were matching her instincts. That night she closed her laptop before 10 pm for the first time in months, feeling both lighter and slightly uneasy.

She decides to keep using the tool as an assistant and reminds herself that she still had the power to override anything she saw as wrong. Mrs. Long was a little worried about what students would think if they found out a "robot" was providing the feedback and decided she did not have to disclose it. After all, she did not disclose every other tool or source she used in her own time.

For each essay, the AI-drafted comments, she skimmed each essay, tweaked some strong language in the constructive feedback, and added one or two personal notes at the end. As time went on, she noticed she was accepting AI comments with minimal edits when tired and promised herself she will pay closer attention next time.

The students were visibly excited. They were getting feedback back in days not weeks, and the rate of rewrites went up as students were still invested in the assignment by the time they got their feedback. Mrs. Long was happy that she may have found a sustainable way to honor her "see every child" promise without burning out.

In February, Mrs. Long overhears a conversation her students are having during a group project. Jonah casually mentions that his high school cousin's essays are "AI graded now." Maya wondered if that is what Mrs. Long used, given how quickly her last essay was graded: "like two seconds after I turned it in."

The next day, Kelsey is the one who brings it up directly with Mrs. Long. "Um, Mrs. Long, are you using a robot to grade our essays now?" The room went quiet, and curious eyes turned toward Mrs. Long as she decided what to say.

Mrs. Long hesitantly admits that she uses a tool that the school was providing teachers to help her give feedback faster, but she always reviewed everything herself. Some students looked puzzled, and others were visibly upset. The rest seemed indifferent. The bell for lunch rang, and they all speedily emptied the classroom, seemingly forgetting about the conversation. Mrs. Long was feeling tense from the conversation but was relieved that it was all out in the open. She opened up a comment box on the LMS that evening to allow students to share their feelings and thoughts openly.

During lunch, Kelsey initiated the conversation again, "I have been doing a rewrite for each essay, and I like not having to wait weeks to know how I did. I guess it is no big deal." Jonah was more concerned, "What is the point of writing if it is all read by a robot anyway? And what if it is wrong?" Andre in particular was upset, "This makes so much more sense. Lately, Mrs. Long has been correcting a lot more of how I speak, but never did that before." Andre preferred to write his personal narratives in African-American Vernacular English, and Mrs. Long had encouraged him to do so early in the semester. "I guess it's a racist robot."

That weekend, Mrs. Long got an email from Maya's mother saying her daughter felt "betrayed" and wondering how there were assurances about the grades being "fair." She was also concerned about the privacy policy, "And, what happens to the work after the algorithm grades it? Do they have her writing forever? I am really disappointed in the school right now and expect a formal response." As she checked the notes, she saw that Andre had conveyed his concerns about the comments on his writing style, and Jonah said he had felt something was different when he asked for her help on the last essay and missed feeling like his writing mattered.

Mrs. Long decides to bring up these issues directly with the school admin and other teachers at the faculty meeting that week. The Vice-Principal assured everyone that the AI tool was district-approved, teachers retained final say on grades, and that the school needed to "model innovation" for the students. Mr. Lopez was unconcerned and called the tool "efficient and harmless." Ms. Brianca on the other hand had decided not to use the tool, "I want to see my students improve based on my comments, and the tool doesn't seem to think about the long term goals for each student the way I do." The Vice-Principal assured that he would respond to any parent inquiries for now and was going to talk to the district about a parent orientation next fall.

Mrs. Long left not really sure about what to do next. She had been relieved to have the tool's support in grading, but the parents' and students' responses had made her feel almost shameful. She thought back to her early days with them, "Writing is about finding your voice, and my job is to listen and help you make it more powerful." She started to lean toward returning to full manual grading but worried about sustaining it. The district was not going to reduce class sizes or workload anytime soon, and she knew if she complained, they would just tell her to use the tool.

By late spring, the principal announced that all teachers must disclose any "AI assistance" to students and families. The directive included a vague note about respecting family concerns and giving students ways to appeal the grade, but there was no clear procedure beyond that. What about families who didn't even know the difference and whether opting out helped or hurt? How much did she have to disclose and at what point? Did she need a form for them to fill? What about her students' concerns? Andre had been right about the aggressive corrections to "formal English," and like Jonah, she had also noticed how much less connected she felt to the students when they asked her follow-up questions.

She decided she would start by drafting a letter to her students and parents about how she was going to approach it, which is exactly what she often told her students to help them think through hard problems. The way she saw it, she had three options: stop using the system entirely, continue but be transparent to students and families about how it is used, or limit her use to certain situations only. Mrs. Long kept wondering what it really meant to help her students find their voices.

VOICES

Mrs. Long, Teacher: I really cannot give the quality of feedback and time that I want to with this many students. I see a clear difference in student writing, and I can focus my time on planning more engaging lessons and finally get some time with my family. I miss feeling like I know my students inside and out, but is that really feasible anymore? I want my students to feel cared for, but my first job is to help their writing.

Maya, Student: I am not really sure about all this. It feels weird to be writing for a robot to read my writing. I do not feel close to Mrs. Long anymore, and my writing feels like it is just busywork.

Kelsey, Student: I like getting feedback so quickly, and the comments are so easy to understand when they are connected to the rubric so clearly. I also like to revise my work when I am still thinking about the essay prompt, rather than think about it again weeks later. It seems like it is worth it to me.

Mr. Dawson, Parent: I send my child to school to be taught by humans. We picked our house and location very carefully to be in this school district, and if they are going to be taught by AI bots anyway, what is the point of all that? I should have at least been told, and I still do not get what happens to the data. My daughter spends enough time on screens; I do not want her to depend so much on robots too.

Vice-Principal, Mr. Kim: I see my teachers drowning in paperwork, and AI will finally allow us to relieve some pressure while maintaining feedback quality. The district tech team has already vetted and approved the tool, and we are leaving humans in the loop. I did not realize families and students would care so much, but I hope I can show them how much better the speed and consistency will be for their education.

COMPLICATIONS

Relational Trust: Middle school classrooms, in particular, rely on fragile relationships between adults and children, where the children both test and crave adult attention. The reactions that came from replacing a human touchpoint with a technological one make sense in that context. We also do not know if the trust would have been as ruptured had disclosure happened earlier.

Uneven Interpretation: With no clear guidance or protocols from the school, individual teachers were left to plan disclosure and consent on their own. The differences between rollout made a school-wide announcement difficult since some were still experimenting and others refused to use the tool at all.

Writing Feedback: Feedback on writing is both evaluative and formative, and it shapes how students see themselves as thinkers and communicators. The speed of feedback makes a huge difference in how receptive students are to the feedback and can incorporate it. We need to figure out the balance between timely feedback and human feedback, and which is pedagogically more valuable.

Algorithmic Bias: Most algorithms that are trained on large datasets center on the average to determine the standard. The program might not be built to the voices, dialects, or linguistic development of all students in the school. Students who write in non-standard English, are multilingual, or have writing-related disabilities, may receive systematically harsher comments.

Professional Identity: Some teachers may see their professional identity rooted in judgment, interpretation, and relationship, not just content delivery or facilitation. At the same time, teacher workloads are increasingly more cumbersome, and burnout rates are not trivial. Offloading a major time-consuming task could help alleviate some of that burden.

YOUR TURN

Reflect

- What was your initial response to Mrs. Long's situation? Would you have felt relief from saved time, discomfort at the secrecy, or something else?
- Have you ever used a tool that made your work easier but left you unsure about how students or families would perceive it?
- What does "authentic" feedback mean in your context? Is it about who writes it, the thought behind it, or how students receive it?
- When does efficiency support learning, and when does it undermine values like honesty, care, and fairness?

Act

- If you use AI for grading or feedback, draft a disclosure statement in age-appropriate language, explaining how, when, and why it is used. You can decide whether to share it or not.
- Revise AI-generated comments so they reflect personal insight, knowledge of the student, and appropriate emotional tone.
- Teachers can model consent by asking whether students are comfortable with AI-assisted review and, when feasible, offering alternatives such as peer conferences or teacher-only handwritten feedback.
- Build a habit of documenting your practices and rationale (i.e., why the tool is used, how human review is layered, what safeguards are in place) in case questions are raised later.

Advocate

- Push for transparent district policies that specify expectations for disclosure of AI use in teaching.
- Recommend establishing stakeholder committees to review AI tools for accuracy, bias, relational impact, and workload implications before adoption.
- Ask for professional development that addresses how to operate AI tools and the ethics of feedback, trust, data privacy, and care.
- Have conversations with your colleagues and students to talk about what forms of automation you all find acceptable in schooling and where you would draw the line.

Case Study 6: Mrs. Greene & How Risk Becomes a Category
NARRATIVE

Mrs. Greene opened her inbox to find the announcement of the new "Student Success Analytics" program just before the school year began. Mrs. Greene worked as a counselor at a large, underfunded inner-city public school with a majority Black and Hispanic population.

The email was sent by Mrs. Riley, one of the other four counselors, who had been in the district for over 15 years. She herself attended the school and was proud to be back after her education. Each counselor was responsible for over 400 students, including managing class registrations, checking graduation requirements, writing letters of recommendation, helping with FAFSA, and handling any special accommodations.

The new program, LearnSight, was going to serve as an early-warning system to help them be more proactive about students who were at risk of dropping out, failing a class, or facing a disciplinary issue. With this new program, Mrs. Greene was hopeful that she could move from putting out fires to proactively protecting students.

LearnSight was powered by a predictive analytics company that started off as a voter outreach data analytics company working for political campaigns. They realized their advanced predictive abilities would be perfect for school settings and were partnering with schools across the country this fall to put the system to test. It would use attendance, grades, disciplinary records, LMS engagement (e.g., clicks, logins, timestamps), teacher notes, and parent emails. It sorted students into color-coded risk categories for each of the three main areas: drop out risk, academic problems, or behavioral threats.

The company's promise to ensure "no child will slip through the cracks" resonated with Mrs. Greene, who had an exceptionally hard time last year, with two unexpected dropouts, a juvenile court referral, and a psychiatric hospitalization. During the demo, the vendor rep had clicked through dashboards with heatmaps and graphs, emphasized the number of indicators used, and promised predictive accuracy and targeted interventions. One of the counselors asked about racial disparities, and the vendor offered a confident reassurance, "We're one of the few providers who has built the system ground-up to avoid bias!"

Mrs. Greene left the meeting attracted to the idea and willing to try it out, but still felt like the connection between the data points and the simple ranking was not super clear to her. As the school year started, the dashboards officially launched, and Mrs. Greene's new morning routine was to open her email, log in to the LearnSight dashboard, and see the list of flagged students generated overnight. The district had a policy of documenting follow-up for any student flagged as red risk within a week, and counselors would be evaluated on the number of students who moved lower on the risk ladder.

Mrs. Greene noticed just how much her rhythm at work had changed. She did not have the time to do her own check-ins with students she was worried about or talk to teachers about any concerning signs. She was constantly relying on the system to keep up with what was happening to her students.

One Tuesday in late September, she noticed Malik, a quiet sophomore from last year, was on her red list. She remembered that he ended his first year with a 2.8 GPA after bringing it up the second semester, had nearly perfect attendance, and was on the junior varsity basketball team. She clicked into the record to see what was being flagged: three recent tardies, two incomplete English assignments, and one absence marked as "family reasons." The red pop-up announced: "Predictive pattern consistent with prior chronic disengagement cohort." She was not sure if she should trust the system or her memory of Malik, but settled on the side of caution.

When Malik came down to her office, he seemed afraid he had gotten in trouble. She started with a gentle, open-ended check-in, "How's school feeling this fall?" Malik explained that the daycare his parents had been using changed their hours, his mom's car had broken down, and he had to help get his little brother to school until it was fixed. She wanted to tell Malik that he had been flagged and just be honest, but the district policy was to not disclose the flags. She decided to just stick to the facts it shared: "I'm a little concerned because our new tool shows some attendance and grade issues." Malik reacted, irritated, "Well, I do not really care what the tool thinks. I have more important stuff to deal with right now." He walked out, and Mrs. Greene felt uneasy about how Malik had left the room.

By November, LearnSight claimed it had recalibrated its threshold based on the new district data, and suddenly there was a surge in yellow and red flags. A third of the students on

Mrs. Greene's list were either yellow or red, and the counselors were all noting that the list seemed to be disproportionately Black and Hispanic.

Mr. Rivas, one of the counselors who was skeptical, started calling it the "digital scarlet letter." It also became clear that teachers were unintentionally disclosing the flagged status of students by suddenly paying them more attention. By the end of the month, students were trying to figure out who was on the list and who was likely to be called in next. Students started to skip check-ins because they did not want to be seen as going to the counselor's office.

At the same time, the principal had concrete data to show at the next meeting. The number of students who failed the first quarter was already the lowest it had ever been, and disciplinary referrals to the district had dropped by 75%. The early intervention seemed to be working.

Next week, Jade popped up on Mrs. Greene's red list. There was a sudden drop in grades, several absences, and a drop in parent logins and late-night logins by her. She called Jade into her office and asked her if she was doing okay. Jade revealed to her that her dad had recently been diagnosed with cancer, and the family was scrambling to figure out what next steps were going to be. Mrs. Greene was thankful she called her in, and reassured her that she would coordinate accommodations from the teachers for any assignments and extra tutoring support when she was ready. Jade was relieved, "Wow, thank you so much. I did not even know I was allowed those things. I have been really worried about falling behind." Mrs. Greene realized that the algorithm caught a student that she might have missed otherwise.

In December, Isabella is the latest yellow-risk flag in Mrs. Greene's list. She was a first-year student with straight A's and perfect attendance but was flagged as a yellow risk on everyone's screen. Mrs. Greene tried to dig deeper and noticed that "low digital engagement" was the primary flag. During their meeting, Isabella calmly explained that the home Wi-Fi was not reliable, so she often uploaded her homework after she got to school. Mrs. Greene told her that that was fine as long as it was working for her, and Isabella did not seem concerned. The yellow flag was impossible to remove though, and Mrs. Greene worried about what conclusions other teachers might draw. She did not want them to stop challenging Isabella or treat her differently in class. When she asked the vendor rep, he just explained that the algorithm just looks at the data, and until that metric improved she would be flagged as yellow.

At the next PTA meeting, some parents seemed to be upset about the new software. Rhonda, Malik's mom, stood up and explained, "Malik was put in a support program and taken out of class and put on probation for the basketball team, but none of his white teammates with the same metrics are being flagged." She added, "The system is creating problems before there are any!" The principal tried to reassure everyone by claiming that the new system ensured that data was the core of helping students equitably. Rhonda retorted, "Do not tell me about your data. Tell me about my son."

The counselors were supposed to vote on whether or not to keep using the system next year at the next board meeting. They needed a majority to support keeping it, and Mr. Rivas had already indicated he was going to vote against it, while the other two were in favor. Mrs. Greene would be the swing vote on what the school did next year. As she debated her vote,

Mrs. Greene ran through all the emotions that had come up: Malik's anger, Jade's relief, Isabella's disadvantage, and Rhonda's fury.

VOICES

Malik, Student: I hate this new system. It makes me feel watched, and it is not even being consistent with who it changes. All my teachers suddenly treat me like I am delicate, and no one gets how hard I am working to keep up with schoolwork, stay on the team, and manage things at home. I am okay, but they keep telling me I am not.

Isabella, Student: I guess it does not really matter, but I feel like I am doing something wrong after Mrs. Greene called me in. I do not want anyone to think I am copying homework or being lazy. I just wish the system understood why I was behaving the way I was.

Mr. Rivas, Counselor: There is clearly a bias in how the system is operating, and I can see the difference in how these students are being treated. I was keeping up with my students just fine, and it did not have to be so systemized and public. I have spent years building my judgment and relationships, and now I feel like I am just an intermediary. I wish they gave us tools that support equity rather than undermine it.

Vice-Principal: We have to keep track of metrics to show the state that we are improving with the additional funding. Hitting our graduation targets with the number of staff we have is close to impossible. Tools like this help us allocate scarce resources more fairly and objectively. The counselors have shared so many stories of successfully catching students, and a few false positives are not enough to give up on it.

COMPLICATIONS

Resource Constraints: The counselors serve extremely large caseloads, which makes it impossible to know every student's situation perfectly. AI triage tools are appealing because they offer a way to prioritize attention in an overburdened system.

Opacity: LearnSight provides more information than some other systems, but it is still largely a black box why some students are flagged and others are not. It is not clear how much weight is given to the students' demographic information, the variables that it collects regularly, and historical information about the student and the school. This lack of explainability makes it difficult to assess fairness or challenge questionable flags.

Label Stickiness: Once a student is flagged, their risk shows up for everyone. This shapes expectations, hypervigilance around their behavior, disciplinary responses, and access to future opportunities. That affects both their self-identity and their career trajectory.

Community Pressures: When students fall through the cracks, it opens up the school to lawsuits and public scrutiny about how they are monitoring and supporting students. A predictive system can be framed as a responsible, modern response. At the same time, community trust is also at stake if parents think their children are being treated unfairly, especially based on protected classes.

YOUR TURN

Reflect

- Imagine yourself in Mrs. Greene's role with her caseload, context, and constraints. What would you choose to do?
- What emotions arise when you think about being required to use a system that you do not fully trust?
- How might your own students be misjudged by similar data?
- What is your moral responsibility when the tools you are required to use are themselves ambiguous?

Act

- Use any digital data as a starting point for inquiry, rather than as the authority on students.
- Collaborate with teachers to identify alternative forms of evidence about engagement and risk that complement or challenge numerical data.
- Be honest with students, at an age-appropriate level, about how their data is used.

Advocate

- Push for your school to regularly audit the equity of any algorithmic systems.
- Recommend forming committees that include educators, students, parents, and community advocates to review and plan technology adoption and vetting.
- Promote professional learning on data ethics so that colleagues can interpret systems critically rather than deferentially.

CHAPTER 19

Cases in Safety

Case Study 7: Dr. Walsh & Help with Critical Support
NARRATIVE

Dr. Walsh is the school psychologist for a mid-sized suburban public high school. He has witnessed a few different waves of mental health crises in his career. Most recently, the pandemic isolation and post-pandemic burnout had left a lasting impact on his students, such as a loss of formative socio-emotional development time during those years.

He is the first line of care for a lot of the students who end up seeking mental health care. As the rate of mental health issues, and awareness of them, has increased, his case load has gotten larger and larger. Because of this, he was struggling to keep up with everything on his plate. He normally did proactive meetings with students whom faculty identified as having a sudden behavior shift or displaying any other signs of distress, but that had all but stopped in the last year as he was spending most of his time seeing students and parents who came to him and coordinating outside care for them.

Besides him, the school had one full-time counselor who helped with students who were not in need of clinical care, but were struggling with things like identity formation, bullying, and academic pressure. Together, they were responsible for over 800 students across all grade levels.

The district had also become increasingly concerned after a few serious incidents that made local news, and state guidance was indicating that all schools needed to be thinking more critically about how they were protecting student mental health. This year, the district had rolled out a new tool for all high school students called MoodRing. It was an AI-driven reflective journaling app that was going to supplement the limited counseling resources the school had.

MoodRing was a "private, evidence-based tool" with aggregated dashboards for "emotional trends" and automated flagging of "high-risk" entries using sentiment and keyword analysis. At the same time, the company reassured administrators that the actual journal entries would never leave the students' device and no one could read them unless there were indicators of a threat to self or others.

Dr. Walsh was skeptical of the idea of an algorithm being able to detect what he had spent decades perfecting, but it did not hurt to have another tool to help manage the growing workload, and so he was curious. Academically, he was interested in what they used for sentiment analysis and keyword analysis, and how they determined trends, but very little information was available to professionals like him.

The IT director had vetted the vendor for basic security checks, FERPA compliance, training data restrictions, and data retention and deletion policies. The IT director could also set alert thresholds, decide who would get automatically notified, and many other settings, but they decided to start out with the default settings that the tool came with.

This year's back-to-school packet included an opt-out form that explained that the app was "private but monitored for safety and trends." Students could choose how much to use or not use the app, and only first-period teachers had to set aside time for students to use it in class. They described it to students as a private journal, like a "techy diary" that would help them track their own emotions and thoughts, and only big picture data would be shared with anyone else. The students were wary of who would read it, but MoodRing's onboarding was full of reassurances about how their entries would not be shared with anyone including their staff.

By mid-October, nearly all the students were using it at least once a week. Dr. Walsh was starting to see "automated alerts" in his dashboard when the system identified someone for possible intervention. It came with a rating between 1 and 5 flags. He was struggling to keep up with the 1 and 2 flag ratings, but made sure he addressed at least all five flag ratings the same day, and four flag ratings by the end of the week.

When he approached one of the students, the student got very defensive about what Dr. Walsh had been able to read. "I thought this was private. It is not like I said I was going to kill myself, so why are you talking to me?" Dr. Walsh calmly reassured him that it was just sentiment analysis that tracked emotional trends in writing patterns, not the actual entries; and he just wanted to offer his support if it would be of help. The student, clearly not convinced, rolled his eyes and walked away.

Next Tuesday morning Dr. Walsh had a red banner pop up: "URGENT CONCERN." When Dr. Walsh opened it, it showed the words, "I do not see the point in waking up anymore. Everyone would be fine if I were no more," highlighted in red along with the ability to view the last 30 days of entries. Dr. Walsh was thrown off by this ability, but he quickly shifted to making sure the student was okay. The student identified was Aiden, a quiet eleventh grader that Dr. Walsh knew from prior social issues his first year. He called Aiden in for a wellness check, and Aiden looked panicked, "Is this about my journal?"

Dr. Walsh did not want to startle him or shut him down from sharing anything, so he tried to approach it with caution. Before Dr. Walsh could ask him anything, Aiden said, "It was just a song lyric I was working on for my band." Dr. Walsh was skeptical at first, but they pulled up the entry together, and Aiden had been working on lyrics for the last few weeks, and Aiden had clearly been trying to write a heartbreak song. "Are you sure this isn't about you?" "Dr. Walsh, my band is called 'The Demons Without,' most of our songs have dark themes. Can I go now?"

Dr. Walsh was apologetic and sent him back to class. He was a little uneasy about the interaction he just had, but told himself it was better to be safe than sorry.

The next day he had another alert. This time the system flagged Lily for possible abuse at home. Dr. Walsh decided it was worth reading the entries this time and read through whatever he could find. It did seem like something was wrong. She was writing about being afraid to go home because of her stepfather. She had multiple entries about him having gotten angry, and even one about him driving recklessly with her in the car. Dr. Walsh was a mandated reporter, and he immediately had to file a case with Child Protective Services.

Lily did not come to school for the next few weeks, but when she returned Dr. Walsh immediately called her in. "How are you doing Lily?" She explained that she was now living with her aunt. "I guess I should thank you. I did not really know what to do or how to talk to anyone." Dr. Walsh was relieved that Lily was doing better: "Are you ready to be at school? We can arrange some more time off." "No, I finally feel like I can focus, so I want to get back to my classes if that's okay."

Dr. Walsh was glad this worked out, but felt uneasy because he had discovered that when the system flagged her file, it had also sent all her entries to Child Protective Services without his involvement. What doors did that open for future problems?

Jordan is one of the students who uses the system every morning. He has logged an entry each day since the roll out, and spends every minute they are allowed in class to reflect in his journal. That week, he was writing about struggles with sexual orientation and not knowing how to label himself. He wrote how he was scared of being bullied and felt alone in figuring out what was right for him.

MoodRing picked up on fear, identity terms (which were high-risk markers), and bullying. Since the default settings were never changed, any alerts flagged for bullying were also sent to the parents. His mom got an email with the subject "Parental Involvement Recommended: Identity-Related Social Distress." When Jordan got home, his mom confronted him with the email on her phone. "What is all this about? Are you being bullied? What identity issues are you having?" Jordan's mom had not yet clicked on the "View Entries" button, but Jordan saw the button in her email and tried to explain to her with as little detail as possible.

Jordan stopped coming to school regularly over the next few days with attendance marked as "illness" while tensions at home escalated. His mom was trying to find a different school to enroll him in, because she did not trust that he was being taken care of properly at his current school. Dr. Walsh gets an alert about the reduced attendance and decides to call Jordan's mom. "Hi Beth, I just wanted to check in and see if everything was okay with Jordan. We have missed him the last few days." "How dare you call me after outing my child to me through an email! Jordan will be attending a different school starting next week. Please leave my family alone."

Dr. Walsh was in shock. He had no idea that an email had gone out to Beth and was caught completely off guard. He felt directly responsible for the harm because he had agreed to lead the pilot at the school. He tried to dig into the settings that allowed this to happen, but there were hundreds of settings with thresholds that made little sense. Was it better to alert a parent at 75% or 76% certainty of bullying at school? Dr. Walsh was confused. He had a lot of positive interventions this fall, including Lily, but his unease over access and automation were at a peak after his interaction with Beth. Should he keep using the system at the school?

VOICES

Dr. Walsh, School Psychologist: I have built a career of being a trusted confidant with some of our most vulnerable students. Lately, it feels like I have become a robot monitoring a dashboard all day long. I barely get to make any decisions that impact my students' care. I know I need the help, but I fear this is going to end up causing more problems.

Dr. Alvarez, Principal: We have had too many crises in the last few years, and finding more psychology staff in our area has proven impossible. We have to do something about our struggling students, and technology feels like the only scalable way to do so. I just do not know where the line is between caring for students or monitoring them.

Aiden, Student: I was really enjoying getting some of my creative energy out in the journal every day, but now I just type "I'm fine" every day. Being flagged made me feel foolish, and I was not even ready to share those lyrics with anyone.

Jordan, Student: I thought MoodRing was the only place I shared my internal struggles without anyone else seeing it, but they did not tell me my parents could be given access. I do not really get why they were told because there was not really "immediate danger." It made more danger after outing me to my parents!

COMPLICATIONS

Professional Judgment: The labels and algorithms can only account for human judgment and relationships so much. Without being able to tinker with every single little setting in a meaningful way, it would be hard to completely capture the reality of a particular school's context into a mathematical formal. This system was making ethical decisions of its own without human intervention, and that caused problems for Jordan.

Informed Consent: Parents were only given an opt out form, which typically have much lower rates of completion. There was not nearly enough information provided to students or parents about what all the triggers were for disclosure and what would be disclosed to whom when. Can consent be meaningful when power dynamics, technical knowledge, and the stakes are so uneven between families, schools, and vendors?

Cultural Bias: The training data encodes assumptions about culture, and uses past data to identify risk, but it was not able to identify that different types of risk might require different types of interventions based on the context of the school and family. Biases like this can flag marginalized youth more and not flag students whose distress does not match "normal" patterns.

Moral & Legal Injury: Dr. Walsh normally has a lot to deal with, but the AI model adds more work and takes away autonomy in a way that makes him feel complicit in the harm the model causes. Beyond that, Dr. Walsh was not told what would happen if he did not act on a flag properly or overreacted, and whether there was professional liability.

YOUR TURN

Reflect

- How should Dr. Walsh balance the duty to protect students from harm with the duty to preserve their privacy and trust?
- Have you ever had sensitive information about a student? How would you feel if an algorithm had seen it first?
- Which ethical principle feels most pressing in this case for you?
- Do you lean toward acting on any possible sign of harm or toward protecting privacy unless danger is clear and present?

Act

- Invite students to co-create norms for how school technologies collect, share, and respond to their data.
- After any serious intervention that involves digital data, set aside time to debrief with the student about what was seen, why adults responded, and how you will try to protect both their safety and their privacy.
- Regularly invite student feedback on how school technologies affect their sense of safety, freedom, and trust, and adjust practices when students report feeling surveilled or silenced.

Advocate

- Push your school to adopt clear principles for any technology that uses student data including strong limits on secondary uses of information.
- Call for consent that distinguishes learning support from safety monitoring, specifies exactly who can access which kinds of data, and gives students and families actual choices.
- Advocate for policies that keep human judgment at the center of high stakes decisions about safety.

Case Study 8: Ms. Nguyen & The Decision to Speak
NARRATIVE

Ms. Nguyen is the journalism teacher at a large, suburban high school right outside a major city. They have a mixed demographic breakdown by race and socioeconomic status, and have a reputation as a "solid" mid-performing school. The diversity lends itself to a politically diverse community spanning the entire polarized political spectrum.

The Comet is the school's long-running, student-led publication that had won regional awards and had a reputation for occasionally pushing edgy, critical pieces that sparked debates among the student body, but never amounted to anything larger.

Ms. Nguyen, in her seventh year as advisor for the group, had worked to build a culture of responsible independence in the newsroom. She allowed the students to pitch, select, and revise stories with minimal adult interference.

Earlier this year, the district adopted SafeWords, an internet filter on all student-facing platforms after several tense board meetings because of a surge in cyberbullying, explicit images, and online threats. Ms. Nguyen had quickly scanned the email, and saw phrases like "proactive liability management" and "early intervention." They were told that SafeWords would monitor and filter on all student emails, LMS messages, and all other school-sponsored digital platforms based on the AI moderation filters. Ms. Nguyen had not really had issues with any of those things, so she quickly deleted the email and moved on.

At the next faculty meeting, the Tech Director was sharing a success story of the new SafeWords rollout. It had picked up a set of late-night searches from a school device that involved searching for self-harm related content. The system instantly flagged the "imminent self-harm" and sent the alerts to the counselor and administrators. The school was able to contact the student's family and arrange for an emergency mental health evaluation. The family sent the staff flowers to thank them for "saving our family." The staff was very reassured by this incident, and saw it as a powerful example of the technology stepping up where the adults never could have.

The next month, the staff heard about another incident where SafeWords flagged a file-sharing attempt that included a screenshot of a student's social media profile annotated with slurs and their phone number. The system did not allow the image to go through, alerted the administrators, and again allowed the adults to step in before the bullying even began online. That same week, SafeWords intercepted an explicit, non-consensual image being sent through the school email system and sent an automatic alert to the Title IX coordinator.

Ms. Nguyen asked the students if they were considering writing an article about the new filter tool, but the editor-in-chief, Bruce, was still unsure about what direction they would take, "Well, I know there are some success stories, but the system is also kind of annoying because it flags harmless jokes, and just makes our group chats bland." China, another columnist, shared that "It also flagged a poster for the Gender & Sexuality Alliance because it had 'fight back' on it." Bruce added, "I hate to harp on this, but it also keeps hiding comments on the art club page because of 'potential bullying,' but these are just inside jokes." They decided they would write up a column to at least start covering the topic.

Next Thursday afternoon, Ms. Nguyen got to the journalism lab expecting to hear the usual bouts of chatter and keyboard clicks, but it seemed ominously quiet. Inside, the student editors were clustered around a computer near the printer, faces angry, some were scrolling on their phones while others were staring at the screen. As she put down her handbag and walked over, she noticed that they were looking at a distorted version of *The Comet*'s homepage. "What's going on?"

Bruce explained that the latest issue of *The Comet* seemed to have disappeared along with their access to edit the website. "It looked fine yesterday, but when my parents tried to read it this morning, it just loaded jumbled up text. China added that it was not just the home page, all of the new stories, photos, and other content they had built for this month's edition seemed to have just vanished.

Ms. Nguyen logged into her email to see if there was anything there, but it turned up empty. She quickly sent off an email to the Tech Director asking for help. He responded instantly:

Hi Ms. Nguyen,

    I am so sorry for the trouble. It seems like SafeWords has marked *The Comet* as "pending review due to sensitive content." They will send us a final report by the end of the day. Just FYI - The flagged content seems to be a post titled, "When the Algorithm Decides: How AI Is Changing Our Classrooms."

    More soon!

Ms. Nguyen shared the email with the students in the room, and they all looked at each other with the realization that the article about AI oversight had been pulled by the AI oversight tool. The article covered more than just SafeWords; it was also a critical take on plagiarism detectors, feedback generators, and student usage of AI tutors. They had interviewed a whole range of people from enthusiastic teachers to skeptical students and parents who were grateful for the protections. They even had an anonymous anecdote from a student who described harassment ending after the introduction of SafeWords. China was livid, "We followed all journalistic best practices you taught us. We fact-checked, verified quotes, offered right-of-reply to the principal and even the vendors, and had addressed the benefits. I just do not get it."

Ms. Nguyen did not really know what to say. She was proud of her students. This was an exceptionally talented group of writers this year, and they had been publishing some great content that led to the highest readership since she had taken over. She did not get why this was dealt with so drastically. The students had published sharp critiques of cafeteria food, dress code enforcement, and unbalanced sports funding in the last year, and no one had raised any issues.

Even when an administrator had asked for small edits to a critical editorial about bathroom access, the students were able to directly talk to him and compromised on including his message as a quote without changing the piece all together. This felt different: there had been no conversation, no warning, just an automated judgment that neither she, nor her students, could even see or understand.

Finally, the tech director wrote back that the system had determined that the article included "sensitive institutional criticism linked to prior high-risk incidents." That did not seem any more helpful than the initial flag, and she decided to speak to Principal Daniels as soon as she could.

She walked into his office, and Principal Daniels seemed sympathetic but exhausted, rubbing his temples and glancing at a stack of discipline reports on his desk, as he listened. "Look Ms. Nguyen, I cannot possibly address every flag that SafeWords puts up. They have this issue under a category involving 'sensitive institutional criticism,' 'safety systems,' and 'recent self-harm/doxxing events' leading to 'elevated risk of misinterpretation and community unrest.'" Ms. Nguyen looked in disbelief. This felt like language used in a national security TV show, not a public school principal's office.

"We have to let the system do what it does. We do not have the resources to deal with appeals, and they have the data to back up their filter. We would not even know where to start!"

Ms. Nguyen asked for permission to speak to the vendor directly, and Principal Daniels was very happy to move on from the conversation by agreeing.

Ms. Nguyen spoke to the vendor representative, Melissa, who referred to the earlier successes at the school, and reassured her that all decisions were made by an advanced algorithm that took school safety very seriously. She mentioned that the algorithm was being extra sensitive right now because similar schools had experienced incidents where student pieces on gender identity, policing, or school safety went viral and produced angry board meetings, national media coverage, and threats against staff.

The students had called an emergency editorial board meeting for their lunch period, and Ms. Nguyen was not really sure what to share with them. When they started, the students shared that they wanted to publish an open letter on the paper's social media accounts calling the takedown "censorship" and naming SafeWords and the district as being complicit in authoritarian policing of student free speech. One of the students expressed concern about the district shutting down The Comet, and another one was concerned they would lose credibility if they did not offer the same balanced viewpoint. They decided to come back to the issue during the next official meeting later that week.

By the end of the week, news got around that the issue was taken down because of SafeWords, and the hashtag, "#LetTheCometSpeak" was floating around everyone's social media posts. The journalism club still had not decided on an official response, and the public narrative was getting heated. "Our free speech rights have to matter!" "SafeWords literally saved my cousin. Be careful what you ask for." As Ms. Nguyen looked through some of the comments on the latest district post saying they would put out a statement shortly, she saw her name tagged as both "the only teacher who cares" and "irresponsible."

The next morning, Ms. Nguyen got an email from the superintendent with the subject line: "Automated Flagging Incident: Please Advise Students to Refrain from Public Commentary." He explained that the district was "committed to student expression within appropriate parameters and consistent with our duty to maintain a safe learning environment and public trust." There was also an email from the union rep sent to all teachers cautioning them not to comment publicly about the incident without consulting the union.

At the editorial meeting, the students all arrived early to see what Ms. Nguyen had decided. "What are we going to do? We cannot just stay quiet while everyone around us is talking about it!"

Ms. Nguyen looked down at her list as she began to explain their options.

VOICES

Ms. Nguyen, Journalism Advisor: The work my students do is important not only to the culture of the school, but also their own sense of civic engagement and empowerment. I always guide them to reframe pieces when they are unfair, under-sourced, or likely to cause targeted harm, but we always have a discussion and come to a consensus. The SafeWords incident feels different and treats my students' work as a threat rather than a learning opportunity. The district seems really serious about not publicly commenting, but I also want to make sure I stand up for my students, both current and future ones.

Bruce, Editor-in-Chief: I am proud of the work we have been doing this year, and our team takes their role seriously. It does not seem fair that a random algorithm gets to decide what is right and wrong when our job is to tell the full story. I want to become a journalist because democracy needs people who speak uncomfortable truths about powerful institutions, especially when others prefer we stay quiet.

PTA President: As a parent, I have been leading the charge on digital safety and online harm prevention for youth in our local community and school. My child was the one of the students who almost got sent an explicit image, and SafeWords successfully helped prevent that. Still, I admire students who care about big issues and speak up thoughtfully. After all, that is why we send our children to schools like this. SafeWords might not be the exact right solution, but it is better than leaving students unprotected in our current digital environment.

District Technology Director: I really had hope that SafeWords would support educators by catching the worst content before they seriously hurt someone. We have seen so much good come of it already, and the same statistical patterns that are causing this controversy are the ones that have prevented serious incidents this year. Building a fast and robust appeals process is what I would prefer, but without the resources to deal with those appeals, I do not want to start second-guessing the algorithm. It is much easier to maintain a bright line of offloading these decisions to SafeWords.

COMPLICATIONS

Risk Management: Administrators have to think about more than just student learning. They also have to avoid scandals, lawsuits, and bad press that could damage the district and their own careers. Systems like SafeWords can bring down the risk profile of using digital tools, and make it easier to bring in innovative tools faster. The language of "safety" and "consistency" can sometimes mask bureaucratic self-protection, even as real harms are prevented.

Student Speech: In the United States, Tinker v. Des Moines established that students retain free speech unless their expression causes or is likely to cause disruption. This gives schools substantial leeway especially if an algorithm provides credible reasoning about the risk of allowing the speech. What exactly counts as "disruption" or "harm" is hard enough for humans to judge, let alone an automated system.

Cultural Polarization: Schools will face criticism no matter how they act in situations like this. Some community members will call for tighter controls on student expression and others will demand uncensored student voices. They might accuse the school of indoctrinating students by being overly permissive with digital policies and media access, but also of censoring honest discussions about race, gender, and school policies under the banners of "safety" and "civility."

Teacher Obligations: Teachers have to think about their own career and contract language like "morals clauses" that limit how much they can stand up for students in situations like this. Employees can face discipline for speech seen as insubordinate, unprofessional, or damaging to the district image. Journalism advisors are sometimes treated as responsible for anything students publish, raising the stakes for higher oversight over school newspapers. This is directly opposed to what many teachers, like Ms. Nguyen, view as their professional obligation to cultivate and model civic courage and transparency, and to show solidarity with students when they are being wronged.

YOUR TURN

Reflect

- If you were Ms. Nguyen, what would you do and say when students ask about how to respond as a group? What options would you present, and which would you encourage?
- What emotions arise as you think about each person's perspective in this case? Do you find yourself starkly on one side or flip flopping as you read each account?
- Think about whether you lean toward sympathizing more with safety-seeking stakeholders or more with those prioritizing student voice.
- Have you ever softened, delayed, or withheld student work out of fear of backlash or harm to them or the school?
- Have commitments to "protect from harm," "empower voice," or "protect the institution," come into tension in your own experience?

Act

- If your school has filters, try to learn exactly what kinds of language or content trigger the system, who is notified, and what happens after a trigger.
- Build explicit lessons on media ethics into writing, journalism, civics, or advisory curricula, including the rights and responsibilities of free expression.
- Co-create classroom norms for online communication that empower students to make the right decisions over being filtered by an algorithm.
- When facing a struggle like Ms. Nguyen, explain to students both what you wish you could do and what you must currently weigh.

Advocate

- Call for policies that distinguish safety monitoring (for threats, harassment, self-harm) from student speech control.
- Form committees of teachers, students, parents, and tech staff to review and revise these policies regularly.
- Document patterns of over- or under-flagging to inform these discussions or to share with relevant staff.
- Encourage your school to develop digital civics curricula that presents free expression, safety, and mutual care as complementary goals.

Case Study 9: Ms. Cipriano & Between Two Fears

Two years after the school shooting the building still carried the weight of fear and grief. In the main hallway, the trophy case stood half empty from the removal of shattered awards, and the smell of disinfectant seemed to intensify around anniversaries. Lockdown drills took on a new meaning and felt ominous with scared faces and palpable tension.

Ms. Cipriano was the Director of Technology and Infrastructure, and the school shooting had happened two years into her career. For those first two years, she mainly focused on device rollouts, Wi-Fi infrastructure, and cybersecurity, things that no one else really thought about.

Over the last couple of years, her work had come to the forefront, with fear, public scrutiny, and expectations for visible security changes dictating what she focused her time on. She herself had a nephew in the school this year and felt the extra weight of feeling responsible for her sister's child.

The school had started doing quarterly open houses to bring in parents and community members to discuss safety concerns, provide grief and anxiety support resources, and generally build trust after the incident. Ms. Cipriano regularly received demands for proof that she was "doing something" and her inbox was full of pitches for various solutions to "stop threats before they even start."

In the last two years, she led the installation of new electronically controlled reinforced doors, metal detectors, and access control systems. This year, the state released a grant for "advanced school safety interventions" that required spending 75% of funds on approved tech products. One of the board members, a local banker, was insisting that the school consider an AI-powered gun detection system, after his bank installed similar technology this spring. The system used a network of cameras with machine learning software that could scan real-time video for weapons and trigger alerts to local law enforcement and initiate school lockdowns.

Ms. Cipriano had been tasked with looking into this as a potential way to spend the grant money this year. Ms. Cipriano started with a visit from the vendor, a former law enforcement officer turned sales representative, who spoke both about policing and school safety. He focused on "proactivity" and emphasized how quickly the system was able to detect a weapon before a first shot. He emphasized that the system was not perfect, but that new data was helping it improve every day, and doing something was better than "being sitting ducks." He explained that he would help write the grant proposal and even include an additional set of cameras for free if they closed the deal before the end of the month.

Ms. Cipriano did not need to be convinced that every second matters. She still wished she had been able to run faster to the security room when she was paged for an issue so she could have alerted the authorities earlier. If this system had done it for her, that might have prevented a catastrophe.

Still, Ms. Cipriano was skeptical of a system that required continuous, building-wide video surveillance to function. The system relied on scanning every student and staff member as they moved through hallways, entrances, and cafeterias. It would establish who was normally in the building, how they behaved, and other signs of normalcy, so it could detect when something was wrong.

The model was trained on a variety of law enforcement contexts, sports stadiums, banks, movie theaters, and political protests, but they were still collecting more data on schools to keep training the model. Ms. Cipriano worried about what it meant to look at children primarily through a lens built for crime control.

She decided to call some local districts and review the case studies before making any more decisions. One of her peers shared that the system had largely been an unnoticed presence, but that one time it flagged a student's collapsible umbrella as a weapon, causing a lockdown and law enforcement to rush over.

As Ms. Cipriano looked further into the company, she found that there had been some criticisms of the higher error rates when subjects had darker skin tones, wore certain clothing (e.g., hijabs), or were in poor lighting, being more likely to mistakenly mark them as having weapons. Independent reports also showed that the false positives largely involved Black and Brown people. She was concerned by these reports but found a page on the vendor's website promising that they were training the algorithm on more diverse datasets to continue to perfect their detection system.

Ms. Cipriano thought about the harm of a false positive. Besides scaring the whole school, she wondered what it would be like for the student who was flagged. Would they be put in danger? How might that shape their trust and sense of belonging in the school?

She closed the websites for now and went back to her inbox. She kept scrolling through the latest batch of messages from parents suggesting all sorts of interventions and security measures. One parent with three children in the school insisted "Please do whatever it takes," to prevent another tragedy.

At the next staff meeting, safety came up again. One teacher was expressing exhaustion with drills and extra security, "What kind of school are we becoming if every safety measure makes us feel more like a prison?" Another chimed in that he would "take ten cameras over one more funeral." When Ms. Cipriano explained the new option, the staff appeared split along those same lines.

As they left the room, the principal pulled Ms. Cipriano aside. "Look, I still cannot forget the image of our school that day, as I am sure you cannot, but I need your professional recommendation that includes a clear plan that the board can defend publicly. I saw the links about false positives, and that is concerning, but I also do not want us to later regret not using technology that might be lifesaving."

Ms. Cipriano returns to her office. One other consideration was the other 25% of funds that came with the grant. She knew the counselors wanted more support, and maybe she could share the extra resources with them if they were chosen for the grant. She began to draft a document, "AI-Enhanced School Safety Proposal." But she struggled to get past the title. Finally, she started writing about "proactive detection of threats while maintaining trust and equity." That still felt like an oxymoron to her given what she had learned about the technology. She quickly jotted down: safety, equity, trust, and harm to remind her of the top things on her mind, and logged off to think it through more.

The morning of the board meeting, she was still thinking through the recommendations she ended up writing. She had drafted one for each possibility to help think through the outcomes, but also give her more time to decide on one. As she walked into the building, she noticed that most students barely noticed the cameras and mindlessly went through the metal detector. Still, there were students who clearly felt uneasy and embarrassed as they walked through the detector and it went off because of spare change or most often, their cellphone.

As she entered the gym, she noticed the seats filled with board members and community members, the bright stadium lights, and two reporters from the local news station set up. The board chair called Ms. Cipriano up to present the grant proposal. "I've reviewed the grant, but I don't see your recommendation attached," they said. Ms. Cipriano started, "The key question is: how do we protect our children without turning them into suspects? Given our current constraints, I recommend we. . ."

VOICES

Ms. Cipriano, Technology Director: I do not want to miss any opportunity to keep students safe again, but safety is many things. I do not want to be complicit in racially targeting our students, and I do not fully trust that the company has figured out how to operate in school contexts. Once AI surveillance is installed, it will be nearly impossible to roll back, but also if we can allocate more money towards counseling, our students would really benefit.

Parent: I have lost one child to a school shooting, and I want us to do everything we possibly can to prevent anyone else from going through that pain. It took me months to allow my other child to leave my sights, and I want the school to do whatever it takes to keep them safe. The fear of surveillance is nothing compared to the pain of loss.

Student Council President: They keep adding new security and tell us it is for our safety, but no one has asked us if we actually feel safer. Coming into school feels like a bad experience at airport security every time, and it starts the day off with a constant reminder of what happened. No one has data on whether this stuff works, and we still hear stories of shootings even when schools have all these gadgets.

School Resource Officer: Responding to calls without knowing if it is a prank, false alarm, or an active shooter is an exhausting and trying experience every time. Good information, about where, what, and who, would be invaluable in these moments. If AI can provide that information, I would be able to approach these situations so much more calmly. On the other hand, I know students of color have a hard time with my presence, and I worry that any false positives will further cause them to feel anxious at school. I have been in the community for decades, know every student personally, and have received extensive training on working in schools, including implicit bias training, it is not clear the AI can match that yet.

COMPLICATIONS

Trauma and Fear: The community experienced a massive shock and is actively grieving. For many parents, visible safety measures are the only tangible proof that the district cares and is acting. Each new layer of security creates a sense of safety for some, but reopens wounds for others.

Bias and Error: Every independent test of AI gun detection systems shows uneven accuracy, especially across different lighting, clothing, and skin tones. Students who might be disproportionately targeted with false positives might quickly change their relationship to the school, seeing themselves as objects of suspicion and feeling fearful of being falsely accused again. Every erroneous alert can trigger lockdowns, police responses, and stigma, all of which dramatically shape the culture of the school.

Funding Incentives: The grant money will be lost if it is not spent on this new technology. The group of approved vendors that they are allowed to spend on is small; and the school already has most of the other recommended technology that is allowed under the grant. The unrestricted 25% of the funding that would allow them to spend on any measures related to school safety would be enough to add two more counselors to a current team of five.

Longevity: Changes to infrastructure like this are hard to pilot and usually require a multi-year investment. Once the technology is introduced, it is hard to remove or change vendors without incurring substantial costs. There are also ongoing costs of paying for monitoring and software updates and replacing the advanced cameras as they break.

YOUR TURN

Reflect

- What would you say if you were Ms. Cipriano? What recommendation would you make and what justification would you share with the board?
- Which voice did you instinctively side with and how do your own experiences with safety, policing, or surveillance shape that reaction?
- Do you think safety and privacy can coexist in schools, or does one inevitably risk sacrificing the other?
- What are the values beyond the ones Ms. Cipriano jots down that you would take into account when making your decision?

Act

- Look into existing safety technologies and protocols and who was consulted when they were adopted.
- Seek trauma-informed professional development so that responses to threats and to false alarms prioritize de-escalation and care.
- Try to help create standing structures, such as student advisory councils or stakeholder committees, which give the students who have to deal with the new protocols a real voice in shaping these policies.

Advocate

- Push at the policy level for clear standards governing surveillance in schools that include requirements for bias and accuracy audits.
- Volunteer with civil rights organizations, student groups, and privacy advocates to demand transparency from vendors about training data and error rates.
- Encourage your school to evaluate new measures through the lens of efficacy and not just perception.

CHAPTER 20

Cases in Policy

Case Study 10: Mr. Khan & AI for All
NARRATIVE

Mr. Khan is a 14-year veteran English teacher at a large, racially, and socioeconomically diverse public high school. The school has had trouble closing the digital divide, with some families having multiple devices and home offices and others sharing a single tablet and relying on school Wi-Fi. Mr. Khan primarily teaches eleventh grade American Literature plus one AP Language section.

Throughout his career, he has experienced all sorts of changes such as new literacy frameworks, standards-based grading, a 1:1 laptop rollout, and more platforms than he could remember. All of these "improvements" came with bold promises, and mixed results, like a reading intervention app that actually improved comprehension for ninth graders and a clicker system for in-class jeopardy that was gathering dust. As he thought about generative AI, he was not sure what to make of it yet.

Last year, it turned out that a handful of students had quietly started using AI tools, and it took the teachers a few months to realize that this is why they suddenly had a surge in polished essays from students who had struggled before. One student was caught after boasting on social media about an A he received thanks to a "bot," which unraveled the whole mystery for the school.

The teachers all panicked, and the district had issued a blanket AI ban that was strongly enforced on the school devices and network. The district added AI detection to their plagiarism software, and the school network created reports of anyone who tried to use AI sites on the Wi-Fi. They insisted that they had to "protect the integrity of our diplomas."

But, they quickly started to notice an issue. The students who relied on school Wi-Fi were getting caught more often, while classmates with private laptops and home Wi-Fi were able to continue using AI with less risk. Mr. Khan was uneasy about the ban because it punished the least resourced and least tech-savvy students, while giving him no way to police the students who had their own devices and were learning all tricks to circumvent the ban.

Soon, the administrators also agreed that the AI ban was not working. They kept hearing stories of students using their own accounts or logging into parents' accounts at home. They even heard from some parents that they were paying extra for the "good version" of AI to help with tutoring and studying, while other parents were upset that the children were being punished for using tools that "most adults in modernized countries" were using.

The ban was unenforceable and inequitable, so they decided to shift to a harm reduction model, bringing AI use into the open and providing controlled access for everyone. As they looked into vendors, they found one that promised guardrails for safety, easy provisioning with the existing LMS, and offered multiple plans. The district could only afford the basic plan that used an older AI model, had stricter limitations on what students could do, and did not have advanced features like web search and voice mode. There was concern from teachers, including Mr. Khan, about introducing a new tool to students that they didn't even know how to use, and more up-to-date teachers were concerned that the equal access promise wasn't really true if they were going to provide a weaker tool to everyone while some students still had premium accounts at home.

The school still released their "AI for All" initiative that was branded with the vendor's logo and came with the promise of a district-managed AI account for all students through their school laptops. The message from the district was that after the failed ban, they wanted to "provide safe AI access for all students, not just those whose families can pay for private tools."

The next few days the hallway was filled with chatter among the students. Some students expressed excitement about getting to play around with the new AI tool finally, and others were muttering about how it was the "baby version" compared to what they had at home.

Mr. Khan hoped the initiative might increase access to AI tools, even if the capabilities remained higher for families who were purchasing more advanced technology.

Along with the new rollout, the school decided to form an AI Implementation Committee that would translate the AI for All initiative into concrete school-wide policies. Mr. Khan was chosen to serve on it as one of the senior members of the staff and a key figure during the rapid switch to digital learning during the pandemic.

The committee consisted of the principal, the instructional technology coach, English, History and Math teachers, the special education coordinator, an ESL teacher, and the school social worker. It was charged with crafting guidelines that "ensure equitable access to district AI tools" while "safeguarding academic integrity and public confidence in our assessments."

As Mr. Khan read the memo, he underlined equitable access, circled academic integrity, and scribbled a question mark about policies regarding students' access to other AI accounts. The principal started the presentation with a slideshow with the opening slide titled, "From Ban to Access." The principal acknowledged that the ban was needed in that moment but not sustainable, and that monitoring what students did at home or on their own devices was difficult, so they hoped more students would use the school-issued AI if they provided it.

The history teacher was relieved that he could see how the students were using the tool instead of relying on detectors and the ESL teacher was excited about the built-in language support. But, the science teacher was still cautious about what it meant for the students critically thinking, especially as they drafted their lab reports. Mr. Khan himself was unsure of what to make of the new tool but thought that the shift from ban to access made sense.

At the next meeting, the instructional technology coach presented a draft policy that distinguished between three categories of AI use: "no AI," "district AI only," and "any AI with disclosure." There was also a clause that students "may not use personal or parent AI accounts during class time" and "should rely on district accounts for schoolwork whenever possible." Mr. Khan was the first to respond, "How exactly do we know if someone used a parent's account at home?" In response, the principal explained that enforcement would never be perfect, but that the goal was to set norms and do what they could. The committee decided that they would start evaluating the policy in their own classrooms to gather information to refine the guidelines.

Mr. Khan was teaching the argumentative essay that week. This was an important part of the year because not only did it cover one of two essays on the state exam, but students' final work was also entered into a district-wide competition for scholarship money.

He gave the final assignment with an explanation of his AI policy. He told them that they may use the district AI for brainstorming and revision but that they should write their drafts themselves. He expected them to primarily use the school-provided AI, so he could print out a report of their usage, and make note of any usage beyond that.

As the students got to work, some students started with outlines on pen and paper, while others immediately began prompting the district's AI to brainstorm possible topics. As the students were leaving the classroom, Mr. Khan overheard one student say, "I am just going to do this at home. My dad's account can, like, write full essays."

As he collected the drafts, he had mixed feelings. He was sure that the students all had used AI to varying degrees, and even though they had a policy and the district provided tools, and he was worried about what it meant in practice for how he evaluated the essays.

As he read the drafts, he could see traces of AI usage, such as polished and generic phrasing and arguments that felt staler than the ones his students normally submitted. Some students had turned in essays that sounded great but seemed to be substantially better than the writing he had seen from them before. Even with the disclosure notes, he was not sure how to grade fairly when he had students who clearly used no AI and submitted only their own thoughts and writing and others who he suspected used AI that was far more advanced than others.

That evening, he saw an email from a parent of a struggling student:

Hi Mr. Khan,
    I just wanted to thank you and the school for providing Bill with the new AI tutor. This was the first time I did not see him shut down over a writing assignment. Bill's dad and I do not really understand all this AI stuff, but we are glad the school is helping, because we did not even know where to start. Hopefully, he will be better prepared than us!

Another email read:

Dear Mr. Khan,
    Juliana told us about the school providing the new AI software to the students. We are a little concerned for two reasons.

First, we are not sure we want her to have access to these tools yet. We have seen studies that it stunts brain development. If her peers are using it, it becomes hard for us to restrict her usage, especially if the school is endorsing the tool.

Second, Juliana shared that some peers have been using their parents' accounts or have personal premium accounts of their own for much stronger models. I do not think it is very fair if Juliana's work is compared to those students, and I hope the school is planning to do something.

Mr. Khan was left even more confused. If the district could not afford the best tools, was it more fair to give everyone a limited tool or to keep trying to keep AI out altogether?

At the next committee meeting, they discussed the issues again. The principal shared that the district could not afford the most advanced AI tier, and that even though the wealthier private schools in the area were subscribing to more powerful AI suites, this just was not something the school had the resources for.

When Mr. Khan brought up the concerns of restricting student usage altogether, the other teachers were skeptical that anything could get students to not use these tools anymore, and that it was better to focus on responsible usage. Mr. Khan retorted that he needed to teach them foundational skills before the students could actually distinguish between responsible and irresponsible usage.

The committee had to produce its policy for the school, and Mr. Khan was not sure what to do. Should he push back on the limited-edition rollout? Or should he accept that there would be uneven access and just grade what he received?

VOICES

Mr. Khan, English Teacher: None of the actual solutions are possible. I do not think the tools are helpful for most of our students at their stage of learning and providing it just to equalize the field does not make sense to me. Even then, we are not actually equalizing anything! Regardless, my students need to be future ready by knowing how to use these tools, and something might be better than nothing. I just do not know what this means for how I grade or enforce policies in my class anymore.

Principal: AI is here to stay. Families are already using it, and we have made the promise to provide "AI for All." That is the only sensible path forward, and the rest will have to be figured out at the classroom level. I tried banning all AI and that was a massive failure, and I know I cannot try to do that again. I guess we do have to figure out how to deal with premium accounts, but at least we gave the students something this year.

Mia, Student: I really enjoy writing and I want to show my teachers that I can write on my own. I also want to make sure that I am prepared for college writing, so I really do not want to use any of these AI tools. But, my classmates keep using the AI tools to help them, and they finish faster and can study harder for other things or spend more time on extracurriculars. I do not want to fall behind.

ESL Teacher: The new AI tool has been a huge help for some of my multilingual students. They can use it to practice writing and get instant feedback, talk to it in their native language when they are struggling with the English, and are starting to build more confidence submitting things when they know the AI has given them an initial round of feedback. I wish they could speak to the tool like the other schools have for their students, but this is already such a big help.

COMPLICATING FACTORS

Economic Pressures: The school cannot realistically provide the advanced AI system to all students. And, as the technology continues to develop there will be multiple tools all with different tiers that can affect what the students can and cannot do with the software. They had to choose the low-tier one if they were going to offer the AI, but the primary motivator, equity, seems unfulfilled.

Assessment: The varied usage of AI and the different AI tools available to students make grading fairly a challenging task. AI detectors are more likely to pick up on basic usage and students with only school tool access are substantially less likely to misuse the tool. That still leaves students with premium access outside of school with a substantial advantage over their peers.

Privacy and Data: Oftentimes, free and low-price tools come at the expense of more data retention and allowance for things like training models on student and teacher usage. Students and teachers who use tools that are not protected by a school vendor contract might be risking more information than they realize, and the school does not have control over that.

YOUR TURN

Reflect
- What policy or combination of policies should Mr. Khan advocate for in the final committee vote?
- How might you balance raising the floor of access with addressing unequal ceilings?
- Do these dynamics (uneven AI access) currently exist at your school? What is your school doing about it?
- What does "cheating" really mean when families pay for tutoring, editing, and now AI subscriptions?

Act
- Establish a clear policy for your classroom on expectations over AI usage. Co-create it with students to encourage them to consider the ramifications of unequal or inappropriate usage.
- Include = "AI-free" activities, like brief in-class writings or debates, which provide a sense of what students can do independently.
- Offer optional workshops or office hours to help students without external support learn how to get the most from the tech tools they do have, so lack of familiarity does not compound lack of access.

Advocate
- Push for district policies that explicitly acknowledge the existence of external AI accounts and articulate what is expected, realistic, and fair.

- Explore ways to narrow, even if you cannot erase, the digital divide.
- Treat AI policy as a living document that can adapt as tools, budgets, and access patterns change.

Case Study 11: Mrs. Sierra & Cellphone Exceptions
NARRATIVE

Mrs. Sierra teaches middle school science in a mid-sized, diverse public school district in a small city center near the coast. She starts each period watching each student add their phone to the shoe hanger that she had converted into a phone "parking lot." Each student had an assigned number, and she stood there at the beginning and end of every period to watch as each student deposited and then took their phone.

A handful of students had a small sticker on their phone labeled "Authorized Device Use," for students who had gotten exceptions to the school-wide cellphone policy. She mostly knew who had exceptions, but the stickers made it easy when there were new exceptions. This had been standard practice since last spring, and the students and staff had gotten fairly accustomed to the procedures.

Lately, the community had taken interest in the amount of screen time students were getting after a contentious battle at the board meeting where the cellphone policy was adopted. Leading up to it, there were multiple scandals from selective filming of teachers, cheating by keeping notes on the lock screen, and multiple state tests interrupted with ringing cellphones.

In response, the board adopted an "off and away" policy that had students make sure their phones were turned off and put in the holders installed in every classroom. This was not a perfect solution, but it was a starting point that was a compromise between parents and the school.

After the initial policy was created, students and parents started to ask for exceptions based on documented medical and disability needs, mostly students with obvious health devices or long-standing IEPs. The district agreed to allow exceptions.

At first, it meant that students could keep their phone if they had gotten permission from the main office. This often led to students shyly looking at their phone to check the glucose monitor, or trying to sit in the back of the classroom to use the speech-to-text feature on their phone. Often, teachers would call them out in the middle of class for still having their device, and they would have to explain that they had prior permission. This repeated any time they rotated classes, had substitute teachers, or a teacher happened to forget who had exceptions.

The stickers were a response to streamline exceptions and honor the accommodation without having the students have to explain their needs again and again. One student explained, "I finally feel like I'm not breaking the rule anymore instead of having to argue with every teacher."

Still, the sticker system led to occasional teasing: "It must be nice to get a pass." This meant that those students had to decide how much to reveal or deflect to avoid having to share their private information to avoid harassment.

As the year went on, more families approached counselors about students with anxiety, OCD, and ADHD who were relying on phone-based support to help them get through the day.

The district sent out a memo to schools encouraging "reasonable support" within existing policies. One student used a Cognitive Behavioral Therapy during passing time, and another used a checklist app to stay organized to help make up for executive functioning deficiencies.

One day, Jordan interrupted the class after he saw a student use their phone under their desk: "How come they get to keep their phones if none of us can? That is not fair." Several students nodded, and eyes turned to Mrs. Sierra to explain. She had anticipated this moment, and shared her rehearsed line, "Some students have private reasons they need different tools to learn. We do not discuss other people's situations." The students with exceptions visibly shifted in their seats, and the rest of the class seemed dissatisfied.

At lunch, Mrs. Sierra heard one student ask another, "So what's wrong with you?" And, she saw the student respond by leaving the cafeteria. Over the next few weeks, she heard students making their own judgments and declaring to each other that some kids are "faking it" and some "obviously need it."

Lila is a quiet, bright, methodical student who always takes a seat near the window and has nearly perfect attendance and grades. She does not have a sticker herself, but wishes she could make use of her support systems that she had built for herself. At home, she updates her medication alarms, task reminders, color-coded to-do lists, and scheduled breathing exercises.

Her mother watches over her with pride as she remembers the constant panic attacks before they found a system that helps Lila feel in control. Lila mentioned the stickers with her mom, "A lot of students have exceptions. Do you think you can reach out now?" Lila's mom had been hesitant of having anything officially recorded because "people look at you differently," especially when you are an immigrant; and she wanted to keep Lila's diagnosis a private matter. She reiterated her concerns, and Lila nodded obediently, still wishing she could convince her mom.

Back in class, Lila was quietly reading along with other students and suddenly felt a panic attack coming on after she came across a part of the story that echoed one of her worst fears. She felt her heart racing and throat tense up, but worked to maintain a composed exterior to avoid anyone seeing something was wrong. Mrs. Sierra, however, noticed that Lila, who was a quick reader, had barely turned more than a page that day.

As the class was leaving, she stopped Lila and checked in with her about why she was struggling to make progress today. Lila broke down crying, and Mrs. Sierra quickly closed the door and sat Lila down. "What is going on Lila? Are you comfortable talking to me?" Lila opened up to Mrs. Sierra about her diagnosis, how she uses her phone for grounding apps or quick distractions to avoid and deal with panic attacks, and how her mom does not want to put anything on her record. She also expressed her own hesitation about having to explain to other students why she had a sticker.

Mrs. Sierra promised to look into it more and offered to walk her to her next class. Back in her classroom, she thought about the complexity of the policy. The policy basically said: "We will help you, but only if you are willing to share private information with everyone." She was not sure what to do. If she pushed Lila to get a badge, it would force her to explain herself and upset Lila's mom, but if she did nothing, then Lila would continue to suffer in silence.

Mrs. Sierra decided to speak to the special education coordinator about the situation. The coordinator explained that expanded exceptions were meant to help students like Lila, but they were tied to diagnoses, documented plans, and visible stickers for tracking and consistency. He also acknowledged that in practice, this process asked students to self-advocate and share publicly if they wanted phone-based support.

Mrs. Sierra was still confused. She saw the difference that the phone ban had made in her classroom. Students were paying attention, less distracted, and interacting with each other instead of their phones. Across the board, her colleagues had shared relief at finally "having their students back."

She went to the principal to talk further about what could be done. She emphasized the pattern of students demanding explanations about who gets exceptions, and how that puts everyone in a weird situation. But he stood firm, arguing that visible stickers were intended to prevent students from accusing teachers of secret favoritism and keep enforcement possible. Mrs. Sierra reiterates the social and emotional cost of the policy onto students with invisible disabilities, who must either accept being visibly marked or forgo support. The principal agreed to revisit communication but makes no commitment to actual change.

Mrs. Sierra was not sure what to do tomorrow. Should she urge Lila to go through official channels without her mother's approval? Should she call Lila's mother and push her to see the cost of not seeking support? Should she push the administrators to find a new system or revoke the cellphone altogether? Or, should she make an exception for Lila and hope no one notices?

VOICES

Mrs. Sierra, Teacher: The policy looked so perfect on paper. There were rules and processes for exceptions to meet everyone's needs. The change in the school's culture was obvious: calmer hallways, deeper discussions, and the absence of mindless scrolling in class. But, now I wonder how many other students are quietly struggling because they do not want to deal with the social stigma or have to explain themselves.

Principal: We had to do something about the phone crisis. It was getting uncontrollable and the exception system is the best we could produce to help students who need accommodations. If we start quietly making exceptions to our exceptions, other students will feel cheated, parents will accuse the school of favoritism, and the policy will unravel.

Special Education Coordinator: I have to work within the systems that exist, and getting official documentation can be life changing for a student. I know that some parents and students fear losing their privacy, but having this information helps us better support the students. It has been particularly helpful to some of my students as it prevents them from constantly thinking about checking their phones or feeling the buzz of their notifications. I also hate that students or families have to self-advocate for any of these accommodations, because we are definitely missing many students whose families do not know where to start even if they want to. I do wish this policy did not also involve having to sacrifice privacy to other students, but I cannot let go of the ban.

Parent: I have spent years trying to help Lila manage her anxiety and panic attacks at home without drawing attention. My husband and I have seen how labels can stick, especially for immigrants, and we do not want a clinical diagnosis to close doors for Lila. I do not want her to feel isolated or become a target of gossip or pity. I do not understand why they cannot just let everyone keep their phones if there are already exceptions for some students. Surely, they can find other ways to deal with the students who use their phones irresponsibly.

COMPLICATIONS

Exceptions: Any policy that is made needs to leave room for exceptions. However, exceptions also draw attention and that can come at a real cost to students and families. It is difficult to determine whether, and how much, schools should adjust a broadly effective policy to protect students who are harmed not by the rule itself but by the way support is accessed.

Invisible Disabilities: Many disabilities are invisible, and often teachers and classmates never even know how hard some students are working just to appear "fine." Forcing them to have to share their diagnosis by attracting attention creates an unnecessary burden on students who might prefer to keep that private. It might open them up to bullying and harassment, or feelings of being different and singled out that can make students struggle to feel like they belong.

Teacher Enforcement: Teachers end up having to defend and enforce these policies that are often made by administrators without educator input. They have to field complaints of fairness and answer questions about how the rule is determined and how exceptions are decided. They have to walk a tight balance of showing understanding and empathy to their students, and fidelity to their school's policies.

Legal Versus Moral: Even if certain accommodations meet the legal requirements, and documentation helps prevent legal scrutiny later, that does not mean that the action is morally defensible. A school policy that is legally compliant but regularly leaves undiagnosed or privacy-oriented students without functioning supports causes real harm.

YOUR TURN

Reflect

- What should Mrs. Sierra do when Lila walks into class tomorrow with her phone and looks to Mrs. Sierra for help?
- In this situation, who should carry more of the burden of making the system work?
- Are you more worried about chaos if rules loosen, injustice if rules stay firm, or the emotional cost to students asked to explain themselves?
- Do you or your school's policies assume that students who need help will speak up?

Act

- Offer low stakes, private ways for students to share needs so that not all help depends on proactive self-advocacy.
- Think ahead about how to answer, "Why do they get to. . .?" in ways that protect privacy while affirming that accommodations are normal and not a sign of favoritism.
- Collaborate with counselors and families to see whether some supports can be delivered through less visible means.

Advocate
- Recommend exploring alternative accommodation structures that rely less on visible markers, even if these require more behind-the-scenes coordination.
- Propose student and family advisory groups to surface how policies feel on the ground and to co-design changes that reduce burdens on our most vulnerable students.
- Consider how you might bring this case into your own school conversations about cellphone policies to help clarify what the risks of a ban include.

Case Study 12: Dr. Rivera & Defending Enrollment
NARRATIVE

Dr. Rivera is an economics and civics teacher at a large, top-performing, public school in a major city. She attended the school herself and has spent her entire teaching career of over 25 years working here. Throughout her time, she has seen all sorts of educational "revolutions": 1:1 laptops, flipped classrooms, personalized dashboards, and online LMS systems that arrived with much fanfare, but often faded away or were cut due to tightening budgets. She has learned to smile through new buzzwords, focus on what helps her reach her pedagogical goals, and remain steadfast in her mission to help develop effective members of civic society.

Over the last few years, her school had been increasingly introducing AI technology, first to help with teacher workflow, and then as engagement tools to use in classes. She had found the workflow tools to be useful, especially to quickly summarize the day's current events for the "In Civics Today" section of her website, and to design inquiry-based learning assignments for each of her major lesson topics. She had yet to use AI directly with her students as she preferred face-to-face contact, but had regularly included topics about AI policy and the impact on misinformation, labor markets, and civic discourse in her classes.

Last year, she noticed that the public narrative was strongly moving toward "AI literacy" or "AI readiness" with headlines warning about students being left behind in the college admissions process, and worse, the job market. One of the local prep schools had redesigned their curriculum to help students be "future-ready" by integrating AI tools across disciplines, showing students how the tools could be used in different academic and professional areas.

Having had a child go through the school system, she was part of many ThatApp groups and FaceStream parent groups. Over the summer, there had been a flood of anxious posts from families asking whether the public schools were keeping up. After the district stood by its policy to allow individual teachers to integrate, or not integrate, AI as they saw fit, the parent backlash got stronger. The district lost 7% of student enrollment, almost exclusively affluent families, to local private and prep schools.

The district had to collapse a few classes down, especially at the high school level, with newly hired faculty being laid off, and senior faculty being moved temporarily to lower grade levels. There was a lot of uncertainty about what would happen if enrollment numbers dropped anymore.

At dismissal one afternoon, a parent pulled Dr. Rivera aside to inquire about her class structure. He asked, "Have you started showing students how to use AI to process data?," clearly expecting a yes.

This was a gentler question than she had received in the past few weeks, with one angry email even accusing her of gross negligence. Dr. Rivera had calmly responded with an explanation of how she needed to help students build fundamental skills before they could fully understand what the AI was producing and accurately judge its output. She also explained that she wanted to make sure they felt empowered to voice their opinion on matters of public policy and learn how to write and speak persuasively. She had yet to receive a response, but Dr. Rivera knew it was not going to be a pleasant one.

In the hallway the next day, she overhead a few students talk about how they were using AI coding tools to create their own apps, while other students did not understand how AI could design an app without human input. She spent her prep period reading through some teaching forums about how other civics and economics teachers were approaching teaching AI, but all of it seemed short-sighted and reactionary.

That evening, Dr. Rivera was scheduled to attend the monthly school board meeting. She was the teacher representative for the union and had not missed a single board meeting since taking on the role. As she walked in, she noticed the aura of anxiety. There were more attendees than normal, a large contingency of parents, two local council members, and a few students who were attending for a government class assignment. During the public comment period, one father, dressed in a tailored suit, stood and identified himself as a tech company executive and parent of two boys in the school system. He explained:

> This is the future workforce. My company is one of the largest employers in the area, and we rely heavily on AI every day. Students need to learn to work with these new tools, not be shielded from them by adults who are uncomfortable with change. I have been a longtime supporter of our public school system, and my wife and I started our family here because of the district's reputation. If the district is not going to keep up with the times, we will have to do what is right for our children, and look elsewhere.

There were murmurs of agreement in the audience, and his remarks were followed by two more parents who expressed a similar concern, a student who worried about being competitive in college compared to her friends who were learning all about AI, and one sole vocal opponent, a child psychiatrist, who wanted stricter AI policies, because of the increase in students relying on AI bots for mental health support.

After the public remarks period was over, the board moved to an executive session with the union to discuss next year's personnel decision. Principal Cho started the conversation, explaining that for each lost student, the district lost thousands in state aid with them, on top of potential losses in local fundraising and grant competitiveness. He warned that if the trend continued the school would be forced to reduce compensation packages during the next contract negotiation and expressed the possibility of another round of layoffs.

Dr. Rivera had a separate meeting scheduled the next day with the faculty where she was to share what she learned from the conversations. She was dreading having to share the news, but also was not sure herself what the way out was.

After sharing the news, she opened up the space for comments. Ms. Zoya, a math teacher, expressed concern over further funding losses. "We would have to cut electives and reduce counselors. On top of that, my after-school homework lab that our vulnerable students rely on is barely staying afloat. There's only so much goodwill can do to keep it open if we cannot compensate faculty members for staying longer." The English department chair was visibly upset, "These are all real risks, but we cannot imitate private schools just to please a handful of parents. We have a duty to build our student's intelligence, not make them reliant on a robot's intelligence."

Two months later, the board finally made a call on next steps. Following a unanimous board vote, they announced a new "AI Integration Initiative." The memo had the words "innovation," "efficiency," "digital natives," and "future-ready" highlighted. It explained that each teacher must incorporate at least one district-approved AI platform into both instruction and assessment by spring. They also had to submit at least one lesson plan a month that directly taught students how to use the latest AI technology.

Dr. Rivera quickly worked with the union to draft a response letter expressing concern about workload, teacher autonomy, and mission alignment with the school's stated values. The district agreed to do something about only the first of those three issues, and planned out a year-long professional development plan to support teachers in the rollout.

The first professional development session was schoolwide. The district had hired one of the AI platform vendors to come in and explain how students could "leverage AI for learning." Teachers left feeling unsure about what this meant for their actual classrooms, and still sitting with the burden of having to redo their curriculum to make room for the new initiative, while being expected to prepare students for state standardized exams.

At lunch, Dr. Rivera was venting to her long-time friend and colleague about the impact of the AI tools on her class. "Ever since the school has allowed the students to use the AI tools, all my students' writing sounds eerily similar. It is all the same bland voice." Mrs. Wam quips back, "I thought these tools were supposed to personalize learning. It feels like they are standardizing their thoughts instead. I understand the teacher's usage benefits, but I still cannot figure out why we have to roll out these apps to our students so fast before any of us even fully understand the impact!"

By the end of the next month, the faculty was divided. Some younger teachers and a special education teacher were praising the time savings, accommodations, and increased student engagement levels since the rollout. Others worried that the lack of human interaction, messy writing processes, and screen-free classrooms were ruining the school's culture. "I just wish we had more say in how much we talked about AI. Why do we all have to talk about it all the time?"

In the same meeting, Principal Cho responded to mixed comments by showing graphs of rising AI usage among students, and parent survey quotes that included language like "impressed by innovative tools" and that they were glad the school was "keeping up." He reminded the staff that they had to stem enrollment losses, and the best way was to show families they were preparing students for a changing world, not clinging to nostalgia of their own educational experiences. He also shared that the district that he lived in had recently collapsed their two high schools, and had to change all electives to online enrollment courses without onsite faculty. "We don't want to fall into the same trap."

Dr. Rivera was struggling to comfort the teachers who were fraught. She reflected on the irony that the public school was being pushed toward market demands. She also worried about the precedent this set. The more the district imitates private schools to appease the families who can leave, the less of a voice our students and families who do not have that option will have.

She decided to speak to the union leadership about her options. The president outlined some possible paths: filing another grievance about workload and autonomy, proposing a smaller pilot-and-review compromise, barely adhering to the AI integration and risking reprimand, or waiting to address AI in the next contract negotiation. The president was skeptical of any of those options though. "We'll defer to you, but at the end of the day, we have to keep those students if we want our members to keep their jobs."

VOICES

Dr. Rivera, Teacher: I became a teacher to help young people learn what democracy can mean for them. I want to help them become autonomous individuals who will help make society better for everyone. I know the AI tools can be useful sometimes, and I understand needing to keep enrollment numbers, but the path we are going down will change the fabric of our school and student learning forever.

Parent: I understand the faculty have been teaching for a while, but it is time for them to adapt with the times. My daughter told me that they were requiring students to handwrite their essays in class this year, and, frankly, that is ridiculous. I want my child to be competitive in the current world, and she needs to learn how to use AI. My law firm is switching our processing over to AI, and my husband's medical office is using it for scribing. I do not understand how we can expect children to survive in the age of artificial intelligence if we insist on archaic teaching methods.

Principal Cho: I have to keep the school's doors open. Every student who leaves means fewer dollars, less political clout, and more pressure to make cuts that disproportionately affect students with the fewest options. I also feel rushed into this, and I am worried that we have not vetted our tools and new curricula enough, but I do not have the luxury of waiting another school year without risking funding loss.

Innovation Coordinator: I know there is a lot of division among the teachers, but AI is not a shiny new fad. The way it is reshaping our economy is drastic, and our students will have to work within those systems. The wealthier students will learn to use AI outside of school or at the private schools, but we have a responsibility to democratize access, so these tools do not become just another private advantage. This is not just about retention; it is also about equity.

COMPLICATIONS

Enrollment Spiral: When district funding is tightly linked to enrollment, the families who can threaten to leave have a disproportionate say in the school's policymaking. These parents are also the ones who bring in higher local tax revenues, fundraising connections, and political clout, which all makes their voices louder. The consequences of wealthy families leaving the public school or local community falls disproportionately on the students who remain, who are often poorer, more diverse, and with greater needs. It leaves schools with less resources to support them, and risks school closures and mergers.

Purpose of Education: Dr. Rivera clearly views the purpose of schooling as being centered on civic engagement and personal flourishing. The parents who are outspoken are mainly concerned with economic aims and career readiness. There is a disconnect between the two aims when they are posed as diametrically opposed goals, but there might be ways to realign the conversation to reduce the zero-sum nature of the narrative.

Grand Openings: New initiatives are often rolled out in a grand, all-hands type of fashion, especially when it is driven by political or community pressure. A school-wide approach like this does not allow for experimentation and impact-testing before exposing all students to new technologies and materials. And it does not allow teachers enough time to adapt materials in ways that actually support their teaching rather than just check off a box for their evaluation.

YOUR TURN

Reflect

- What would you do if you were Dr. Rivera? Would you fully comply with, partially adapt, collectively challenge, or openly refuse the AI mandate?
- What lies within your sphere of influence versus what would require coalition-building to change?
- When have you felt pressured to adopt a policy or tool for the sake of optics, competition, or compliance rather than for reasons grounded in your own educational values?
- How do you define "readiness for the future" in your classroom?

Act

- Go through your curriculum and tools and decide which things you think are for political or community reasons versus pedagogical reasons. Is there a way to bring them in alignment?
- Instead of redesigning everything around a new tool, choose a single lesson, project, or routine and think about how you might experiment with it to solve one concrete need.
- Invite students to share their own reflections on how a tool or policy is affecting their learning, motivation, and identity.

Advocate

- Advocate for funding formulas that cushion schools from sudden enrollment swings.
- Collaborate with peers, administrators, and community organizations to define "future readiness" that includes digital ethics, critical media literacy, and civic reasoning, and not just technical proficiency.
- Consider writing op-eds, attending community forums, or posting on social media about what you think it means for education to be a public good.

CHAPTER 21

Our Ethical Reality

I started the book by explaining the fears that motivated me: the threats to our students' humanity, the continued risk of national civic fracture, and the struggle to maintain the relevancy of our schools. These fears still very much sit with me, and in fact, writing this book has only heightened my sense of urgency.

But, I also see a path forward. I truly believe that if we all reason together, care deeply, and deliberate responsibly, we can move our educational institutions toward the reform they will need to survive and function in the next era of humanity.

Change like this happens incrementally; it requires all of us to do our part in our spheres of influence while building a coalition of fellow educators who are dedicated to more ethical practice in education. By now, you know that I do not take a prescriptive stance on what ethical practice looks like. My work here was to help all of us build the shared knowledge, dispositions, and skills that will allow us to define it both collectively for all of us and individually in our own contexts.

As technology continues to rapidly evolve, and bring those promises and perils, we will need this collective force more than ever to make our schools sites of empowerment and flourishing for each generation that passes through them.

This final chapter is not a triumphant end to our conversation, but a realistic beginning to what we must all set out to do.

My goals for this chapter are to answer any lingering questions that the rest of the book has left you with. To that end, I first address our ethical reality and obvious constraints to fully realizing the goals of this book. I then address some complaints that I anticipate will come up from my approach. Finally, I suggest next steps for how you might translate the new knowledge and skills you have gained through this book into your daily practice.

Definite Constraints

Our educational systems are far less than perfect. And, throughout the book, I have addressed various constraints that our ethical reality brings. Within those constraints, we are likely to feel like ethics is "one more thing" on an already impossible workload. But, as the book has hopefully shown, slow, deliberate, ethical reasoning is becoming increasingly necessary as the risk of harm from rushed decisions in a fast-paced technological world rises.

Structural Constraints: Our ethical agency is exercised inside systems that are in need of reform. As we saw in Chapter 12, the external constraints span from district procurement policies to state and federal policies, which sometimes support, but also restrict ethical action. Individual educators cannot solve these systemic injustices on their own, but they can advocate for change to influence them.

Teacher Burnout: The framework in this book is not enough for teachers to be able to do the sort of deliberate reasoning called for. Leaders must reduce burdens and provide institutional support for teachers to exercise their professional judgment without further fatigue.

Tragic Choices: This book exists because we have to make imperfect decisions where some trade-off will inevitably have to be accepted. Thus, given how we have built our framework, we might define "ethical" to mean the "most philosophically defensible, transparently shared, and stakeholder-justifiable option available." You will still make mistakes. Acting ethically means being willing to revisit decisions, to repair when possible, and to keep learning.

This is not meant to be a pessimistic concession. Instead, acknowledging our ethical reality allows us to act in sustainable ways that prevent burnout and enables us to act strategically.

Possible Critiques

I stand on the shoulders of giants to build the argument offered here. I have translated relevant philosophical and organizational scholarship to be as accessible as possible for practitioners around the world to make use of immediately. However, no framework is perfect.

Good Actors: The book largely presumes that people *want* to act ethically. In reality, we will face actors who are self-interested and behave opportunistically, commercially, or politically. This is precisely why shared commitments and processes among those of us committed to acting ethically become so important. Together, we can defend and build more ethical institutions, so that "bad actors" are limited in their ability to cause harm.

Unresolvable Tensions: I have addressed the fact that the framework does not work like an algorithm and will not provide a single right answer every time. So, what happens when principles point to opposite policy mandates? Can the framework still produce actionable outcomes? To that, I say yes, because we must still act despite competing reasons. The framework, then, provides us the tools to reason and deliberate rigorously to minimize harm and build consensus. Some tensions cannot be fully resolved, but by naming them, we can responsibly manage them.

Power Dynamics: When stakeholders fundamentally disagree and ethical reasoning does not produce consensus, transparency about the decision and documentation of dissent matters most. We cannot always convince everyone, and sometimes we have to exercise the authority we have as educators given our best judgment. Other times, we will be overridden by those who have more power than us, and we must reevaluate what acting ethically means given those constraints and choose from a narrower set of options.

Measurement: Measuring ethical outcomes is not as easy as measuring test scores or graduation rates. We have to look for meaningful signs when possible that we are making progress. We might notice cultural shifts in how discussions are had, the pace at which new tools and policies are introduced, or how much different stakeholders are being consulted for decision-making. Ultimately, ethical school culture is built over years, and we have to celebrate incremental progress rather than seek a dramatic shift. The right question to focus on is "Are we acting more ethically?" rather than "Are we ethical yet?"

What's Next?

This book has argued that ethical education in a technological age depends on three things: shared language, shared processes for reasoning together, and shared commitments to act within our spheres of influence.

The work of this book is a starting point. You will continue to face changing technology, contested values, and new dilemmas. The goal in the meantime is to continue to internalize the habits of ethical reasoning, and support your colleagues, and your students, in building those skills. An ethically serious school is one where decisions are made transparently, reasons are shared, harms are minimized, and students see adults wrestling openly and humbly with what is right.

Once you are done with the book, one possible next step is to start a peer group. This can be a group of any size, even meeting informally, that wants to practice more case studies together, reflect on real scenarios together, and recruit more members as time goes on. Together, you can share a commitment to ethical reflection and advocacy that can slowly push for change in your school and build your practical wisdom.

There will be times that you see injustices that you do not have the power to fix. Some inequities are structural problems that demand structural change. The framework equips you to see when incremental change is adequate and when transformation is needed because the harms are too great. In those instances, advocacy and action through solidarity are the right move, not individual steps.

We Are Not Alone

It is easy to feel alone when we approach these issues with a critical lens and suggest deep ethical reflection. One definite thing that I have learned in researching for this book is that we are not alone. Teachers, policymakers, educational technology companies, students, and parents are out there trying to think about the same questions and issues that we have raised here. Wherever you sit in this ecosystem, you have some corner of influence. Whether that is a classroom, a product road map, a policy, a family conversation, a student organizing space, etc., the framework belongs in all of those places.

Our goal is to find each other and work toward these ethical ends. That possibility gives me hope and has kept me going when I feel like I am fighting an avalanche of uncritical change. When we feel like we are fighting unwinnable battles, we have to focus on doing what we can to keep our institutions "good" enough until conditions change and open the door for more drastic action.

I leave you with the vocabulary to name what matters, a process to reason together, a community of fellow readers, and a recognition of your agency to act ethically in your daily practice. The conversations in this book are a beginning; and my hope is that you will adapt, critique, and improve this framework in ways I could not anticipate, and then share what you learn with others. Learning can remain a human endeavor in our increasingly technological age when we keep listening, questioning, and reflecting together. So, let's talk!

Exit Ticket

Reflect

- Which of the principles and values we have discussed feel most protected in your current school? Which feel most neglected?
- What is one ethical problem that you have been avoiding that you now feel ready to name?
- How has your understanding of "ethical" in education changed throughout this book?

Act

- Identify one technology decision in which you will consciously use this framework.
- Choose one element of ethical infrastructure (normative, procedural, or cultural) you can begin building, even informally.
- Pick one case study or scenario you will bring to your colleagues for practice.

Advocate

- Decide how you will incorporate at least one student voice and one parent voice into a technology decision this year.
- Identify one ally in your school or district who shares your commitment to ethical ed tech.
- What is one structural barrier you will name publicly even if you cannot change it immediately?

Bibliography

Aamodt, Agnar, and Enric Plaza. "Case-Based Reasoning: Foundational Issues, Methodological Variations, and System Approaches." *AI Communications* 7, no. 1 (1994): 39–59. https://doi.org/10.3233/AIC-1994-7104.

Abry, Tashia, Sara E. Rimm-Kaufman, and Timothy W. Curby. "Are All Program Elements Created Equal? Relations Between Specific Social and Emotional Learning Components and Teacher–Student Classroom Interaction Quality." *Prevention Science* 18, no. 2 (2017): 193–203. https://doi.org/10.1007/s11121-016-0743-3.

Adams, Catherine, Patti Pente, Gillian Lemermeyer, and Geoffrey Rockwell. "Ethical Principles for Artificial Intelligence in K-12 Education." *Computers and Education: Artificial Intelligence* 4 (2023): 100131. https://doi.org/10.1016/j.caeai.2023.100131.

Aguilar, Stephen J., William Swartout, Benjamin Nye, Gale Marie Sinatra, Changzhao Wang, and Eric Bui. "Critical Thinking and Ethics in the Age of Generative AI in Education." Preprint, EdArXiv, January 29, 2024. https://doi.org/10.35542/osf.io/7dr9j.

Akgun, Selin, and Christine Greenhow. "Artificial Intelligence in Education: Addressing Ethical Challenges in K-12 Settings." *AI and Ethics* 2, no. 3 (2022): 431–440. https://doi.org/10.1007/s43681-021-00096-7.

Allen, Danielle S. *Education and Equality*. Paperback edition. With Tommie Shelby, Marcelo M. Suárez-Orozco, Michael A. Rebell, and Quiara Alegría Hudes. The University of Chicago Press, 2018.

American Psychological Association. "Health Advisory: Use of Generative AI Chatbots and Wellness Applications for Mental Health." November 2025. https://www.apa.org/topics/artificial-intelligence-machine-learning/health-advisory-chatbots-wellness-apps.

American Psychological Association. "Developing Responsible and Autonomous Learners: A Key to Motivating Students." Accessed November 17, 2025. https://www.apa.org/education-career/k12/learners.

Anderson, Elizabeth S. "What Is the Point of Equality?" *Ethics* 109, no. 2 (1999): 287–337. https://doi.org/10.1086/233897.

Anderson, Elizabeth. "Fair Opportunity in Education: A Democratic Equality Perspective." *Ethics* 117, no. 4 (2007): 595–622. https://doi.org/10.1086/518806.

Andoh, Efuah. "Many Teens Are Turning to AI Chatbots for Friendship and Emotional Support." *Monitor on Psychology*, October 1, 2025.

Apple, Michael W. *Education and Power*. 2nd ed. Reprinted. Routledge, 2009.

Aristoteles, and Jonathan Barnes. *The Nicomachean Ethics*. Further revised edition, edited by Hugh Tredennick. Penguin Classics. Penguin Books, 2004.

ASCL Editor. "AI's 'Black Box' Problem." *American Society of Comparative Law*, September 29, 2021. https://ascl.org/ais-black-box-problem/.

Ashman, Helen, Tim Brailsford, Alexandra I. Cristea, et al. "The Ethical and Social Implications of Personalization Technologies for E-Learning." *Information & Management* 51, no. 6 (2014): 819–832. https://doi.org/10.1016/j.im.2014.04.003.

Au, Wayne. *Unequal by Design: High-Stakes Testing and the Standardization of Inequality*. Second edition. Critical Social Thought. Routledge, 2022. https://doi.org/10.4324/9781003005179.

Autor, David, David A. Mindell, and Elisabeth B Reynolds. *The Work of the Future: Building Better Jobs in an Age of Intelligent Machines*. MIT Press, 2022.

Baker, Ryan S., and Aaron Hawn. "Algorithmic Bias in Education." *International Journal of Artificial Intelligence in Education* 32, no. 4 (2022): 1052–1092. https://doi.org/10.1007/s40593-021-00285-9.

Balaskas, Stefanos, Ioanna Yfantidou, Theofanis Nikolopoulos, and Kyriakos Komis. "The Psychology of EdTech Nudging: Persuasion, Cognitive Load, and Intrinsic Motivation." *European Journal of Investigation in Health, Psychology and Education* 15, no. 9 (2025): 179. https://doi.org/10.3390/ejihpe15090179.

Barnes, Megan. "Cognitive Neuroscience, Educational Technology, and Ethics: Ethical Considerations on the Adoption of Educational Technology Using Cognitive Neuroscience." Paper presented at the Society for Information Technology and Teacher Education (SITE) Conference 2024, Las Vegas, NV, March 2024. https://academicexperts.org/conf/site/2024/papers/63115/share/

Barnes, Megan. "Soft Systems Analysis: Digital Tool Selection in K–12 Classrooms." Paper presented at the University of North Texas Education Research Exchange 2024, Denton, TX, September 2024.

Barreda-Ángeles, Miguel, Sophie Horneber, and Tilo Hartmann. "Easily Applicable Social Virtual Reality and Social Presence in Online Higher Education during the Covid-19 Pandemic: A Qualitative Study." *Computers & Education: X Reality* 2 (2023): 100024. https://doi.org/10.1016/j.cexr.2023.100024.

Batanero, Monica D., and Ellie R. Austin. "Microsoft PowerPoint - Part II - Conducting Title IX Investigations." December 9, 2019. https://sclscal.org/wp-content/uploads/2020/10/FINAL-MDB-ERA-12-09-19-Title-IX-Part-II-Conducting-TIX-Investigations-K-12-COMPLETE.pdf.

Bates, A. W. (Tony). "8.3 Ease of Use." In *Teaching in a Digital Age*. Tony Bates Associates Ltd, 2015. https://opentextbc.ca/teachinginadigitalage/chapter/9-3-the-sections-model-ease-of-use/.

BBC. "'Degree Inflation': How the Four-Year Degree Became Required." January 28, 2021. https://www.bbc.com/worklife/article/20210126-degree-inflation-how-the-four-year-degree-became-required.

Beach, Josh M. "Why We Can't Measure What Matters Most in Education." *New England Board of Higher Education*, January 11, 2022. https://nebhe.org/journal/why-we-cant-measure-what-matters-most-in-education/.

Beauchamp, Tom L, and James F. Childress. *Principles of Biomedical Ethics*. Oxford University Press, 2013.

Bender, Emily M., Timnit Gebru, Angelina McMillan-Major, and Shmargaret Shmitchell. "On the Dangers of Stochastic Parrots: Can Language Models Be Too Big?" *Proceedings of the 2021 ACM Conference on Fairness, Accountability, and Transparency* (New York, NY, USA), FAccT '21, Association for Computing Machinery, March 1, 2021, 610–623. https://doi.org/10.1145/3442188.3445922.

Berlin, Isaiah. *Four Essays on Liberty*. Oxford University Press, 1989.

Bernal, Raquel. "Education Can Help Prepare Learners for Tomorrow's Demands." World Economic Forum, January 17, 2025. https://www.weforum.org/stories/2025/01/future-of-education-and-skills/.

Biesta, Gert. "What Is Education for? On Good Education, Teacher Judgement, and Educational Professionalism." *European Journal of Education* 50, no. 1 (2015): 75–87. https://doi.org/10.1111/ejed.12109.

Binns, Reuben, and Michael Veale. "Is That Your Final Decision? Multi-Stage Profiling, Selective Effects, and Article 22 of the GDPR." *International Data Privacy Law* 11, no. 4 (2021): 319–332. https://doi.org/10.1093/idpl/ipab020.

Birch, Sondra H., and Gary W. Ladd. "The Teacher-Child Relationship and Children's Early School Adjustment." *Journal of School Psychology* 35, no. 1 (1997): 61–79. https://doi.org/10.1016/S0022-4405(96)00029-5.

Bird, Kelli A., Benjamin L. Castleman, and Yifeng Song. "Are Algorithms Biased in Education? Exploring Racial Bias in Predicting Community College Student Success." *Journal of Policy Analysis and Management* 44, no. 2 (2025): 379–402. https://doi.org/10.1002/pam.22569.

Blouin, Lou. "AI's Mysterious 'Black Box' Problem, Explained | University of Michigan-Dearborn." *Dearbon News*, March 6, 2023. https://umdearborn.edu/news/ais-mysterious-black-box-problem-explained.

Blum, Susan D. *Ungrading: Why Rating Students Undermines Learning (and What to Do Instead)*. First edition. Teaching and Learning in Higher Education. West Virginia University Press, 2020.

Blum, Susan D. *Schoolishness: Alienated Education and the Quest for Authentic, Joyful Learning*. Cornell University Press, 2024.

Boateng, Obed, and Bright Boateng. "Algorithmic Bias in Educational Systems: Examining the Impact of AI-Driven Decision Making in Modern Education." *World Journal of Advanced Research and Reviews* 25, no. 1 (2025): 2012–2017. https://doi.org/10.30574/wjarr.2025.25.1.0253.

Bolón-Canedo, Verónica, Laura Morán-Fernández, Brais Cancela, and Amparo Alonso-Betanzos. "A Review of Green Artificial Intelligence: Towards a More Sustainable Future." *Neurocomputing* 599 (September 2024): 128096. https://doi.org/10.1016/j.neucom.2024.128096.

Boninger, Faith, and T. Philip Nichols. *Fit for Purpose? How Today's Commercial Digital Platforms Subvert Key Goals of Public Education*. National Education Policy Center, 2025.

Brackett, Marc. *Permission to Feel: Unlock the Power of Emotions to Help Yourself and Your Children Thrive*. Quercus Publishing, 2021.

Brake, Elizabeth, and Joseph Millum. "Parenthood and Procreation." In *The Stanford Encyclopedia of Philosophy*, Winter 2025, edited by Edward N. Zalta and Uri Nodelman. Metaphysics Research Lab, Stanford University, 2025. https://plato.stanford.edu/archives/win2025/entries/parenthood/.

Brighouse, Harry. *On Education. Thinking in Action*. Routledge, 2006.

Brighouse, Harry, and Adam Swift. "Parents' Rights and the Value of the Family." *Ethics* 117, no. 1 (2006): 80–108. https://doi.org/10.1086/508034.

Brighouse, Harry, and Adam Swift. "Legitimate Parental Partiality." *Philosophy & Public Affairs* 37, no. 1 (2009): 43–80. https://doi.org/10.1111/j.1088-4963.2008.01145.x.

Brighouse, Harry, Helen F. Ladd, Susanna Loeb, and Adam Swift. *Educational Goods: Values, Evidence, and Decision-Making*. University of Chicago Press, 2018. https://press.uchicago.edu/ucp/books/book/chicago/E/bo27256234.html.

Brighouse, Harry, Helen Ladd, Susanna Loeb, and Adam Swift. "Good Education Policy Making: Data-Informed but Values-Driven." *Phi Delta Kappan* 100, no. 4 (2018): 36–39. https://doi.org/10.1177/0031721718815671.

Bryk, Anthony, and Barbara Schneider. *Trust in Schools: A Core Resource for Improvement*. Russell Sage Foundation, 2002.

Bryk, Anthony S., Louis M. Gomez, Alicia Grunow, and Paul G. LeMahieu. *Learning to Improve: How America's Schools Can Get Better at Getting Better*. Harvard Education Press, 2015.

Busiek, Julia. "Three Fixes for AI's Bias Problem." *The University of California*, March 21, 2024. https://www.universityofcalifornia.edu/news/three-fixes-ais-bias-problem.

Calabresi, Guido, and Philip Bobbitt. *Tragic Choices*. W. W. Norton & Company, 1978.

Callahan, Raymond E. *Education and the Cult of Efficiency: A Study of the Social Forces That Have Shaped the Administration of the Public Schools*. Paperback ed., [Nachdr.]. University of Chicago Press, 2007.

Carroll, Aaron E., Linda A. DiMeglio, Stephanie Stein, and David G. Marrero. "Using a Cell Phone-Based Glucose Monitoring System for Adolescent Diabetes Management." *The Diabetes Educator* 37, no. 1 (2011): 59–66. https://doi.org/10.1177/0145721710387163.

Center for Democracy & Technology. "State Student Privacy Law Compendium." October 2016. https://cdt.org/wp-content/uploads/2016/10/CDT-Stu-Priv-Compendium-FNL.pdf.

Center for Democracy & Technology. *State Student Privacy Laws – Public Interest Privacy Center*. June 24, 2025. https://publicinterestprivacy.org/resources/state-student-privacy/.

Chai, Fangyuan, Jiajia Ma, Yi Wang, Jun Zhu, and Tingting Han. "Grading by AI Makes Me Feel Fairer? How Different Evaluators Affect College Students' Perception of Fairness." *Frontiers in Psychology* 15 (February 2024): 1221177. https://doi.org/10.3389/fpsyg.2024.1221177.

Chandra, Bilva, and Todd Helmus. *Generative Artificial Intelligence Threats to Information Integrity and Potential Policy Responses*. RAND Corporation, 2024. https://doi.org/10.7249/PEA3089-1.

Chang, Michael Alan, Mike Tissenbaum, Thomas M. Philip, and Sidney K. D'Mello. "Co-Designing AI with Youth Partners: Enabling Ideal Classroom Relationships through a Novel AI Relational Privacy Ethical Framework." *Computers and Education: Artificial Intelligence* 8 (June 2025): 100364. https://doi.org/10.1016/j.caeai.2025.100364.

Chapman, Robert, and Havi Carel. "Neurodiversity, Epistemic Injustice, and the Good Human Life." *Journal of Social Philosophy* 53, no. 4 (2022): 614–631. https://doi.org/10.1111/josp.12456.

Chen, Ruishi, Victor R. Lee, and Monica G. Lee. "A Cross-Sectional Look at Teacher Reactions, Worries, and Professional Development Needs Related to Generative AI in an Urban School District." *Education and Information Technologies* 30, no. 11 (2025): 16045–16082. https://doi.org/10.1007/s10639-025-13350-w.

Chew, Stephen L. "Student Engagement Is Not Student Learning." *The Teaching Professor*, November 14, 2022. https://www.teachingprofessor.com/topics/student-learning/student-engagement-is-not-student-learning/.

Chisom, Onyebuchi N., Preye W. Biu, Aniekan A. Umoh, Bartholomew O. Obaedo, Abimbola O. Adegbite, and Ayodeji Abatan. "Reviewing the Role of AI in Environmental Monitoring and Conservation: A Data-Driven Revolution for Our Planet." *World Journal of Advanced Research and Reviews* 21, no. 1 (2024): 161–171. https://doi.org/10.30574/wjarr.2024.21.1.2720.

Chory-Assad, Rebecca M., and Michelle L. Paulsel. "Classroom Justice: Student Aggression and Resistance as Reactions to Perceived Unfairness." *Communication Education* 53, no. 3 (2004): 253–273. https://doi.org/10.1080/0363452042000265189.

Chouldechova, Alexandra. "Fair Prediction with Disparate Impact: A Study of Bias in Recidivism Prediction Instruments." *Big Data* 5, no. 2 (2017): 153–163. https://doi.org/10.1089/big.2016.0047.

Common Sense Media. "Our K-12 Digital Citizenship Curriculum." July 21, 2016. https://www.bgcsedu.org/media/s2udjyqm/csmdigitalliteracycurriculum.pdf.

Communications Workers of America. "Ghost Workers in the AI Machine." July 2025. https://cwa-union.org/ghost-workers-ai-machine.

Congressional Research Service. "What Is Disparate-Impact Discrimination?" Legislation. July 9, 2025. https://www.congress.gov/crs-product/IF13057.

Corbett, Brooklyn J., and Jason M. Tangen. "AI Tutors vs. Tenacious Myths: Evidence from Personalised Dialogue Interventions in Education." *Computers in Human Behavior* 175 (February 2026): 108828. https://doi.org/10.1016/j.chb.2025.108828.

Coşkun, Başak, Sevda Katıtaş, and Barış Eriçok. "Emotional Labor, Job-Related Stress, and Burnout in School Leadership: Insights from Educational Administrators." *BMC Psychology* 13, no. 1 (2025): 818. https://doi.org/10.1186/s40359-025-02987-4.

Cossio, Samantha, Stefania Chiappinotto, Sara Dentice, et al. "Cybersickness and Discomfort from Head-Mounted Displays Delivering Fully Immersive Virtual Reality: A Systematic Review." *Nurse Education in Practice* 85 (May 2025): 104376. https://doi.org/10.1016/j.nepr.2025.104376.

Cuban, Larry. *Oversold and Underused: Computers in the Classroom*. Harvard University Press, 2001.

Cuban, Larry. *Confessions of a School Reformer*. Harvard Education Press, 2021.

Deci, Edward L., Richard Koestner, and Richard M. Ryan. "A Meta-Analytic Review of Experiments Examining the Effects of Extrinsic Rewards on Intrinsic Motivation." *Psychological Bulletin* 125, no. 6 (1999): 627–668; discussion 692–700. https://doi.org/10.1037/0033-2909.125.6.627.

Dewey, John. *Democracy and Education - An Introduction to the Philosophy of Education*. Foreman Press, 2011.

Dewey, John. *Experience and Education*. Free Press, 2015.

Dexter, Phillips R., Taslikyah Stewart-Fox, Simone Phillips, Mischka Griffith, and Jimmy Bhojedat. "Distributed Leadership in Education: A Systematic Review of Its Role in Fostering Innovative Practices and Enhancing School Performance." *International Journal of Science and Research (IJSR)* 12, no. 11 (2023): 2083–2089. https://doi.org/10.21275/SR231128014118.

Dienlin, Tobias, and Niklas Johannes. "The Impact of Digital Technology Use on Adolescent Well-Being." *Dialogues in Clinical Neuroscience* 22, no. 2 (2020): 135–142. https://doi.org/10.31887/DCNS.2020.22.2/tdienlin.

Dietrich, Frank. "Critical Reflection and the Limits of Parental Authority." *Journal of Applied Philosophy* 39, no. 4 (2022): 562–580. https://doi.org/10.1111/japp.12555.

Diliberti, Melissa K., Lisa Chu, Lydia R. Rainey, Samantha E. DiNicola, Robin J. Lake, and Heather L. Schwartz. *Chronic Absenteeism Still a Struggle in 2024–2025: Selected Findings from the American School District Panel and the American Youth Panel.* 2025. https://www.rand.org/pubs/research_reports/RRA956-34.html.

Doan, Sy, and Julia Kaufman. "What Role Do States Play in Selecting K-12 Textbooks?" *NASBE – National Association of State Boards of Education* 24, no. 1 (2024): n1. https://www.nasbe.org/what-role-do-states-play-in-selecting-k-12-textbooks/.

Douglas, Thomas. "Parental Partiality and the Intergenerational Transmission of Advantage." *Philosophical Studies* 172, no. 10 (2015): 2735–2756. https://doi.org/10.1007/s11098-015-0442-0.

DPM. "What Are 8 Data Subject Rights According to the GDPR." *Data Privacy Manager*, October 16, 2022. https://dataprivacymanager.net/what-are-data-subject-rights-according-to-the-gdpr/.

De Dreu, Carsten K. W. and Laurie R. Weingart. "Task Versus Relationship Conflict, Team Performance, and Team Member Satisfaction: A Meta-Analysis." *Journal of Applied Psychology* 88, no. 4 (2003): 741–749. https://doi.org/10.1037/0021-9010.88.4.741.

Drimmer, Sonja. "'The Printing Press Democratized Knowledge': When Slogans Masquerade as History." September 10, 2025. http://sonjadrimmer.com/blog-1/2025/9/10/the-printing-press-democratized-knowledge-a-slogans-masquerading-as-history.

Eaton, Lance. "Recent Talk: Student EngAIgement." Substack newsletter. *AI + Education = Simplified*, November 18, 2023. https://aiedusimplified.substack.com/p/recent-talk-student-engaigement.

Edmondson, Amy. "Psychological Safety and Learning Behavior in Work Teams." *Administrative Science Quarterly* 44, no. 2 (1999): 350–383. https://doi.org/10.2307/2666999.

Effing, Robin, and Michael Hinz. "Are Children Ready for the Metaverse? The Minefield of Virtual Participation in Digital Social Spaces with Harmful Content and Behavior." In *Electronic Participation*, edited by Marius Rohde Johannessen, Csaba Csáki, Lieselot Danneels, et al., vol. 14891. Lecture Notes in Computer Science. Springer Nature Switzerland, 2024. https://doi.org/10.1007/978-3-031-70804-6_1.

Eisenstein, Elizabeth. *The Printing Press as an Agent of Change: Communications and Cultural Transformations in Early-Modern Europe.* Cambridge University Press, 1991.

Emanuel, Ezekiel J. "MOOCs Taken by Educated Few." *Nature* 503, no. 7476 (2013): 342. https://doi.org/10.1038/503342a.

Epley, Nicholas, and Amit Kumar. "How to Design an Ethical Organization." *Harvard Business Review*, May 2019. https://hbr.org/2019/05/how-to-design-an-ethical-organization.

Erikson, Erik H. *Childhood and Society*. 1st ed. W. W. Norton & Company, Incorporated, 1993.
Eskelson, Tyrel C. "States, Institutions, and Literacy Rates in Early-Modern Western Europe." *Journal of Education and Learning* 10, no. 2 (2021): 109. https://doi.org/10.5539/jel.v10n2p109.
Eubanks, Virginia. *Automating Inequality: How High-Tech Tools Profile, Police, and Punish the Poor*. New York, 2018.
European Commission. What rules apply if my organisation transfers data outside the EU? Last modified unknown. Accessed November 1st, 2025. https://commission.europa.eu/law/law-topic/data-protection/rules-business-and-organisations/obligations/what-rules-apply-if-my-organisation-transfers-data-outside-eu_en
Feathers, Todd. "Flawed Algorithms Are Grading Millions of Students' Essays." *VICE*, August 20, 2019. https://www.vice.com/en/article/flawed-algorithms-are-grading-millions-of-students-essays/.
Feinberg, Joel. "The Child's Right to an Open Future." In *Whose Child? Children's Rights, Parental Authority, and State Power*, edited by William Aiken and Hugh LaFollette. Littlefield Adams, 1980.
Feinberg, Joel. "The Child's Right to an Open Future." In *Justice, Politics, and the Family*. Routledge, 2014.
Fishkin, Joseph. "*Bottlenecks: A New Theory of Equal Opportunity*." Oxford University Press, 2014.
Fleming, James. "Participation vs. Engagement in Education." *Renaissance*, June 7, 2018. https://www.renaissance.com/2018/06/07/blog-dont-confuse-participation-and-engagement-in-middle-and-high-school/.
Freire, Paulo. *Pedagogy of Hope: Reliving Pedagogy of the Oppressed*. Bloomsbury Academic, 2021.
Freire, Paulo, and Donaldo P. Macedo. *Pedagogy of the Oppressed: 30th Anniversary Edition*. 30th anniversary edition. Translated by Myra Bergman Ramos. Bloomsbury Publishing, 2000.
Fricker, Miranda. *Epistemic Injustice: Power and the Ethics of Knowing*. Reprinted. Oxford University Press, 2007a.
FTC. "Children's Online Privacy Protection Rule ('COPPA')." Federal Trade Commission, July 25, 2013. https://www.ftc.gov/legal-library/browse/rules/childrens-online-privacy-protection-rule-coppa.
Furze, Leon. *Practical AI Strategies: Engaging with Generative AI in Education,* 1st ed. Amba Press, 2024. https://www.amazon.com/Practical-AI-Strategies-Generative-Education/dp/1923116355/.
Ganapini, Marianna B., and Enrico Panai. "AI-Enhanced Nudging: A Risk-Factors Analysis." *American Philosophical Quarterly* 62, no. 3 (2025): 263–278. https://doi.org/10.5406/21521123.62.3.05.
Garcia, Adan. "It's Easy to Mistake Engagement for Learning. Here's How I Learned the Difference." *Leading Educators*, October 27, 2020. https://leadingeducators.org/blog/its-easy-to-mistake-engagement-for-learning-heres-how-i-learned-the-difference/.
García-López, Iván M., and Laura Trujillo-Liñán. "Ethical and Regulatory Challenges of Generative AI in Education: A Systematic Review." *Frontiers in Education* 10 (June 2025): 1565938. https://doi.org/10.3389/feduc.2025.1565938.
Gary, Mercer. "Relational Approaches in Bioethics: A Guide to Their Differences." *Bioethics* 37, no. 8 (2023): 733–740. https://doi.org/10.1111/bioe.13200.

Georgieff, Alexandre. "Artificial Intelligence and Wage Inequality." *OECD Artificial Intelligence Papers*, ahead of print, OECD Publishing, April 9, 2024. https://doi.org/10.1787/bf98a45c-en.

Geron, Tatiana. "'Creating Justice in My Practice': Supporting Teachers' Values Through Professional Development in Educational Ethics." *Teachers College Record: The Voice of Scholarship in Education* 127, no. 3 (2025): 40–66. https://doi.org/10.1177/01614681251336676.

Geron, Tatiana, and Meira Levinson. "The Ethics of World-Building in Normative Case Studies." *Educational Theory* 74, no. 3 (2024): 293–300. https://doi.org/10.1111/edth.12612.

Ghai, Bhavya, and Klaus Mueller. "D-BIAS: A Causality-Based Human-in-the-Loop System for Tackling Algorithmic Bias." arXiv:2208.05126. Preprint, arXiv, August 10, 2022. https://doi.org/10.48550/arXiv.2208.05126.

Gheaus, Anca. "Children's Vulnerability and Legitimate Authority Over Children." *Journal of Applied Philosophy* 35 (2018): 60–75.

Gilligan, Carol. *In a Different Voice: Psychological Theory and Women's Development*. 38. print. Harvard University Press, 2003.

Gilmore, Linda. "Understanding and Supporting Student Motivation for Learning." In *Positive Schooling and Child Development: International Perspectives*, edited by Sibnath Deb. Springer, 2018. https://doi.org/10.1007/978-981-13-0077-6_4.

González, Javier López, Francesca Casalini, and Juan Porras. *A Preliminary Mapping of Data Localisation Measures*. OECD Trade Policy Papers No. 262. Vol. 262. OECD Trade Policy Papers. 2022. https://doi.org/10.1787/c5ca3fed-en.

Gordon, Nora. "Block Granting Federal Education Funds Comes with Trade-Offs." *Brookings Institution*, July 15, 2025. https://www.brookings.edu/articles/block-granting-federal-education-funds-comes-with-trade-offs/.

Gordon, Hava Rachel, Kate Willink, and Keeley Hunter. "Invisible Labor and the Associate Professor: Identity and Workload Inequity." *Journal of Diversity in Higher Education* 17, no. 3 (2024): 285–296. https://doi.org/10.1037/dhe0000414.

Goswami, Gaurav. *AI Echo Chambers: How Algorithms Shape Reality, Influence Democracy, and Fuel Misinformation*. February 26, 2025. https://www.authorea.com/doi/full/10.36227/techrxiv.174059950.03385147/v1?commit=874ec27e1203a6a72bc26f0a7af8ff78f7dd4ee0.

Goulas, Sofoklis. "Making AI Work for Schools." *Brookings Institution*, July 31, 2025. https://www.brookings.edu/articles/making-ai-work-for-schools/.

Grant, David G., Jeff Behrends, and John Basl. "What We Owe to Decision-Subjects: Beyond Transparency and Explanation in Automated Decision-Making." *Philosophical Studies* 182, no. 1 (2025): 55–85. https://doi.org/10.1007/s11098-023-02013-6.

Gulya, Jason. "The Age of Chat: Education and the Rise of No-Code Chatbots." In *Teaching and Learning in the Age of Generative AI*. Routledge, 2025.

Gupta, Vanita. "Office of Public Affairs | Ensuring Equal Educational Opportunities for English Learner Students." July 1, 2015. https://www.justice.gov/archives/opa/blog/ensuring-equal-educational-opportunities-english-learner-students.

Gutmann, Amy. "Children, Paternalism, and Education: A Liberal Argument." *Philosophy & Public Affairs* 9, no. 4 (1980): 338–358.

Gutmann, Amy. *Democratic Education*. Princeton Paperbacks. Princeton University Press, 1999.

Gutterman, Lucas. "'Chromebook Churn' Report Highlights Problems of Short-Lived Laptops in Schools." *U.S. PIRG Education Fund*, April 18, 2023. https://pirg.org/edfund/resources/chromebook-churn-report-highlights-problems-of-short-lived-laptops-in-schools/.

Habermas, Jürgen. *Justification and Application: Remarks on Discourse Ethics*. Wiley. Wiley.Com, 1993. https://www.wiley.com/en-us/Justification+and+Application%3A+Remarks+on+Discourse+Ethics-p-9780745616391.

Halat, Rasha, and Lina Kahir Rahme. *Addressing Inequities in Education: AI as a Double-Edged Sword (Part II) – Middle East Professional Learning Institute*. June 30, 2024. https://mepli.gse.harvard.edu/our-fellows-at-work/addressing-inequities-in-education-ai-as-a-double-edged-sword-2/.

Hall, Rachel. "Heavy ChatGPT Users Tend to Be More Lonely, Suggests Research." Technology. *The Guardian*, March 25, 2025. https://www.theguardian.com/technology/2025/mar/25/heavy-chatgpt-users-tend-to-be-more-lonely-suggests-research.

Hanna, Alex, and Emily M. Bender. "The Hidden Labor That Makes AI Work." Rest of World, July 1, 2025. https://restofworld.org/2025/the-ai-con-book-invisible-labor/.

Hanus, Michael D., and Jesse Fox. "Assessing the Effects of Gamification in the Classroom: A Longitudinal Study on Intrinsic Motivation, Social Comparison, Satisfaction, Effort, and Academic Performance." *Computers & Education* 80 (January 2015): 152–161. https://doi.org/10.1016/j.compedu.2014.08.019.

Harvard. "Mission, Vision, & History | Harvard." n.d. https://college.harvard.edu/about/mission-vision-history.

Harvard Graduate School of Education. "How to Make Mission Matter at Your School | Harvard Graduate School of Education." September 8, 2022. https://www.gse.harvard.edu/ideas/usable-knowledge/22/09/how-make-mission-matter-your-school.

Hendrick, Carl, and Jim Heal. "Just Because They're Engaged, It Doesn't Mean They're Learning." *My College*, September 14, 2020. https://my.chartered.college/impact_article/just-because-theyre-engaged-it-doesnt-mean-theyre-learning/.

Hendrie, Mary. "Cellphones in Schools: Addiction, Distraction, or Teaching Tool?" Technology, Classroom Technology. *Education Week*, June 21, 2024. https://www.edweek.org/technology/opinion-cellphones-in-schools-addiction-distraction-or-teaching-tool/2024/06.

Herbener, Arthur B., and Malene F. Damholdt. "Are Lonely Youngsters Turning to Chatbots for Companionship? The Relationship Between Chatbot Usage and Social Connectedness in Danish High-School Students." *International Journal of Human-Computer Studies* 196 (February 2025): 103409. https://doi.org/10.1016/j.ijhcs.2024.103409.

Hernandez, Stephen J. "Collaboration in Special Education: Its History, Evolution, and Critical Factors Necessary for Successful Implementation." *US-China Education Review*, June 2013.

Herold, Benjamin. "Ed-Tech Supporters Promise Innovations That Can Transform Schools. Teachers Not Seeing Impact." Technology, Classroom Technology. *Education Week*, April 24, 2019. https://www.edweek.org/technology/ed-tech-supporters-promise-innovations-that-can-transform-schools-teachers-not-seeing-impact/2019/04.

Herold, Benjamin. "All That Ed Tech Schools Bought During the Pandemic Won't Improve Equity. Here's Why." *Education Week*, November 28, 2022.

Herold, Benjamin, and Michelle R. Davis. "'De-Identifying' Student Data Is Key for Protecting Privacy." Technology, Privacy & Security. *Education Week*, August 26, 2015. https://www.edweek.org/technology/de-identifying-student-data-is-key-for-protecting-privacy/2015/08.

Hinduja, Sameer, and Justin W. Patchin. "Metaverse Risks and Harms Among US Youth: Experiences, Gender Differences, and Prevention and Response Measures." *New Media & Society*, October 12, 2024, 14614448241284413. https://doi.org/10.1177/14614448241284413.

Hofmann, Valentin, Pratyusha R. Kalluri, Dan Jurafsky, and Sharese King. "AI Generates Covertly Racist Decisions About People Based on Their Dialect." *Nature* 633, no. 8028 (2024): 147–154. https://doi.org/10.1038/s41586-024-07856-5.

Holland, Beth, and Nate Kellogg. "How Phones Can Facilitate Distance Learning." Edutopia, May 15, 2020. https://www.edutopia.org/article/how-phones-can-facilitate-distance-learning/.

hooks, bell. *Teaching to Transgress: Education as the Practice of Freedom*. Routledge, Taylor & Francis Group, 1994.

Horowitz, Juliana M., Kim Parker, and Luona Lin. "How Teachers Manage Their Workload." *Pew Research Center*, April 4, 2024. https://www.pewresearch.org/social-trends/2024/04/04/how-teachers-manage-their-workload/.

IBM. "What Is Data Residency? | IBM." October 21, 2025. https://www.ibm.com/think/topics/data-residency.

ICO. "A Guide to Lawful Basis." ICO, December 2, 2024. https://ico.org.uk/for-organisations/uk-gdpr-guidance-and-resources/lawful-basis/a-guide-to-lawful-basis/.

ICO. "What Is Valid Consent?" ICO, September 22, 2025. https://ico.org.uk/for-organisations/uk-gdpr-guidance-and-resources/lawful-basis/consent/what-is-valid-consent/.

Idowu, Jamiu A. "Debiasing Education Algorithms." *International Journal of Artificial Intelligence in Education* 34, no. 4 (2024): 1510–1540. https://doi.org/10.1007/s40593-023-00389-4.

Idrees, Blal, Hugues Sampasa-Kanyinga, Hayley A. Hamilton, and Jean P. Chaput. "Associations Between Problem Technology Use, Life Stress, and Self-Esteem Among High School Students." *BMC Public Health* 24, no. 1 (2024): 492. https://doi.org/10.1186/s12889-024-17963-7.

Information Technology Industry Council. "VPAT - Information Technology Industry Council." February 2013. https://www.itic.org/policy/accessibility/vpat.

Institute of Education Sciences. *Total Cost of Ownership*. 2014. https://nces.ed.gov/programs/slds/pdf/TotalCostofOwnership.pdf

Ireh Maduakolam. "Budgeting and Funding School Technology: Essential Considerations." September 2010. https://files.eric.ed.gov/fulltext/EJ914657.pdf.

Jacob, Brian A., and Cristina Stanojevich. "Rewiring the Classroom: How the COVID-19 Pandemic Transformed K-12 Education." *Brookings*, August 26, 2024. https://www.brookings.edu/articles/rewiring-the-classroom-how-the-covid-19-pandemic-transformed-k-12-education/.

Jaikla, Paiboon, and Araya Piyakun. "Teachers' Emotional Labor: A Systematic Review." *Journal of Education and Learning* 14, no. 2 (2024): 159. https://doi.org/10.5539/jel.v14n2p159.

James, Kirsten. "Semiconductor Manufacturing and Big Tech's Water Challenge." World Economic Forum, July 19, 2024. https://www.weforum.org/stories/2024/07/the-water-challenge-for-semiconductor-manufacturing-and-big-tech-what-needs-to-be-done/.

Jeffries, Adrianne. "Machine Learning Is Racist Because the Internet Is Racist." The Outline, April 2017. https://theoutline.com/post/1439/machine-learning-is-racist-because-the-internet-is-racist.

Jencks, Christopher. "Whom Must We Treat Equally for Educational Opportunity to Be Equal?" *Ethics* 98, no. 3 (1988): 518–533. https://doi.org/10.1086/292969.

Johns Hopkins Engineering Online. "Unseen Dangers Lurking in Storing Student Data in the Cloud." *Johns Hopkins Engineering Online*, September 18, 2024. https://ep.jhu.edu/news/cloudy-with-a-chance-of-breach-unseen-dangers-lurking-in-storing-student-data-in-the-cloud/.

Johnson, Paula N. *Using Equity Audits to Assess and Address Opportunity Gaps Across Education.* 2020. https://files.eric.ed.gov/fulltext/ED605706.pdf

Johnson, Harlan R. "Printing and Censorship | Research Starters | EBSCO Research." EBSCO, 2023. https://www.ebsco.com.

Johnson, Robert, and Adam Cureton. "Kant's Moral Philosophy." In *The Stanford Encyclopedia of Philosophy*, Winter 2025, edited by Edward N. Zalta and Uri Nodelman. Metaphysics Research Lab, Stanford University, 2025. https://plato.stanford.edu/archives/win2025/entries/kant-moral/.

Jonker, Alexandra, and Julie Rogers. "What Is Algorithmic Bias? | IBM." IBM, September 20, 2024. https://www.ibm.com/think/topics/algorithmic-bias.

Jonsen, Albert R., and Stephen Toulmin. *The Abuse of Casuistry: A History of Moral Reasoning.* University of California Press, 1989.

Judge, Sharon, Kathleen Puckett, and Burcu Cabuk. "Digital Equity: New Findings from the Early Childhood Longitudinal Study." *Journal of Research on Technology in Education* 36, no. 4 (2004): 383–396. https://doi.org/10.1080/15391523.2004.10782421.

Justice in Schools. "Case Discussion Protocol." Justice in Schools | EdEthics, n.d.. https://www.justiceinschools.org/protocols.

Kannan, Prabha. "How Harmful Are AI's Biases on Diverse Student Populations? | Stanford HAI." *Stanford HAI*, October 3, 2024. https://hai.stanford.edu/news/how-harmful-are-ais-biases-on-diverse-student-populations.

Kaptein, Muel. "Developing and Testing a Measure for the Ethical Culture of Organizations: The Corporate Ethical Virtues Model." *Journal of Organizational Behavior* 29, no. 7 (2008): 923–947. https://doi.org/10.1002/job.520.

Kariou, Anna, Panagiota Koutsimani, Anthony Montgomery, and Olga Lainidi. "Emotional Labor and Burnout Among Teachers: A Systematic Review." *International Journal of Environmental Research and Public Health* 18, no. 23 (2021): 12760. https://doi.org/10.3390/ijerph182312760.

Karran, Alexander J., Patrick Charland, Joé Martineau, et al. "Multi-Stakeholder Perspective on Responsible Artificial Intelligence and Acceptability in Education." arXiv:2402.15027. Preprint, arXiv, February 28, 2024. https://doi.org/10.48550/arXiv.2402.15027.

Kestigian, Aidan. *Democratic Decisions in a Critical Thinking Crisis.* 1st ed. Lexington Books, 2025. https://doi.org/10.5040/9781978748514.

Kharvi, Prakash L. "Understanding the Impact of AI-Generated Deepfakes on Public Opinion, Political Discourse, and Personal Security in Social Media." *IEEE Security & Privacy* 22, no. 04 (2024): 115–122. https://doi.org/10.1109/MSEC.2024.3405963.

Kidron, Baroness, Alexandra Evans, Jenny Afia, et al. *Disrupted Childhood: The Cost of Persuasive Design*. 87589, 2018. https://5rightsfoundation.com/wp-content/uploads/2024/08/5rights_DisruptedChildhood_G.pdf

Kim, Soyeon, and Eunjoo Kim. "Emergence of the Metaverse and Psychiatric Concerns in Children and Adolescents." *Journal of the Korean Academy of Child and Adolescent Psychiatry* 34, no. 4 (2023): 215–221. https://doi.org/10.5765/jkacap.230047.

Kizilcec, René F., Justin Reich, Michael Yeomans, et al. "Scaling up Behavioral Science Interventions in Online Education." *Proceedings of the National Academy of Sciences* 117, no. 26 (2020): 14900–14905. https://doi.org/10.1073/pnas.1921417117.

Klein, Alyson. "Ed Tech Usage Is Up. So Are Parent Privacy Concerns." Technology, Privacy & Security. *Education Week*, November 16, 2021. https://www.edweek.org/technology/ed-tech-usage-is-up-so-are-parent-privacy-concerns/2021/11.

Koenig, Rebecca. "Is There Still Time to Build Equity into Virtual Reality Edtech? - EdSurge News." EdSurge, September 21, 2022. https://www.edsurge.com/news/2022-09-21-is-there-still-time-to-build-equity-into-virtual-reality-edtech.

Kohn, Alfie. "Emphasis on Testing Leads to Sacrifices in Other Areas." *USA Today*, August 21, 2001. https://www.alfiekohn.org/article/emphasis-testing-leads-sacrifices-areas/?print=print.

Kolowich, Steve. "MOOCs Are Largely Reaching Privileged Learners, Survey Finds." *The Chronicle of Higher Education*, November 20, 2013. https://www.chronicle.com/blogs/wiredcampus/moocs-are-reaching-only-privileged-learners-survey-finds.

Kools, Marco, and Louise Stoll. *What Makes a School a Learning Organisation?* OECD Education Working Papers No. 137. Vol. 137. OECD Education Working Papers. 2016. https://doi.org/10.1787/5jlwm62b3bvh-en.

Kraut, Richard. "Aristotle's Ethics." In *The Stanford Encyclopedia of Philosophy*, Fall 2022, edited by Edward N. Zalta and Uri Nodelman. Metaphysics Research Lab, Stanford University, 2022. https://plato.stanford.edu/archives/fall2022/entries/aristotle-ethics/.

Krumova, Milena, and Ashish Kataria. "Education Cybersecurity: Learning Management System, Data and Tools." *Proceedings of the 16th International Conference on Theory and Practice of Electronic Governance*, ACM, September 26, 2023, 318–323. https://doi.org/10.1145/3614321.3614364.

Kucirkova, Natalia I. "Opinion: AI Must Heed Benefits, Drawbacks of Personalized Learning." GovTech, June 16, 2023. https://www.govtech.com/education/k-12/opinion-ai-must-heed-benefits-drawbacks-of-personalized-learning.

Kulowiec, Greg. "Cell Phones as Classroom Tools." TeachingHistory.Org, 2018. https://teachinghistory.org/digital-classroom/tech-for-teachers/25273.

Kuo, Tsai C., Chien Y. Kuo, and Liang W. Chen. "Assessing Environmental Impacts of Nanoscale Semi-Conductor Manufacturing from the Life Cycle Assessment Perspective." *Resources, Conservation and Recycling* 182 (July 2022): 106289. https://doi.org/10.1016/j.resconrec.2022.106289.

Labaree, David F. *Someone Has to Fail: The Zero-Sum Game of Public Schooling*. First Harvard University Press paperback edition. Harvard University Press, 2012.

Laestadius, Linnea, Andrea Bishop, Michael Gonzalez, Diana Illenčík, and Celeste Campos-Castillo. "Too Human and Not Human Enough: A Grounded Theory Analysis of Mental Health Harms from Emotional Dependence on the Social Chatbot Replika." *New Media & Society* 26, no. 10 (2024): 5923–5941. https://doi.org/10.1177/14614448221142007.

Laird, Elizabeth, Maddy Dwyer, and Hannah Quay-de la Vallee. "Hand in Hand: Schools' Embrace of AI Connected to Increased Risks to Students." Center for Democracy & Technology, October 2025. https://cdt.org/wp-content/uploads/2025/10/FINAL-CDT-2025-Hand-in-Hand-Polling-100225-accessible.pdf.

Lake, Robin. "AI Is Coming to U.S. Classrooms, but Who Will Benefit?" *Center on Reinventing Public Education*, May 16, 2024. https://crpe.org/ai-is-coming-to-u-s-classrooms-but-who-will-benefit/.

Langreo, Lauraine, and Kaylee Domzalski. "Cellphone Policies in Schools, Explained." *Education Week*, May 21, 2024. https://www.edweek.org/technology/video-cellphone-policies-in-schools-explained/2024/05.

Lareau, Annette. *Unequal Childhoods: Class, Race, and Family Life, 2nd Edition with an Update a Decade Later.* University of California Press, 2011.

Latta, Laura. "Equity and Standardization: Are They Compatible?" *Impact Tulsa*, January 3, 2020. https://impacttulsa.org/2020/01/02/impacttulsa-equity-in-education-defining-equity-2/.

Lazovich, Tomo. "ChatGPT's Hidden Bias and the Danger of Filter Bubbles in LLMs | Institute for Experiential AI." The Institute for Experiential AI. March 1, 2024. https://ai.northeastern.edu/news/chatgpts-hidden-bias-and-the-danger-of-filter-bubbles-in-llms.

Lee, Nicol T. "Bridging Digital Divides Between Schools and Communities." *Brookings Institution*, March 2, 2020. https://www.brookings.edu/articles/bridging-digital-divides-between-schools-and-communities/.

Lee, Carol D., and Alessandra E. Ward. *The Role of SEL in Improving Literacy Development Introductory Brief.* Collaborative for Academic, Social, and Emotional Learning, 2024. https://casel.org/role-of-sel-in-improving-literacy-development-introductory-brief/.

Lee, Victor R., Denise Pope, Sarah Miles, and Rosalía C. Zárate. "Cheating in the Age of Generative AI: A High School Survey Study of Cheating Behaviors Before and After the Release of ChatGPT." *Computers and Education: Artificial Intelligence* 7 (December 2024): 100253. https://doi.org/10.1016/j.caeai.2024.100253.

Lefstein, Adam, and Hamutal Perath. "Empowering Teacher Voices in an Education Policy Discussion: Paradoxes of Representation." *Teaching and Teacher Education* 38 (February 2014): 33–43. https://doi.org/10.1016/j.tate.2013.11.001.

Lepper, Mark R., David Greene, and Richard E. Nisbett. "Undermining Children's Intrinsic Interest with Extrinsic Reward: A Test of the 'Overjustification' Hypothesis." *Journal of Personality and Social Psychology* (US) 28, no. 1 (1973): 129–137. https://doi.org/10.1037/h0035519.

Levinson, Meira. *The Demands of Liberal Education.* Oxford University Press, 1999.

Levinson, Meira. *No Citizen Left Behind.* First paperback edition. Harvard University Press, 2014.

Levinson, Meira. "Moral Injury and the Ethics of Educational Injustice." *Harvard Educational Review* 85, no. 2 (2015): 203–228. https://doi.org/10.17763/0017-8055.85.2.203.

Levinson, Meira. "Theorizing Educational Justice." In *Handbook of Philosophy of Education*. Routledge, 2022.

Levinson, Meira. "We Need a Field of Educational Ethics." *Theory and Research in Education* 21, no. 2 (2023): 197–215. https://doi.org/10.1177/14778785231187193.

Levinson, Meira, and Jacob Fay. *Dilemmas of Educational Ethics: Cases and Commentaries*. Harvard Education Press, 2016.

Levy, Brian. *How Political Contexts Influence Education Systems: Patterns, Constraints, Entry Points*. Research on Improving Systems of Education (RISE), 2022. https://doi.org/10.35489/BSG-RISE-WP_2022/122.

Light, Jennifer. "Rethinking the Digital Divide." *Harvard Educational Review* 71, no. 4 (2001): 709–734. https://doi.org/10.17763/haer.71.4.342x36742j2w4q82.

Lim, Tristan, Swapna Gottipati, and Michelle Cheong. "What Students Really Think: Unpacking AI Ethics in Educational Assessments Through a Triadic Framework." *International Journal of Educational Technology in Higher Education* 22, no. 1 (2025): 56. https://doi.org/10.1186/s41239-025-00556-8.

Lin, Luona, and Kim Parker. "U.S. Workers Are More Worried Than Hopeful About Future AI Use in the Workplace." *Pew Research Center*, February 25, 2025. https://www.pewresearch.org/social-trends/2025/02/25/u-s-workers-are-more-worried-than-hopeful-about-future-ai-use-in-the-workplace/.

Loewus, Liana. "Houston District Settles Lawsuit with Teachers' Union over Value-Added Scores." Teaching & Learning, Teaching Profession. *Education Week*, October 26, 2017. https://www.edweek.org/teaching-learning/houston-district-settles-lawsuit-with-teachers-union-over-value-added-scores/2017/10.

Luccioni, Sasha, Bruna Trevelin, and Margaret Mitchell. "The Environmental Impacts of AI — Primer." September 23, 2024. https://huggingface.co/blog/sasha/ai-environment-primer.

Luckowski, Jean A. "A Virtue-Centered Approach to Ethics Education." *Journal of Teacher Education* 48, no. 4 (1997): 264–270. https://doi.org/10.1177/0022487197048004004.

Lundin, Robert M., Yuhern Yeap, and David B. Menkes. "Adverse Effects of Virtual and Augmented Reality Interventions in Psychiatry: Systematic Review." *JMIR Mental Health* 10 (May 2023): e43240. https://doi.org/10.2196/43240.

Macleod, Colin M. "Just Schools and Good Childhoods: Non-Preparatory Dimensions of Educational Justice." *Journal of Applied Philosophy* 35 (2018): 76–89.

Marshall, Denise. "When School Policy Limits Access to Assistive Technology for Students with Disabilities - Council of Parent Attorneys and Advocates, Inc." Council of Parent Attorneys and Advocates, September 10, 2024. https://www.copaa.org/news/681778/When-School-Policy-Limits-Access-to-Assistive-Technology-for-Students-with-Disabilities.htm.

McClain, Jessica, and Dianne Wellington. "A PSA I'm Here Too: Exploring the Harmful Experiences of Black Students Through Critical Narratives." *International Journal on Social and Education Sciences* 6, no. 3 (2024): 427–438. https://doi.org/10.46328/ijonses.681.

McGlynn, Clare, and Carlotta Rigotti. "From Virtual Rape to Meta-Rape: Sexual Violence, Criminal Law and the Metaverse." *Oxford Journal of Legal Studies* 45, no. 3 (2025): 554–582. https://doi.org/10.1093/ojls/gqaf009.

McKenzie, Lindsay. "Common App Ditches High School Discipline Question." *Inside Higher Ed*, October 4, 2020. https://www.insidehighered.com/admissions/article/2020/10/05/common-app-stop-asking-students-about-their-high-school-disciplinary.

Medina, José. *The Epistemology of Resistance: Gender and Racial Oppression, Epistemic Injustice, and Resistant Imaginations*. Studies in Feminist Philosophy. Oxford University Press, 2013.

Menashy, Francine. "The End of Efficiency: Implications for Democratic Education." *Journal of Educational Thought/Revue de La Pensée Educative* 41, no. 2 (2018): 165–177. https://doi.org/10.55016/ojs/jet.v41i2.52515.

Mill, John S., and Roger Crisp. *Utilitarianism*. Reprint. paperback. Oxford Philosophical Texts. Oxford University Press, 2010.

Miller, Sterling. "The Basics, Usage, and Privacy Concerns of Biometric Data." Thomson Reuters, July 20, 2022. https://legal.thomsonreuters.com/en/insights/articles/the-basics-usage-and-privacy-concerns-of-biometric-data.

Minow, Martha. "Sources of Difference." In *Making All the Difference*. Inclusion, Exclusion, and American Law. Cornell University Press, 1990. JSTOR. http://www.jstor.org/stable/10.7591/j.ctt1tm7j8t.6.

Mitchell, Dolisha. "Lessons from TikTok: Make E-Learning Videos That Engage Learners." *Articulate*, May 23, 2025. https://www.articulate.com/blog/lessons-from-tiktok-how-to-make-e-learning-videos-that-engage-learners/.

Moore, Raeal, Dan Vitale, and Nycole Stawinoga. "The Digital Divide and Educational Equity: A Look at Students with Very Limited Access to Electronic Devices at Home." ACT's Center for Equity in Learning, August 2018. https://www.act.org/content/dam/act/unsecured/documents/R1698-digital-divide-2018-08.pdf.

Mowreader, Ashley. "Report: Predictive Models May Have Bias Against Black and Hispanic Learners." *Inside Higher Ed*, July 19, 2024. https://www.insidehighered.com/news/student-success/academic-life/2024/07/19/predictive-models-higher-ed-disadvantage-some.

MSU Libraries. "Timeline | Advancing Accessibility: A Timeline | Exhibits | MSU Libraries." MSU Libraries. https://lib.msu.edu/exhibits/advancing-accessibility/timeline.

NARA. "Civil Rights Act (1964)." National Archives, October 5, 2021. https://www.archives.gov/milestone-documents/civil-rights-act.

Naseer, Aliza, Naveed R. Ahmad, and Muhammad A. Chishti. "Psychological Impacts of AI Dependence: Assessing the Cognitive and Emotional Costs of Intelligent Systems in Daily Life." *Review of Applied Management and Social Sciences* 8, no. 1 (2025): 291–307. https://doi.org/10.47067/ramss.v8i1.458.

National Association of Secondary School Principals. "Position Statement: Student Data Privacy." 2021. https://www.nassp.org/wp-content/uploads/2021/12/Student-Data-Privacy-2021-revised.pdf.

National Education Association. "Educator Rights to Report Wrongdoing | NEA." Accessed November 17, 2025. https://www.nea.org/resource-library/educator-rights-report-wrongdoing.

National Education Association. "Environmental Impact of AI | NEA." June 20, 2025. https://www.nea.org/professional-excellence/student-engagement/tools-tips/environmental-impact-ai.

NEA. "Code of Ethics for Educators | NEA." 1975. https://www.nea.org/resource-library/code-ethics-educators.

NEA. "Code of Ethics for Educators | NEA." Accessed November 17, 2025. https://www.nea.org/resource-library/code-ethics-educators.

Neumann, Peter J. "The Death of QALYs Is Greatly Exaggerated - Center for the Evaluation of Value and Risk in Health." March 17, 2025. https://cevr.tuftsmedicalcenter.org/news/the-death-of-qalys-is-greatly-exaggerated.

New York State Education Department. "Graduation Requirements." New York State Education Department. n.d.. https://www.nysed.gov/standards-instruction/graduation-requirements.

New York State Office of Information Technology Services. *Use of Biometric Identifying Technology in Schools*. New York State Office of Information Technology Services, 2023. https://its.ny.gov/system/files/documents/2023/08/biometrics-report-final-2023.pdf.

Nguyen, Andy, Ha N. Ngo, Yvonne Hong, Belle Dang, and Bich-Phuong T. Nguyen. "Ethical Principles for Artificial Intelligence in Education." *Education and Information Technologies* 28, no. 4 (2023): 4221–4241. https://doi.org/10.1007/s10639-022-11316-w.

Nicoletti, Leonardo, and Dina Bass. "Humans Are Biased. Generative AI Is Even Worse." *Bloomberg.Com*, June 9, 2023. https://www.bloomberg.com/graphics/2023-generative-ai-bias/.

Noble, David F. *Digital Diploma Mills: The Automation of Higher Education*. Monthly Review Press, 2002.

Noble, Safiya U. *Algorithms of Oppression: How Search Engines Reinforce Racism*. New York University Press, 2018.

Noddings, Nel. "An Ethic of Caring and Its Implications for Instructional Arrangements." *American Journal of Education* 96, no. 2 (1988): 215–230.

Noddings, Nel. *The Challenge to Care in Schools: An Alternative Approach to Education*. 2nd ed. Teachers College Press, 2005.

Noddings, Nel. *Caring: A Relational Approach to Ethics and Moral Education*. University of California Press, 2013.

Noveck, Beth S. "Artificial Intelligence Can Help Us Create a More Efficient Government." *TheGovLab*, November 16, 2023. https://rebootdemocracy.ai/blog/artificial-intelligence-can-help-us-create-a-more-efficient-government.

Noveck, Beth S. Digital Mirror to Our Deliberation." *TheGovLab*, February 28, 2024. https://rebootdemocracy.ai/blog/AI-transcription.

Nussbaum, Martha C. *Women and Human Development: The Capabilities Approach*. The Seeley Lectures 3. Cambridge University Press, 2000. https://doi.org/10.1017/CBO9780511841286.

Nussbaum, Martha C. "Education and Democratic Citizenship: Capabilities and Quality Education." *Journal of Human Development* 7, no. 3 (2006): 385–395. https://doi.org/10.1080/14649880600815974.

O'Donnell, Kaeli, Hao J. Luh, Margaret Floress, and Assegedetch H. Mariam. "The Effects of Online Anti-Bias Training on Educators' Multicultural Competence." *Contemporary School Psychology* 29, no. 3 (2025): 472–483. https://doi.org/10.1007/s40688-024-00510-x.

O'Neill, John, and Roseanna Bourke. "Educating Teachers About a Code of Ethical Conduct." *Ethics and Education* 5, no. 2 (2010): 159–172. https://doi.org/10.1080/17449642.2010.516633.

Oberg, Glenys. "Moral Injury in Teaching: The Systemic Roots of Ethical Conflict and Emotional Burnout in Education." *Educational Review* (2025): 1–24. https://doi.org/10.1080/00131911.2025.2504523.

OECD. *Students, Computers and Learning*. OECD, 2015. https://doi.org/10.1787/9789264239555-en.

OECD. "Digital Divide in Education." OECD. Accessed November 9, 2025a. https://www.oecd.org/en/topics/digital-divide-in-education.html.

OECD. "Education Economic and Social Outcomes." OECD. Accessed November 19, 2025b. https://www.oecd.org/en/topics/education-economic-and-social-outcomes.html.

OECD. "Public Returns from Education." OECD. Accessed June 21, 2025c. https://www.oecd.org/en/topics/public-returns-from-education.html.

OECD. "Artificial Intelligence and Education and Skills." OECD, n.d. https://www.oecd.org/en/topics/artificial-intelligence-and-education-and-skills.html.

Office of Educational Research and Improvement. "Internet Access in U.S. Public Schools and Classrooms: 1994-99." *U.S. Department of Education*, National Center for Education Statistics, February 2000.

Office of Educational Technology. "Artificial Intelligence and the Future of Teaching and Learning." U.S. Department of Education, May 2023. https://www.ed.gov/sites/ed/files/documents/ai-report/ai-report.pdf.

Office of the Law Revision Counsel. "20 USC Ch. 39: Equal Educational Opportunities and Transportation of Students." August 21, 1974. https://uscode.house.gov/view.xhtml?edition=prelim&path=%2Fprelim%40title20%2Fchapter39.

Oinas-Kukkonen, Harri, Sami Pohjolainen, and Eunice Agyei. "Mitigating Issues With/of/for True Personalization." *Frontiers in Artificial Intelligence* 5 (April 2022): 844817. https://doi.org/10.3389/frai.2022.844817.

Okin, Susan M. *Justice, Gender, and the Family*. Basic Books, 1998.

Olson, Rebecca E., Jordan McKenzie, Kathy A. Mills, Roger Patulny, Alberto Bellocchi, and Fiona Caristo. "Gendered Emotion Management and Teacher Outcomes in Secondary School Teaching: A Review." *Teaching and Teacher Education* 80 (April 2019): 128–144. https://doi.org/10.1016/j.tate.2019.01.010.

Papert, Seymour. "Computers and Computer Cultures." In *Mindstorms: Children, Computers, and Powerful Ideas*, Reprint. Harvester Studies in Cognitive Science 14. Harvester Press, 1982.

Pawelec, Maria. "Deepfakes and Democracy (Theory): How Synthetic Audio-Visual Media for Disinformation and Hate Speech Threaten Core Democratic Functions." *Digital Society* 1, no. 2 (2022): 19. https://doi.org/10.1007/s44206-022-00010-6.

Perkins, Mike, Leon Furze, Jasper Roe, and Jason MacVaugh. "The Artificial Intelligence Assessment Scale (AIAS): A Framework for Ethical Integration of Generative AI in Educational Assessment." *Journal of University Teaching and Learning Practice* 21, no. 06 (2024). https://doi.org/10.53761/q3azde36.

Pew Research Center. *Teens and Cyberbullying 2022*. December 2022. https://www.pewresearch.org/wp-content/uploads/sites/20/2022/12/PI_2022.12.15_teens-cyberbullying-2022_FINAL.pdf

Photopoulos, Panos, and Dimos Triantis. "Think Twice: First for Tech, Then for Ed." *Sn Computer Science* 4, no. 2 (2023): 123. https://doi.org/10.1007/s42979-022-01538-7.

Pirie, Madsen. *How To Win Every Argument: The Use and Abuse of Logic*. Bloomsbury Academic, 2016.

Postman, Neil. *Technopoly: The Surrender of Culture to Technology*. Knopf Doubleday Publishing Group, 2011.

Poth, Rachelle D. "Developing Students' Digital Citizenship Skills." Edutopia, October 3, 2023. https://www.edutopia.org/article/teaching-digital-citizenship-skills/.

Prothero, Arianna. "Student and Teacher Motivation, in Charts." Leadership, Student Well-Being & Movement. *Education Week*, February 21, 2023. https://www.edweek.org/leadership/student-and-teacher-motivation-in-charts/2023/02.

Prothero, Arianna. "Parents Want Cellphones in the Classroom. Here's Why." Leadership, Student Well-Being & Movement. *Education Week*, September 13, 2024. https://www.edweek.org/leadership/parents-want-cellphones-in-the-classroom-heres-why/2024/09.

Quay-de la Vallee, Hannah, and Maddy Dwyer. "Students' Use of Generative AI: The Threat of Hallucinations." *Center for Democracy and Technology*, December 18, 2023. https://cdt.org/insights/students-use-of-generative-ai-the-threat-of-hallucinations/.

Ramineni, Chaitanya, and David Williamson. "Understanding Mean Score Differences Between the E-Rater® Automated Scoring Engine and Humans for Demographically Based Groups in the GRE® General Test." *ETS Research Report Series* 2018, no. 1 (2018): 1–31. https://doi.org/10.1002/ets2.12192.

Ramsey, Clayton. "Ghost in the Chatbot: The Perils of Parasocial Attachment | UNESCO." UNESCO, July 9, 2025. https://www.unesco.org/en/articles/ghost-chatbot-perils-parasocial-attachment.

Randles, Julie. "3 Ways to Bring Student Voice to Digital Citizenship." *ISTE*, April 14, 2017. https://iste.org/blog/3-ways-to-bring-student-voice-to-digital-citizenship.

Rawls, John. *A Theory of Justice*. Rev. ed., 5.-6. printing. Belknap Press of Harvard University Press, 1999.

Rawls, John. *Political Liberalism*. Expanded ed. Columbia Classics in Philosophy. Columbia University Press, 2005.

Reich, Justin. *Failure to Disrupt: Why Technology Alone Can't Transform Education*. Harvard University Press, 2020.

Reich, Justin. "Ed Tech's Failure during the Pandemic, and What Comes After." Phi Delta Kappan 102, no. 6 (February 21, 2021) 20–24.

Riaz, Rimsha, Aurora Vasconcelos, and Pedro Pinto. "An Overview of User Psychological Manipulation Techniques in UI/UX Web Design." *2024 Cyber Awareness and Research Symposium (CARS)*, October 2024, 1–6. https://doi.org/10.1109/CARS61786.2024.10778887.

Robeson, Richard, and Nancy M. P. King. "Performable Case Studies in Ethics Education." *Healthcare* 5, no. 3 (2017): 3. https://doi.org/10.3390/healthcare5030057.

Rogow, Faith. "Media Literacy for Students in a Digital Age | Citizenship." *Carnegie Corporation of New York*, April 10, 2024. https://www.carnegie.org/our-work/article/media-literacy-for-students-in-a-digital-age/.

Romanishyn, Alexander, Olena Malytska, and Vitaliy Goncharuk. "AI-Driven Disinformation: Policy Recommendations for Democratic Resilience." *Frontiers in Artificial Intelligence* 8 (July 2025): 1569115. https://doi.org/10.3389/frai.2025.1569115.

Rose, Todd. *The End of Average: How We Succeed in a World That Values Sameness*. 1st ed. HarperOne, 2016.

Rucinski, Christina L., Joshua L. Brown, and Jason T. Downer. "Teacher–Child Relationships, Classroom Climate, and Children's Social-Emotional and Academic Development." *Journal of Educational Psychology* 110, no. 7 (2018): 992–1004. https://doi.org/10.1037/edu0000240.

Rudin, Cynthia. "Stop Explaining Black Box Machine Learning Models for High Stakes Decisions and Use Interpretable Models Instead." *Nature Machine Intelligence* 1, no. 5 (2019): 206–215. https://doi.org/10.1038/s42256-019-0048-x.

Rudin, Cynthia, and Joanna Radin. "Why Are We Using Black Box Models in AI When We Don't Need To? A Lesson from an Explainable AI Competition." *Harvard Data Science Review* 1, no. 2 (2019). https://doi.org/10.1162/99608f92.5a8a3a3d.

Ruhter, Lindsay, and Meagan Karvonen. "The Impact of Professional Development on Data-Based Decision-Making for Students with Extensive Support Needs." *Remedial and Special Education* 45, no. 1 (2024): 44–57. https://doi.org/10.1177/07419325231164636.

Ruiz, Eugie, and Elizabeth Geib. "Writing Statements of Teaching Philosophy - Purdue OWL® - Purdue University." 2019. https://owl.purdue.edu/owl/job_search_writing/preparing_an_application/documents/ss19_teaching-philosophy_ruiz-geib.pdf.

Sacasas, L. M. "Resistance Is Futile: The Myth of Tech Inevitability." Substack Newsletter. *The Convivial Society*, April 21, 2021. https://theconvivialsociety.substack.com/p/resistance-is-futile-the-myth-of.

Saettler, L. Paul. *The Evolution of American Educational Technology*. 2nd ed. IAP, 2004.

Sailer, Michael, and Lisa Homner. "The Gamification of Learning: A Meta-Analysis." *Educational Psychology Review* 32, no. 1 (2020): 77–112. https://doi.org/10.1007/s10648-019-09498-w.

Sallay, David. *Vetting Generative AI Tools for Use in Schools*. April 2024. https://fpf.org/wp-content/uploads/2024/10/Ed_AI_legal_compliance.pdf_FInal_OCT24.pdf

Salles, Arleen, and Abel W. Paz. "Anthropomorphism in Social AIs: Some Challenges." In *Developments in Neuroethics and Bioethics*, vol. 7. Academic Press, 2024. https://doi.org/10.1016/bs.dnb.2024.02.007.

Satz, Debra. "Equality, Adequacy, and Education for Citizenship." *Ethics* 117, no. 4 (2007): 623–648. https://doi.org/10.1086/518805.

Schmitz, Dagmar, Dominik Groß, Charlotte Frierson, Gerrit A. Schubert, Henna Schulze-Steinen, and Alexander Kersten. "Ethics Rounds: Affecting Ethics Quality at all Organisational Levels." *Journal of Medical Ethics* 44, no. 12 (2018): 805–809. https://www.ovid.com/journals/jmede/fulltext/10.1136/medethics-2018-104831~ethics-rounds-affecting-ethics-quality-at-all-organisational.

Schouten, Gina. "On Meeting Students Where They Are: Teacher Judgment and the Use of Data in Higher Education." *Theory and Research in Education* 15, no. 3 (2017): 321–338. https://doi.org/10.1177/1477878517734452.

Scott, W. Richard. *Institutions and Organizations: Ideas, Interests, and Identities*. SAGE Publications, Inc, 2014.

Selwyn, Neil. *Distrusting Educational Technology: Critical Questions for Changing Times*. Routledge, 2013. https://doi.org/10.4324/9781315886350.

Selwyn, Neil. *Is Technology Good for Education?* Polity Press, 2016.

Selwyn, Neil. *Should Robots Replace Teachers? AI and the Future of Education*. Digital Futures Series. Cambridge Medford, MA Polity, 2019.

Selwyn, Neil. "Ed-Tech Within Limits: Anticipating Educational Technology in Times of Environmental Crisis." *E-Learning and Digital Media* 18, no. 5 (2021): 496–510. https://doi.org/10.1177/20427530211022951.

Selwyn, Neil. *Education and Technology*. 3rd ed. Bloomsbury, 2021.

Sen, Amartya. "Capability and Well-Being." In *The Quality of Life*, edited by Martha Nussbaum and Amartya Sen. Oxford University Press, 1993. https://doi.org/10.1093/0198287976.003.0003.

Shah, Priten. *AI and the Future of Education: Teaching in the Age of Artificial Intelligence*. Jossey-Bass, 2023.

Shah, Priten. "I Was an AI Optimist. Now I'm Worried It's Making Teacher Burnout Worse." Technology, Artificial Intelligence. *Education Week*, June 5, 2024. https://www.edweek.org/technology/opinion-i-was-an-ai-optimist-now-im-worried-its-making-teacher-burnout-worse/2024/06.

Shaller, Sabreena. "How to Craft Your Teaching Philosophy | NEA." June 28, 2022. https://www.nea.org/professional-excellence/student-engagement/tools-tips/how-craft-your-teaching-philosophy.

Shapiro, Joan P., and Jacqueline A. Stefkovich. *Ethical Leadership and Decision Making in Education*. Routledge, 2016. https://doi.org/10.4324/9781315773339.

Shelton, Ken, and Dee Lanier. "Thinking About Equity and Bias in AI." Edutopia, August 30, 2024. https://www.edutopia.org/article/equity-bias-ai-what-educators-should-know/.

Sherwin, Susan, and Katie Stockdale. "Whither Bioethics Now? The Promise of Relational Theory." *International Journal of Feminist Approaches to Bioethics* 10, no. 1 (2017): 7–29. JSTOR.

Shortt, Mitchell, Shantanu Tilak, Irina Kuznetcova, Bethany Martens, and Babatunde Akinkuolie. "Gamification in Mobile-Assisted Language Learning: A Systematic Review of Duolingo Literature from Public Release of 2012 to Early 2020." *Computer Assisted Language Learning* 36, no. 3 (2023): 517–554. https://doi.org/10.1080/09588221.2021.1933540.

Skipper, Yvonne, and Karen Douglas. "The Influence of Teacher Feedback on Children's Perceptions of Student–Teacher Relationships." *British Journal of Educational Psychology* 85, no. 3 (2015): 276–288. https://doi.org/10.1111/bjep.12070.

Skovron, Liz. "AI Literacy in the Workplace: Essential Skills for Every Professional." *Denison Edge*, April 4, 2025. https://edge.denison.edu/blog/ai-literacy-in-the-workplace-essential-skills-for-every-professional.

Slate, John R. "School Mission Statements and School Performance: A Mixed Research Investigation." *New Horizons in Education* 56, no. 2 (2008): 17–27.

Slavin, Robert E. "Evidence-Based Education Policies: Transforming Educational Practice and Research." *Educational Researcher* 31, no. 7 (2002): 15–21. https://doi.org/10.3102/0013189X031007015.

Smith, Molly G., Thomas N. Bradbury, and Benjamin R. Karney. "Can Generative AI Chatbots Emulate Human Connection? A Relationship Science Perspective." *Perspectives on Psychological Science* 20, no. 6 (2025): 1081–1099. https://doi.org/10.1177/17456916251351306.

Sourati, Zhivar, Farzan Karimi-Malekabadi, Meltem Ozcan, et al. "The Shrinking Landscape of Linguistic Diversity in the Age of Large Language Models." arXiv:2502.11266. Preprint, arXiv, February 16, 2025. https://doi.org/10.48550/arXiv.2502.11266.

Sparks, Sarah D. "What Teachers Get Wrong About 'Productive Failure'—and How to Get It Right." Teaching & Learning, Teaching. *Education Week*, September 6, 2024. https://www.edweek.org/teaching-learning/what-teachers-get-wrong-about-productive-failure-and-how-to-get-it-right/2024/09.

Spector, J. Michael. "Ethics in Educational Technology: Towards a Framework for Ethical Decision Making in and for the Discipline." *Educational Technology Research and Development* 64, no. 5 (2016): 1003–1011. https://doi.org/10.1007/s11423-016-9483-0.

Spector, Carrie. "High School Students Are Unequipped to Spot 'Fake News.'" Stanford Report, November 18, 2019. https://news.stanford.edu/stories/2019/11/high-school-students-unequipped-spot-fake-news.

Stanford, Libby. "The Good (and the Bad) of Using Apps to Connect with Parents." Leadership, Families & the Community. *Education Week*, April 25, 2024. https://www.edweek.org/leadership/the-good-and-the-bad-of-using-apps-to-connect-with-parents/2024/04.

Stangl, Fabian J., René Riedl, Wolfgang J. Weitzl, and Sebastian Martin. "Fatigue and Stress Levels in Digital Collaboration: A Pilot Study with Video Conferencing and the Metaverse." In *Information Systems and Neuroscience*, edited by Fred D. Davis, René Riedl, Jan Vom Brocke, Pierre-Majorique Léger, Adriane B. Randolph, and Gernot R. Müller-Putz, vol. 68. Lecture Notes in Information Systems and Organisation. Springer Nature Switzerland, 2024. https://doi.org/10.1007/978-3-031-58396-4_9.

Starratt, Robert J. "Building an Ethical School: A Theory for Practice in Educational Leadership." *Educational Administration Quarterly* 27, no. 2 (1991): 185–202. https://doi.org/10.1177/0013161X91027002005.

Staudt Willet, K. Bret, and Dan He. "Educators' Invisible Labour: A Systematic Review." *Review of Education* 12, no. 2 (2024): e3473. https://doi.org/10.1002/rev3.3473.

Stephens, Caitlynn P. "Politics, Funding Threaten Schools' Focus on Student Learning, Leaders Say." Leadership, School & District Management. *Education Week*, November 10, 2025. https://www.edweek.org/leadership/politics-funding-threaten-schools-focus-on-student-learning-leaders-say/2025/11.

Stevens, Kaylene M., Erin Fife, and Christopher C. Martell. "'It Has a Chilling Effect': How Secondary Social Studies Teachers Across the Country Are Navigating Discriminatory Censorship Laws." *Journal of Curriculum and Pedagogy* (2025): 1–20. https://doi.org/10.1080/15505170.2025.2549839.

Suarez, Victoria D., Videsha Marya, Mary Jane Weiss, and David Cox. "Examination of Ethical Decision-Making Models Across Disciplines: Common Elements and Application to the Field of Behavior Analysis." *Behavior Analysis in Practice* 16, no. 3 (2023): 657–671. https://doi.org/10.1007/s40617-022-00753-1.

Sunday, Oluwafemi J., Olusola O. Adesope, and Patricia L. Maarhuis. "The Effects of Smartphone Addiction on Learning: A Meta-Analysis." *Computers in Human Behavior Reports* 4 (August 2021): 100114. https://doi.org/10.1016/j.chbr.2021.100114.

Swanson, Sean. "Education Funding for K-12 Schools." *Discovery Education*, September 30, 2024. https://www.discoveryeducation.com/resources/featured-topics/education-funding/.

Ta, Vivian, Caroline Griffith, Carolynn Boatfield, et al. "User Experiences of Social Support from Companion Chatbots in Everyday Contexts: Thematic Analysis." *Journal of Medical Internet Research* 22, no. 3 (2020): e16235. https://doi.org/10.2196/16235.

Ta, Tina, Tatiana Geron, Meira Levinson, and Megan Bogia. "'The Power of Open Dialogue': Using Normative Case Studies to Facilitate Ethical Dilemmas Discussions Among School Teachers." *Teaching and Teacher Education* 132 (October 2023): 104237. https://doi.org/10.1016/j.tate.2023.104237.

Tabron, Lolita A., Abigail Bachofer, Natalie Lewis, Tracie Trinidad, and Stephen F. Fusco. "Curriculum Wars: A Critical Policy Analysis of K-12 Critical Race Theory Bills in State Legislatures in the United States." *Education Policy Analysis Archives* 32 (December 2024). https://doi.org/10.14507/epaa.32.8534.

Tate, Kathleen. "The Benefits of Personalized Learning: How It Helps Students." *American Public University*, April 1, 2025. https://www.apu.apus.edu/area-of-study/education/resources/the-benefits-of-personalized-learning/.

Tatter, Grace. "A Toolkit for Digital Civics | Harvard Graduate School of Education." *Harvard Graduate School of Education*, October 7, 2018. https://www.gse.harvard.edu/ideas/usable-knowledge/18/10/toolkit-digital-civics.

Thiel, Chase E., Shane Connelly, Lauren Harkrider, et al. "Case-Based Knowledge and Ethics Education: Improving Learning and Transfer Through Emotionally Rich Cases." *Science and Engineering Ethics* 19, no. 1 (2013): 265–286. https://doi.org/10.1007/s11948-011-9318-7.

ThinkerAnalytix. "ThinkCulture." ThinkerAnalytix, n.d.. https://thinkeranalytix.org/.

Thompson, Carolyn. "New York Bans Facial Recognition in Schools After Report Finds Risks Outweigh Potential Benefits." Education. *AP News*, September 27, 2023. https://apnews.com/article/facial-recognition-banned-new-york-schools-ddd35e004254d316beabf70453b1a6a2.

Tugtekin, Ufuk. "The Dark Side of Metaverse Learning Environments: Potential Threats and Risk Factors." In *Advances in Educational Technologies and Instructional Design*, edited by Gürhan Durak and Serkan Cankaya. IGI Global, 2023. https://doi.org/10.4018/978-1-6684-6513-4.ch004.

Turk, Victoria. "How AI Reduces the World to Stereotypes." Rest of World, October 10, 2023. https://restofworld.org/2023/ai-image-stereotypes/.

U.S. Department of Education. "Racial Incidents and Harassment Against Students | U.S. Department of Education." 1994. http://www.ed.gov/laws-and-policy/civil-rights-laws/harassment-bullying-and-retaliation/racial-incidents-and-harassment-against-students.

U.S. Department of Education. "Protecting Student Privacy While Using Online Educational Services: Requirements and Best Practices | Protecting Student Privacy." February 2014. https://studentprivacy.ed.gov/resources/protecting-student-privacy-while-using-online-educational-services-requirements-and-best.

U.S. Department of Education. "Frequently Asked Questions: Disability Discrimination | U.S. Department of Education." January 17, 2025. http://www.ed.gov/laws-and-policy/civil-rights-laws/disability-discrimination/frequently-asked-questions-disability-discrimination.

U.S. Department of Education. "Frequently Asked Questions: Section 504 Free Appropriate Public Education (FAPE) | U.S. Department of Education." June 30, 2025. http://www.ed.gov/laws-and-policy/civil-rights-laws/disability-discrimination/frequently-asked-questions-section-504-free-appropriate-public-education-fape.

U.S. Department of Education. "Regulations Enforced by the Office for Civil Rights | U.S. Department of Education." n.d.. http://www.ed.gov/about/ed-offices/ocr/regulations-enforced-by-the-office-for-civil-rights.

U.S. Department of Education. *Responsibilities of Third-Party Service Providers Under FERPA*. n.d.. https://studentprivacy.ed.gov/sites/default/files/resource_document/file/Vendor%20FAQ.pdf

U.S. Department of Education. "Title IX and Sex Discrimination | U.S. Department of Education." n.d.. http://www.ed.gov/laws-and-policy/civil-rights-laws/title-ix-and-sex-discrimination.

UN General Assembly. "Convention on the Rights of the Child." *United Nations, Treaty Series* 1577, no. 3 (1989): 1–23.

UNESCO. "Recommendation on the Ethics of Artificial Intelligence." With UNESCO. UNESCO, 2022. https://digitallibrary.un.org/record/4062376.

UNESCO. "Ethical Impact Assessment: A Tool of the Recommendation on the Ethics." July 3, 2023. https://www.unesco.org/en/articles/ethical-impact-assessment-tool-recommendation-ethics-artificial-intelligence.

UNESCO. "Media and Information Literacy: A Critical Skill for All | UNESCO." October 27, 2023. https://www.unesco.org/en/articles/media-and-information-literacy-critical-skill-all.

UNESCO. "Inclusion in Education | UNESCO." December 3, 2025. https://www.unesco.org/en/inclusion-education.

UNESCO. "Education 2030: Incheon Declaration and Framework for Action for the Implementation of Sustainable Development Goal 4: Ensure Inclusive and Equitable Quality Education and Promote Lifelong Learning Opportunities for All - UNESCO Digital Library." n.d.. https://unesdoc.unesco.org/ark:/48223/pf0000245656.

United Nations. General Assembly. *Universal Declaration of Human Rights*. Vol. 3381. Department of State, United States of America, 1949.

US Department of Education. "What Is FERPA? | Protecting Student Privacy." n.d.. https://studentprivacy.ed.gov/faq/what-ferpa.

USC. *Critical Thinking and Ethics in the Age of Generative AI in Education*. 2024. https://today.usc.edu/wp-content/uploads/2024/02/USC_GenerativeAI_011624_FINAL.pdf?fbclid=IwAR12PD0mDGuJ5aMUB9r3QWNDhr8XDZvQV8bcPsRY8Li7rFHEPXfRbqrHtpo

Vaccari, Cristian, and Andrew Chadwick. "Deepfakes and Disinformation: Exploring the Impact of Synthetic Political Video on Deception, Uncertainty, and Trust in News." *Social Media + Society* 6, no. 1 (2020): 2056305120903408. https://doi.org/10.1177/2056305120903408.

Valdez, Amber. *Getting Better at Getting More Equitable: Opportunities and Barriers for Using Continuous Improvement to Advance Educational Equity*. 2020. https://www.carnegiefoundation.org/wp-content/uploads/2020/10/Getting-Better-at-Getting-More-Equitable-Opportunities-and-Barriers-for-Using-Continuous-Improvement-to-Advance-Educational-Equity.pdf

Valenzuela, Jorge. "Teaching the Environmental Impact of AI Through PBL." Edutopia, August 2025. https://www.edutopia.org/article/teaching-environmental-impact-ai-pbl/.

Van der Sloot, B., and Yvette Wagensveld. "Deepfakes: Regulatory Challenges for the Synthetic Society." *Computer Law & Security Review* 46 (September 2022): 105716. https://doi.org/10.1016/j.clsr.2022.105716.

Van Geel, Marieke, Trynke Keuning, Adrie J. Visscher, and Jean P. Fox. "Assessing the Effects of a School-Wide Data-Based Decision-Making Intervention on Student Achievement Growth in Primary Schools." *American Educational Research Journal* 53, no. 2 (2016): 360–394. https://doi.org/10.3102/0002831216637346.

Villegas Dominguez, J., C. Jimenez Recinos, K. I. Gómez De La Cruz, et al. "Cell Phone Addiction and Its Impact on Students' Mental Health." *European Journal of Public Health* 33, no. Supplement_2 (2023): ckad160.1596. https://doi.org/10.1093/eurpub/ckad160.1596.

Walker, Tim. "'Technology Isn't the Hero, Educators Are' | NEA." *National Education Association*, March 5, 2021. https://www.nea.org/nea-today/all-news-articles/technology-isnt-hero-educators-are.

Walker, Kalie. "AI 'Deepfakes': A Disturbing Trend in School Cyberbullying | NEARI." August 2025. https://www.neari.org/advocating-change/new-from-neari/ai-deepfakes-disturbing-trend-school-cyberbullying.

Walker, Tim. "Dismantling the Myth of the 'Average' Student | NEA." Accessed November 17, 2025. https://www.nea.org/nea-today/all-news-articles/dismantling-myth-average-student.

Watkins, Marc. "AI Is Unavoidable, Not Inevitable." Substack Newsletter. *Rhetorica*, January 17, 2025. https://marcwatkins.substack.com/p/ai-is-unavoidable-not-inevitable.

Watson, Cole F. "Protecting Children in the Frontier of Surveillance Capitalism." *Richmond Journal of Law & Technology* XXVII, no. 2 (2021): 1.

Watters, Audrey. "The-Monsters-of-Education-Technology." 2014. https://www.amazon.com/Monsters-Education-Technology-Audrey-Watters/dp/1505225051#detailBullets_feature_div

Watters, Audrey. "Ed-Tech Agitprop." Hack Education, November 28, 2019. http://hackeducation.com/2019/11/28/ed-tech-agitprop.

Watters, Audrey. *Teaching Machines: The History of Personalized Learning*. The MIT Press, 2021.

Weaver, Matthew. "One in Four Unconcerned by Sexual Deepfakes Created Without Consent, Survey Finds." Technology. *The Guardian*, November 24, 2025. https://www.theguardian.com/technology/2025/nov/24/one-in-four-unconcerned-by-sexual-deepfakes-created-without-consent-survey-finds.

Weill, Warren. "Balancing Standardization and Personalization in Education: A Guide." EHL Hospitality Business School. June 20, 2024. https://hospitalityinsights.ehl.edu/personalization-standardization-education.

Weinstein, Milton C., and William B. Stason. "Foundations of Cost-Effectiveness Analysis for Health and Medical Practices." *The New England Journal of Medicine* 296, no. 13 (1977): 716–721. https://doi.org/10.1056/NEJM197703312961304.

Wentzel, Kathryn R., Ann Battle, Shannon L. Russell, and Lisa B. Looney. "Social Supports from Teachers and Peers as Predictors of Academic and Social Motivation." *Contemporary Educational Psychology* 35, no. 3 (2010): 193–202. https://doi.org/10.1016/j.cedpsych.2010.03.002.

West, Darrell M. *The Future of Work: Robots, AI, and Automation*. Brookings Institution Press, 2019.

WHO. "Electronic Waste (e-Waste)." June 15, 2023. https://www.who.int/news-room/fact-sheets/detail/electronic-waste-(e-waste).

Wilkins, Natalie J., Jorge M. V. Verlenden, Leigh E. Szucs, and Michelle M. Johns. "Classroom Management and Facilitation Approaches That Promote School Connectedness." *The Journal of School Health* 93, no. 7 (2023): 582–593. https://doi.org/10.1111/josh.13279.

Winner, Langdon. "Do Artifacts Have Politics?" *Daedalus* 109, no. 1 (1980): 121–136.

Wolford, Ben. "What Is GDPR, the EU's New Data Protection Law?" *GDPR.Eu*, November 7, 2018. https://gdpr.eu/what-is-gdpr/.

Woo, Ashley, Melissa K. Diliberti, and Elizabeth D. Steiner. *Policies Restricting Teaching About Race and Gender Spill Over into Other States and Localities: Findings from the 2023 State of the American Teacher Survey*. 2024. https://www.rand.org/pubs/research_reports/RRA1108-10.html.

Yan, Lixiang, Lele Sha, Linxuan Zhao, et al. "Practical and Ethical Challenges of Large Language Models in Education: A Systematic Scoping Review." *British Journal of Educational Technology* 55, no. 1 (2024): 90–112. https://doi.org/10.1111/bjet.13370.

YMCA of Greater Toronto. "Gamification in Education: Does It Present Risks to Youth?" *YMCA of Greater Toronto*, March 6, 2025. https://www.ymcagta.org/blog.

Young, Iris M., and Danielle S. Allen. *Justice and the Politics of Difference*. Princeton University Press, 2011.

Zhao, Vivian, and Ariel H. Kim. "The Harvard Crimson | Class of 2024 By the Numbers." May 12, 2024. https://features.thecrimson.com/2024/senior-survey/.

Zhu, Haotian, Yao Sun, and Junfeng Yang. "Towards Responsible Artificial Intelligence in Education: A Systematic Review on Identifying and Mitigating Ethical Risks." *Humanities and Social Sciences Communications* 12, no. 1 (2025): 1111. https://doi.org/10.1057/s41599-025-05252-6.

Zuboff, Shoshana. "The Age of Surveillance Capitalism." In *Social Theory Re-Wired*, 3rd ed. Routledge, 2023.

About the Author

Priten Kadakia Soundararajan-Shah is an educator, philosopher, and entrepreneur working at the intersection of technology and education.

He is the CEO of Pedagogy Ventures, where he integrates cutting-edge technology with proven teaching strategies to help educational organizations.

He also supports three nonprofits: PedagogyFutures, as Executive Director, which provides professional development resources to build a responsible, ethical, human-centered future for educational technology; Academy 4 Social Civics, as Chair, which is dedicated to civics education that prepares students to tackle future challenges; and ThinkerAnalytix, as CTO, which is working to scale critical thinking instruction at educational institutions around the world.

Priten is the author of *AI & The Future of Education: Teaching in the Age of Artificial Intelligence* (Wiley, 2023), which was translated into Arabic, Simplified Chinese, Turkish, and Vietnamese. He also teaches courses on the Ethics of Ed Tech, Family & Society, and Epistemic Justice at College Unbound, a bachelor's degree-granting institution focused on adult learners.

He holds a B.A. in Philosophy from Harvard College and an M.Ed. in Education Policy and Management from the Harvard Graduate School of Education.

Acknowledgments

This book is the result of over a decade of relationships, experiences, and conversations, and so I worry that any expression of gratitude will be incomplete. Nonetheless, I will attempt to do so. I extend my deepest appreciation to all of the following:

To Professor Gina Schouten, for introducing me to the field of educational justice, and philosophy more broadly, and for her mentorship, support, and scholarship that have forever shaped my thinking and life. Much of the foundational literature used in this book was first introduced to me by her.

To my wife, for being my sounding board, reasoning checker, and trusted critic. Without her support, this project would not have been possible, and her patience, selflessness, and love have fueled me to the finish line.

To my siblings, Kasish for his love, Chandani for being the first editor of all my work, Shilpa for her deliberative support, and Sinduri for her research guidance and jumpstart.

To my parents, Jalpa and Hiten, for instilling in me the value of education, and to my parents-in-law, Krishnasamy and Suganthi, for continuing to nurture that value.

To my dog, Piku, for staying by my side through late nights and early mornings and reminding me that there is always time to slow down and play fetch.

To my students at College Unbound, for being test subjects for my approach, detectors of unclear thoughts, and examples of the spirit I hope all readers bring to the book.

To Nina Bamberg, for spending the last half decade discussing many of the ideas and arguments in this book, challenging me to refine them, and being my companion in bringing them to educators all around the world.

To my staff at Pedagogy Ventures, especially Eden, Reuben, and Michelle for helping in the tedious but necessary work of conducting literature research, brainstorming ideas and themes, editing with speed and precision, and helping manage moving pieces that I surely would have lost were it not for their diligent efforts.

To the team at ThinkerAnalytix, especially Anne and Aidan, for sharing my vision for educational technology that supports teachers and serves students, and for using it to scale reasoning skills globally.

To Professor Meira Levinson, for unknowingly shaping my thinking, setting the foundation of the field of Eduethics, and inspiring me to see the connection between my ideals and my reality.

To the attendees of my past talks, interviewees for my research, and the countless teachers, students, and researchers whom I have spoken to for sharing their own thinking and experiences and for providing voices to ground my ideas in lived experiences.

To the Wiley Team, for not only trusting me once, but now twice, with the ambitious tasks of helping educators navigate difficult transitions. Ashante Thomas, my editor, has been a steadying voice, helping me keep the big picture in mind, advocated for my work, and been a champion of my strongest convictions.

Index

A

academic integrity, 176–178, 205
access vs productive use, 92–94
access constraints, 119
   accessibility requirements, 124
   civil rights protections in schools, 125
   human rights, 126
   in unequal societies, 123–126
adequacy heuristic, 62–63
adequacy threshold, 57
administrators and school boards, as stakeholders, 47
advocacy, 44
alternative heuristic, 65
Americans with Disabilities Act (ADA), 124
analysis paralysis, 68
Anderson, Elizabeth, 57, 62
anthropomorphic simulation, 101
Aristotle, 16, 34, 55
artificial intelligence (AI), 74–75, 97, 98, 178. *See also related topics*
   academic integrity in age of, 176, 177
   accessibility potential, 74
   adoption in schools, 2
   advanced AI in schools, 75
   blanket bans, 74, 152
   ChatGPT, 74
   civic threats, 105
   designing AI handoff to humans, 102
   disclosure and attribution of usage, 149
   economic implications of, 3
   emotional dependence on, 101–102
   environmental impact of, 103–104
   ethical and responsible usage, 149
   ethics recommendations, 127
   explainable AI advocacy, 99
   fabricated AI-generated content, 105
   feedback to students, 181–185
   -generated curricular content, 147
   generative, 204
   harm reduction model for, 205
   integration vs AI-proof curriculum, 149
   labor and job displacement, 104–105
   literacy, 74, 149, 213
   malicious media creation, 105
   -powered personalized learning platforms, 4
   professional development in literacy, 104–105
   tutoring systems, 147
   unequal AI displacement across schools, 104
   writing detection in assessment, 176, 179
   writing tools in English instruction, 4
artificial predictability, preference for, 101
assistive technologies, 124
asymmetric power
   dynamics, in education, 37
   relationships, 22
audits, 98, 141, 167, 171, 189, 203
   trail logging, 120
automated grading bias, 83, 84, 97, 99, 181–185, 208
automation, of educational tasks, 82, 126
autonomy, 3, 29, 63, 81, 88, 90, 91, 154
   in child development, 21, 23, 25–26
   developmental needs vs, 39–40
   duty-based reasoning, 32
   and informed participation, 154
   and personalization, 86
   vs standardization, 42

B

backup requirements, 121
Beauchamp, Tom L., 21, 22, 112
behavioral engineering
   in ed tech, 100–101
   as non-maleficence concern, 96

behavioral manipulation, in engagement systems, 90
beneficence, 21, 88
   vs autonomy, 28
   vs care, 28
   demonstration requirement, 155
   in education, 24–25
   and innovation, 81
   vs justice, 28
   vs non-maleficence, 28
   in procurement, 154
   as promoting good, 23
bias, 44, 61, 96, 202
   from AI, 74
   in algorithmic systems, 97–98, 184
   as justice concern, 96
Biesta, Gert, 145
bioethics, 1, 9, 21
biometric monitoring, in schools, 76
black box and opacity, 98–99, 188
breach notification requirements, 121
Brighouse, Harry, 3, 14, 24, 26, 39, 45, 50, 56, 62, 67
broadband disparities, 92

C

capabilities approach, 55, 85, 92, 148, 205
care, 34, 81
   vs autonomy, 28
   disability and expanded networks of, 40
   duty-based reasoning, 32, 44
   emotional dimension of, 166
   and emotional labor of teachers, 155
   as relational governance principle, 21, 23, 26–27, 154–155
career preparedness and fairness, 52–53
career readiness, 52, 59, 62, 72, 217
caregiving role of educators, 27
cases
   in assessment, 176–189
   in learning, 163–175
   in policy, 204–217
   in safety, 190–203
categorical imperatives, 32
cellphone ban, school-wide, 152, 209–213

cellphone governance, in schools, 72–73
censorship and control of printed knowledge, 70
ChatGPT, 74
childhood dignity, respecting, 32, 56
Children's Online Privacy Protection Act (COPPA), 120, 126, 165
Childress, James F., 21, 22, 112
civic aims of education, 53–55, 57, 85, 131
civic engagement beyond voting, 55, 59
civic participation, baseline for, 49, 57
civic responsibility, of schools, 5
civic threats, from algorithmic silos, 105
Civil Rights Act of 1964, 125
classroom policies, 145–152
   artificial intelligence, 149
   assessment, 148
   classroom-level ethical decision-making, 145
   communication, 148–150
   curriculum, 146–147
   and decisions, 146–150
   device policies, 149
   disagreements, 151
   first steps in drafting, 150
   ground-up policy making, 152
   homework, 147–148
   inclusion, 151
   vs lived policies, 145, 150
   mission statement, 146
   modeling, 151
   pedagogy, 147
cloud storage safeguards, 121
code of conduct, for students and faculty, 130
commercial incentives vs student wellbeing, 47
Common Sense Media, 127
communication, 148–150
   boundaries with parents, 148–149
   decision, 115
   with families, 46
   parent feedback on, 141
   plan for stakeholders, 158
   transparency, 159
community alignment, in technology implementation, 7

Index

complaint mechanisms, 125
compliance and ethics, distinction between, 14
compulsory education and labor preparation, 51
compulsory schooling, 51
   constraints, 38
   and ethical responsibility, 5
consensus-building, through ethical language, 31
consent policies, 120
consequentialism, 30, 33, 34
contextual judgments, in ethical reasoning, 8
Convention on the Rights of the Child, UN, 126
COVID-19 pandemic, 92
   and remote learning acceleration, 2
critical consciousness, 59
critical evaluation of generated information, 106
critical pedagogy, 59
critical technology literacy, 91
critical thinking, 54, 106
Cuban, Larry, 2, 69, 71, 77, 123
cultural impact of technology, 3
cultural infrastructure, 116, 134–136
culture of care, in schools, 27, 34
curricular integration, of ethical reasoning, 135–136
curricular pressure, 122
curriculum authority, 146–147
cycles of technological adoption, in schools, 2

D

data
   aggregation, in educational systems, 74
   constraints, 119–122
   export and certified deletion, 160
   infrastructure regulation, 121–122
   minimization, 120
   misuse, 76
   qualitative and quantitative, 141
   residence requirements, 121
   retention policies, 120
   safeguarding for student devices, 149
   systems and student labeling, 28–29

data-driven decision-making, 87–89
data governance, 119
decision-tree for technology proposals, 156–158
   decision rules for rejection or pilot, 157
   ethical review through eight-step process, 157
   initial proposal pedagogical purpose statement, 157
   pilot monitoring and evaluation, 157–158
   risk screening, 157
deepfakes technology, 105–106
dehumanization risks, 82
deidentification requirements, 120
deliberative ethics, in education, 7–8
democratic processes, technology and, 3
deontology, 30, 31, 34
design risks, 96–102
   behavioral engineering, 100–101
   bias, 97–98
   black box and opacity, 98–99
   emotional dependence, 101–102
destructive harms, 25
developmental appropriateness, in schooling, 39
developmental attachment concerns, 102
developmental heuristic, 63–64
developmental limits of autonomy, 26
developmental readiness, in schooling, 63
developmental stages and autonomy, 39–40
device inequality, 92
device policies, in classrooms, 149
Dewey, John, 24, 46, 54
dialogic communication, 135
digital citizenship, 73, 136
digital communication, 148
digital divide, 3, 71, 72, 92, 204, 209
digital equity, 72
digital literacy, in AI era, 106
digital natives, 91, 92, 215
direct authority for students, 41
disability and expanded networks of care, 40
disagreement, 37, 46
   as ethical infrastructure, 114, 143
   moral, 151
discernment, 16, 104

discussion norms, balancing respect and rigor, 136
disparate impact analysis, 125
district-level protection policies, 155
documentation
  for accountability, 115
  of deliberation, 139
  of expectations and norms, 150
  of harm and trade-offs, 142
duties as non-negotiable commitments, 30
duty-based ethics, 31–32
duty of care, in teaching, 32, 44
duty to protect, 43, 80, 194
dyslexia, 18

E

economic aims, of education, 51–53, 62, 131, 217
economic opportunity, genuine access to, 53
ed tech. *See also specific entries*
  contemporary challenges, 72–75
  defined, 69–78
  future horizons, 75–77
  governance, 153–160
  historical foundations of, 70–72
  justifications, 91–94
  measurements, 87–90
  never neutral, 77–78
  philosophical foundations of, 6
  promises of improvements to education, 80–87
  themes, 79–94
  vendors, 36
educational decision-making
  ethical implications of, 13
  hard limits in, 32
  philosophy as foundation for, 2
educational ethics, 13–20
  approaching practice, 18–19
  case-studies method, 17–18
  field of, 13
  practical wisdom, 15–16
  questions, in school leadership, 13
  shared commitments, 16–17
  tragic choices, 14–15
educational outcomes, linking ethical practice to, 141–142
educational power dynamics, 4
educational technology. *See* ed tech
educators
  autonomy vs standardization, 42
  coalition-building among, 218
  core ethical obligations toward, 42
  dilemmas faced by, 4
  loyalty to students vs obedience to systems, 42
  personal judgment vs institutional policies, 42–43
  perspectives, in decision-making, 41–44
  professional duties, 44
  protection for ethical dissent, 43
  recognition of hidden labor, 43–44
  role in shaping future citizens, 1
  shared governance, 43
educator–student relationships, length and impact of, 22–23
efficiency
  vs relational impact, 4
  in schooling, 82–83
egalitarianism, 37
emotional dependence, on AI, 101–102
employer influence, on curriculum, 47
employment instability, from automation, 104
encryption and security stipulations, 121
ends vs means
  balancing, 59
  in schooling, 49–50
engagement
  civic engagement, 55, 59, 72, 73
  vs distraction, 4
  as educational goal, 89–90
  emotional engagement, 163, 165
  student engagement, 54, 87, 90, 145
epistemic injustice, 58
Equal Educational Opportunities Act of 1974, 125
equality of access vs equality of outcome, 57
equality of moral standing, 32
equality protections, 126
equality vs equity, 28
equal opportunity, in education, 57

equitable distribution verification, 155
equity, 3, 39, 75, 169, 201
   audits, 125
   community infrastructure for, 9
   digital equity, 72
   equality vs, 28
   gaps, in education systems, 3
   innovation vs, 4
   workload, 42
Erikson, Erik, 39
error correction, 17
ethical approaches, complementing ethical principles, 30–35
ethical baselines, in schools, 127
ethical dissent, protection for, 43
ethical frameworks, in education, 3, 21, 32, 114, 146. *See also* consequentialism; deontology; virtue ethics
ethical governance, 106
   as continuous learning, 138
   evaluation of, 140–141
ethical imperative, in technology integration, 1–9
ethical infrastructure, 142
   vs bureaucratic control, 129–130
   phased implementation of, 136
ethically complex questions, criteria for, 15
ethical obligations, in education, 36, 38, 42, 44, 45
ethical practices, sustaining, 138–144
   agendas, 139
   assessments, 141–142
   evaluation of ethical governance, 140–141
   facilitation, 140
   grand rounds and committees, 139
   potential roadblocks, 142–143
   revision after ethical failure, 142
   starting small with ethical routines, 143–144
ethical principles, 21–29
   autonomy (*see* autonomy)
   beneficence (*see* beneficence)
   building the five principles, 22–24
   care (*see* care)
   carrying ethical lenses into practice, 29
   justice (*see* justice)

   non-maleficence (*see* non-maleficence)
   tensions among, 28–29
ethical progress, measurement of, 220
ethical reasoning, 111
   emotional labor in, 142
   heuristics (*see* reasoning heuristics)
   implementation challenges to, 19
   as institutional habit, 129
   as iterative practice, 115
   limits of law in, 127
   modeling, 151
   pedagogical modeling of, 136
   shared language for, 220
   thinking habits in, 68
ethical reflection, 17, 78, 96, 104, 116, 155, 220
   culture, in schools, 8
   as school norm, 134
ethical schools, 41
   cultural infrastructure, 134–136, 220
   designing, 129–137
   normative infrastructure, 130–132
   phased implementation, 136
   procedural infrastructure, 132–134
ethical tensions, in learning and assessment, 18, 21, 22, 29, 30
ethics
   as professional habit, 116
   technology review committee, 133
ethics committee, 139
   evaluation, 159
   in professional practice, 13
Eubanks, Virginia, 97
eudaimonia. *See* flourishing (eudaimonia)
evidence heuristic, 67–68
e-waste generation, 103
exit rights in classroom decisions, 40
explicit vs implicit institutional values, 16
external constraints, in ethical decision-making, 118–128
   access constraints, 123–126
   data constraints, 119–122
   ethical baselines, 127
   governance constraints, 122–123
external validation vs internal curiosity, 90
extrinsic rewards systems, 89, 100

F

fair equality of opportunity, 53
fairness, 18, 21, 23, 27, 31, 42, 44, 58, 59, 87, 93, 179
   career preparedness and, 52–53
   individualization vs collective fairness, 38–39
   procedural, 84
   systemic transformation toward, 28
false binary avoidance, 114
Family Educational Rights and Privacy Act (FERPA), 120, 126, 165
feedback channels, 135
fiduciary duties of educators, 19
finance and procurement cost analysis, 159
fiscal constraints, 123
flexibility vs rigid rule application, 8
flourishing (eudaimonia), 3, 55, 58, 59, 77, 78, 82, 83, 85, 217, 218
follow-up communication of outcomes, 140
formal training, in disagreement management, 143
Freire, Paulo, 37, 38, 40, 54, 55, 59
funding, 93, 122, 123, 143, 167, 170, 202, 217
future generations, as hypothetical stakeholders, 47

G

gamification, 89, 154
gendered and racialized labor burdens, 43–44
General Data Protection Regulation (GDPR), 119–120
governance architecture, 155–156
governance constraints, 119, 122–123
grand rounds model, in schools, 139
grants and funding limitations, 123
green AI, 103
ground-up policy making, 152
Gutmann, Amy, 3, 8, 24, 37–39, 46, 54, 133, 134

H

habituation, 16
hallucination (AI), 105
harassment protections, 125
harm minimization, 3, 15, 39, 82, 97–98, 220
   of destructive harms, 25
harm reduction model, 205
hermeneutical injustice, 58
heuristics. *See also specific entries*
   as practical decision aids, 61
hidden labor, recognition of, 43–44
homework purpose (grades vs practice), 147–148
hooks, bell, 59
human dignity, 126
human override functions, 155
human rights, 54, 105, 126
human values, in educational technology, 9

I

identity formation, in adolescence, 39, 56
ideological constraints, 122
immediate pause triggers, 158
immediate pressures vs long-term consequences, 19
impact heuristic, 65–66
improvements to education
   innovation, 80–82
   efficiency, 82–83
   standardization, 84–85
   personalization, 85–87
incident response policy, 159
inclusion and belonging, in classrooms, 151
indirect costs, of technology adoption, 123
individual ethical reflection, 18, 141
Individualized Education Programs (IEPs), 40
individualized ethical decision-making, in education, 14
inequality, reproduction through credentials, 52
inevitability rhetoric, 91–92
informed consent, 26, 45, 46, 76, 81, 120, 154, 167, 193
informed understanding vs information sharing, 46
inherent human dignity, 32
inherent risks of technology, 95–106
innovation, 4, 77, 79–82, 94, 181, 182, 215
   vs equity, 4

ethical responsibility in, 1
inequity of, 166
instant feedback conditioning, 100, 175, 181, 207
instinct vs deliberative reasoning, 21
institutional commitments, in technology policy, 7
institutional culture sustaining policy, 160
institutional memory, 116, 129, 136, 142
institutional review boards, 13
instructional and technology staff collaboration, 159
integrity, in digital spaces, 43, 44, 74
intellectual humility, 17, 40
internal trade-offs, among educational aims, 24
International Society for Technology in Education (ISTE), 127
internet adoption, in schools, 71–72
intrinsic goods of childhood, 27, 56
intrinsic vs extrinsic motivation, 89
involvement vs interference, 45
iteration
    in ethical decision-making, 8
    of procedures, 133
    reflective, 115

J

joint decision-making with students, 40–41
judgment, 18, 19, 22, 31, 54, 196
    analysis vs, 61
    ethical, 16, 29
    personal judgment vs institutional policies, 42–43
    professional, 81, 85, 88, 116, 145, 174, 193, 219
    teacher professional, 145
jurisdictional control over data, 121
justice, 19, 31, 33, 36, 55, 57, 81, 84, 88
    vs autonomy, 28
    vs care, 28
    duty-based reasoning, 32
    labor justice, 104
    as systemic fairness, 21, 23, 27–28
    in technology design, 155

K

Kant, Immanuel, 31–32
knowledge as power, in education, 59

L

Labaree, David, 51, 52
labor, 43–44
    emotional labor, 142, 155
    and job displacement, 104–105
    justice, 104
    macroeconomic need for skilled, 52
language access requirements, 46, 125
learning, cases in, 163–175
learning management systems (LMSs), 73, 147
legal compliance, 127, 159
legitimacy and trust, in schools, 135
legitimacy crisis, from opacity, 99
legitimacy heuristic, 64
Levinson, Meira, 13
likelihood vs severity distinction, 66
lived policies, classroom policies vs, 145, 150
loyalty to students
    vs loyalty to community, 5
    vs obedience to systems, 42

M

Macedo, Donaldo, 37, 38, 40, 54, 55, 59
machine-mediated instruction, 75
mandated reporter, 192
mandatory anti-bias training, 125
massive open online courses (MOOCs), 73, 74
maxims in moral reasoning, 32
media ethics education, 106
media literacy, 54, 217
mental health, 25, 190, 195, 214
Mill, John Stuart, 33
mirroring and sycophancy, 101
misinformation and deepfakes, 105–106
mission and vision statements, 16, 80, 116, 130–132, 146
mitigation vs adaptation, 95
modeling ethical reasoning, 151
moral agency, in classroom practice, 147, 160

moral and intellectual excellence, 55
moral commitments, systematic review of, 129, 138
moral content, disciplinary, 136
moral injury, 42
moral responsibility, maximizing in decision-making, 5
moral uncertainty, shared procedure under, 112
moral vocabulary
  in education, 111
  normalization of, 133
motivation, 89–90
  extrinsic motivation, 90
  intrinsic motivation, 89
  student motivation, 75, 89, 100
mutual inclusivity heuristic, 64–65

N

necessity heuristic, 63
negative autonomy, 26
neurodiversity, 58
neutral facilitation, in ethical dialogue, 140
never-neutral thesis, 77–78
Noble, Safiya Umoja, 72, 82
Noddings, Nel, 23, 26, 55, 56, 151
non-maleficence, 21, 25, 89, 91
  vs autonomy, 28
  vs care, 28
  duty-based reasoning, 32
  as harm avoidance, 23
  vs justice, 28
  mitigation plan, 155
  in selection, 154
normative infrastructure, 116, 130–132
normative problems, in educational practice, 18
nudging, algorithmic, 100
Nussbaum, Martha C., 24, 55

O

opacity, as autonomy concern, 96, 98–99
operational infrastructure for scale, 158–160
  continuous oversight review questions, 159
  coordination requirements, across actors, 159
  incident response policy, 159
  permanent discontinuation process, 160
  professional learning infrastructure, 159
opportunity gap, 79
opportunity harms, 25
opt-out rights, 166, 191
organizational reflection, on decision processes, 141

P

paper trail documentation of decisions, 133
parental and student consent, 154, 167
parental autonomy, in schooling, 45
parental trust, in schools, 6, 166
participation rights, 126
payment structure implications, 123
pedagogical access, 124
pedagogical norms, 98
pedagogical style, as ethical choice, 147
personal aims of education, 55–56, 131
personal computer, in schools, 71
personalization
  in education, 85–87
  vs standardization, 59
personal judgment vs institutional policies, 42–43
perspectives heuristic, 67
philosophical vocabulary into institutional language, translation of, 130
philosophy
  as foundation for educational decision-making, 2
  to praxis transition, 111–117
phronēsis. *See* practical wisdom
physical access, 124
physical harms, 25
pluralism
  in ethical practice, 134
  in moral reasoning, 31
plurality heuristic, 62
policies. *See also related policies*
  as ethical guardrail, 111
  as institutional anchors, 115–116
  as structural guardrail, 7
policymaker accountability frameworks, 47

policymaker influence, on educational technology, 6
positive autonomy, 26
Postman, Neil, 69, 77
power imbalance, between schools and technology companies, 118
practical wisdom, 16, 34
   in classroom decisions, 145
   in decision-making, 61
   in ethical dilemmas, 15–16
practice system
   eight-step ethical decision process, 112–115
   for ethical reasoning, 112–115
predictive analytics, 88, 154, 185
preliminary vetting criteria, 155
principal, role in ed tech decisions, 4, 13, 64, 155, 156, 169–171, 183, 187, 205–207, 211
principlism, 21
printing press and educational change, 70–71
privacy
   as human right, 126
   vs personalization, 4
   regulations, in schools, 119–121
probability heuristic, 66, 82
procedural fairness, 84
procedural infrastructure, 116, 132–134
procurement policies, for new technologies, 133
procurement requirements, 123, 133
"productive struggle," 25
professional codes of ethics, 132
professional development, 104–105, 123, 139, 159, 167, 180, 181, 185, 203, 215
professional duties, of teachers, 44
professional expertise of teachers, 42
profiling restrictions, 121
proof heuristic, 66
proprietary opacity, 98
psychological harms, 25
psychological safety, in disagreement, 140
public reasoning, in schools, 21
public scrutiny, of school decisions, 5
public vs private domains of teaching, 42

R
racial bias, in disciplinary policy, 19
Rawls, John, 18, 47, 52–53, 57, 64
raw material extraction, 103
readiness, narrow vs broad definitions of, 53
reasonable accommodations, 124
reasoning heuristics, 33, 111
   apply, 114–115
   in educational ethics, 61–68
   framing, 62–64
   thinking habits, 68
   validating, 66–68
   weighing, 64–66
(re)calibration heuristic, 67
recognition
   vs response, in ethical governance, 106
   and voice, 58–59
reflective equilibrium, 18
   between classroom and school policy, 152
   in education, 8
   in policymaking, 138
reflective iteration, 115
Rehabilitation Act of 1973, 124
Reich, Justin, 156, 159
relational decision-making, in education, 47–48
representation in policy-building, 135
reputational harms, 25
resource distribution fairness, 28
resource scarcity, in education, 19
responsiveness vs consistency, 45
revision after ethical failure, 142
rights and responsibilities of free expression, 106
right to education, 126
right to work, in technological transition, 126
rubric-based evaluation, 181–185

S
safe and fulfilling work environments, 42
school charters, defining educational aims, 130
school leadership and system-wide technology decisions, 5
school-level technology norms, 156

school-wide cellphone ban ("off and away"), 152, 209–213
screen time, 4, 6, 209
security stipulations, 121
self-fulfilling prophecies, 97
Selwyn, Neil, 69, 79, 80, 85, 91
Sen, Amartya, 55
shared civic knowledge, 54
shared civic reasons, 64
shared commitments, in education, 16–17
shared ethical vocabulary, 8, 134
shared governance, in schools, 43
shared leadership model, 134
shared moral vocabulary, with parents, 46
shared obligation, 27
shared power, in deliberation, 140
shared reasoning methods, in schools, 8
shared values, in schooling, 8
social-emotional learning, 56
social media, 12, 70, 73, 77, 90, 195, 197, 204, 217
sorting function of schooling, 52
stakeholder(s), 36–48
  access, 93
  authentic engagement, 37
  balancing interests, 36
  complexity, in ed tech decisions, 4
  consultation, 67, 116, 155
  data, 88
  deliberative engagement, 37
  diversity of moral frameworks among, 8
  educator perspectives, in decision-making, 41–44
  efficiency, 83
  engagement, 90
  expectations, 131
  identify, 113
  inevitability, 91
  innovation, 81
  interest identification, 18
  involvement in revisions, 132
  mapping, 111, 139
  negotiation of readiness, 53
  parents/guardians, 44–46
  personalization, 86
  power and powerlessness, 37–38
  relational decision-making, 47–48
  role of, 37–38
  students, 38–41
  surfacing tensions, 36
stakes
  access, 93
  balancing the, 59
  clarify the, 113
  data, 88
  of educational decision-making, 49
  engagement, 90
  inevitability, 92
  personalization, 86
  preparation vs protection tension, 81–82
  of process, 56–57
  of purpose, 50–51
  as sacrificing elements of schooling, 83
standardization
  in education, 84–85
  through textbooks, 70
stewardship, of public funds, 46
sticky engagement design, 100
structural constraints, in ethical agency, 219
structural disadvantage, in schooling, 38
student(s)
  agency in personalization, 86–87
  appeals process for educators and, 133
  balancing control and needs, 73
  belonging, dignity, and emotional safety, 155
  core ethical obligations toward, 38
  data, as digital commodity, 4
  data protection in social media, 73
  developmental needs vs autonomy, 39
  development and identity formation, 3
  disability and expanded networks of care, 40
  fiduciary duties to, 136
  health and cybersickness, 76
  individualization vs collective fairness, 38–39
  interest surveys, 164
  as least institutionally powerful stakeholders, 38–41

maintaining autonomy, 101
mislabeling risks, 76
-owned smartphone policies, 4
practical strategies, 40–41
as primary technology stakeholders, 5
privacy concerns, 2
privacy laws, 120
support tools for marginalized, 151
voice, 5, 38, 40, 54, 59, 175, 198, 199, 216
wellbeing, 47, 56
Student Data Privacy Consortium (SDPC), 127
student voice, 5, 38, 40, 54, 59, 175, 198, 199, 216
student wellbeing, 37, 44, 45, 47, 51, 56, 81, 88
substantive equality, 84, 93
surveillance, 5, 45, 76, 179, 200, 202, 203
surveillance capitalism, 76, 99
synthetic media, 105
systematic ethical reasoning, 5, 19
systemic barriers, in schooling, 143
systemic harm shifting to teachers, 44
systemic risks, 102–106

T
teacher(s), 145
    autonomy, loss of, 84
    burnout, 219
    collaboration with special education staff, 124
    decision-making authority, 43
    emotional labor of, 155
    handbook ethics codes, 132
    professional duties of, 44
    professional judgment in technology use, 5
    systemic harm shifting to, 44
    unions as ethical stakeholders, 43
teacher–student trust, erosion of, 99
technology. *See also specific technologies*
    companies and commercial incentives, 6
    decisions and civic impact, 36
    in education vs for education, 69
    governance, in schools, 153
    implementation, without critical assessment, 2
    intensifying educator labor, 44
    as neither all good nor all bad, 95
    serving human flourishing, 78
    as value-laden, 77
    vendor responsibilities, 47
termination rules for data access, 120
termination triggers, 158
testimonial injustice, 58
textual authority vs oral authority, 70
thinking habits, in ethical reasoning, 68
thoughtful engagement, with technological change, 8
tiered access to data, 120
time constraints and hierarchical structures, 19
Title IX protections, 124
tokenism, 135
trade-offs
    and alternatives, recording, 139
    explicit reference to principles and, 141
    as inevitable, 219
    resource, 123
    among themes, 79
tragic choices, in decision-making, 14–15, 219
transformative educational practice, 59
transparency, 99, 143
    about AI limitations, 102
    for classroom policies, 146
    in communication, 159
    vs confidentiality, 45
    in decision and dissent, 219–220
    demand, 98
    in documenting trade-offs, 116
    in institutional decision-making, 17
    in limits of participation, 135
    and stakeholder inclusion, 133
    about structural constraints, 143
trust
    and belonging, disposition toward, 34
    erosion of, 99, 105
    legitimacy and, 135
    parental trust, 6, 166
    relational trust, 184
    and respect, in classrooms, 27
    teacher–student trust, erosion of, 99
tyranny of the majority in schooling, 37

U

uncertainty, 22, 61, 68
uncontestable algorithmic decisions, 99
UNESCO, 54
United Nations, 126
United Nations Convention on the Rights of the Child, 126
Universal Declaration of Human Rights, 126
unsustainable energy consumption, 103

V

value-laden pedagogy, 49
values
   balancing competing educational, 8
   conflict, 113
   defining, 24
   implicit, 69
   judgments, in defining good, 25
vendor vetting process, 122
virtual communities of learning, 78
virtual reality (VR), in classrooms, 75–76
virtue ethics, 30, 34

voice and recognition, in schooling, 58–59
vulnerable users, monitoring, 102

W

Watson, Cole F., 76
Watters, Audrey, 69, 79, 80, 85
web platforms, in education, 73–74
wellbeing
   maximizing, 33, 38
   student, 37, 44, 45, 47, 51, 56, 81, 88
whistleblowing, as ethical obligation, 43
wholesale adoption vs wholesale rejection, 9
workload equity, 42
work volatility, future of, 104

Y

youth, developmental vulnerability of, 4

Z

Zhao, Vivian, 131
Zuboff, Shoshana, 99